# Knowledge and the Search for Understanding Among Nations

# Knowledge and the Search for Understanding Among Nations

## DICKSON A. MUNGAZI

Westport, Connecticut
London

**Library of Congress Cataloging-in-Publication Data**

Mungazi, Dickson A.
    Knowledge and the search for understanding among nations / Dickson A. Mungazi.
        p.  cm.
    Includes bibliographical references and index.
    ISBN 0–275–97193–7 (alk. paper)
    1. International education.  2. Peace—Study and teaching.  3. World politics—20th
century.  I. Title.
    LC1090.M85   2001
    370.116—dc21            2001016359

British Library Cataloguing in Publication Data is available.

Library of Congress Catalog Card Number: 2001016359
ISBN: 0–275–97193–7

First published in 2001

Praeger Publishers, 88 Post Road West, Westport, CT 06881
An imprint of Greenwood Publishing Group, Inc.
www.praeger.com

Printed in the United States of America

The paper used in this book complies with the
Permanent Paper Standard issued by the National
Information Standards Organization (Z39.48–1984).

10 9 8 7 6 5 4 3 2 1

*To the memory of Edith H. Parks,*
*missionary and teacher,*
*whose contribution to the advancement of Africans is invaluable.*

*A general association of nations must be formed under specific covenants for the purpose of affording mutual guarantees of political independence and territorial integrity to great and small states alike.*
Woodrow Wilson, Fourteen Points, 1918


*When communication is between people with different world views, special skills are required if the messages received are to resemble the messages sent. The most important overriding skill is understanding the context within which the communication takes place.*
H. Ned Seelye, 1993

# Contents

# Contents

# *Illustrations*

# Preface

## THE PURPOSE

The purpose of this book is to present a line of thinking that leads to the conclusion that the acquisition of education is a critical factor of the search for understanding among nations. It is based on the assumption that in this nuclear age nations have few options other than to initiate good relationships among themselves to initiate peace, cooperation, and trade that they need to make progress. Before they initiate these relationships, nations need knowledge of people in other nations on which to base them. Knowledge is usually a product of education.

Among features of education that yield this knowledge is the study of culture as a critical foundation of national institutions, such as political systems, social structures, economic systems, legal practices, family systems, and such. The important thing to study about culture is that in societies culture goes through change. A nation cannot have meaningful relationships with other nations if its leadership is ignorant of the cultures of other nations. This study discusses the importance of culture in designing relationships among nations.

This approach yields a clear picture of the problems of education in the world and presents the need to solve them in order to improve those relationships. The knowledge, for example, that as of January 1992 the Soviet Union no longer existed as a nation as it had since 1918 offers a unique opportunity to study the main characteristics of its education as a major component of its national character compared to that of the

United States. In this approach the study focuses on variations in education across the world and examines areas of critical importance to the development of relationships among them. These relationships in turn constitute major conditions of education in the world beginning at the conclusion of World War II in 1945.

## THE APPROACH

The book begins with a discussion of the legacy of Woodrow Wilson to efforts among nations to establish relationships so as to avoid conflict and ensure peace. In his effort to help establish the nature of these relationships at the end of World War I, Wilson tried to help create the organization known as the League of Nations. When his efforts failed, derailed by the rejection of it by the U.S. Senate, there ensued serious consequences for both the United States and Europe. Among these consequences is the rise of the Nazi party in Germany in 1919, initiated as soon as extreme political elements knew that the United States was not going to be involved in the formation and operations of the League.

Immediately the Nazi party began formulating components of a policy that led its government to confrontation with other nations, caring nothing about the consequences of that confrontation except its obsession with power to rule the world. By the time it was all over in May 1945, Europe lay in ruins. The Nazi party itself paid the ultimate price, leaving behind chaos for other nations to sort out. The Nazi party was quite willing to sacrifice human life to rule the world. Understanding and proper behavior toward other nations were not an option. The book discusses these consequences to show that U.S. Senate rejection of the proposed League of Nations contributed to the causes of World War II beginning in September 1939.

The book goes on to discuss conditions that influenced education at the end of the war in 1945 and what nations did to improve the situation in order to initiate understanding among them. This discussion suggests reasons why nations made a concerted effort to initiate collective diagnosis of the causes of the outbreak of the war in 1939 and to set an agenda to avoid such conflict in the future. The book discusses the formation of the United Nations at the San Francisco conference and the creation of Unesco, which has played a critical role in seeking to implement the goals that the United Nations set for the future. The action that the San Francisco conference took, the objectives it set, and their results are discussed in this book.

The book then goes on to discuss aspects related to various practices in education pertinent to the influence of historical developments to contemporary educational settings, and why it is important to have a functional knowledge of the past to understand other nations as a condition of establishing relationships needed to have peace and security. It then discusses the importance of national leadership to making efforts to gain knowledge as the basis for effective good relationships between it and the people. The problems that arise out of these efforts are indicative of the problems that arise among nations.

The relationship that exists between society and the individual as the primary recipient of education translates into the benefit of society as a second recipient of the education of the individual. When the needs of these two recipients have been met, then the world community becomes a third recipient. This order of recipients cannot be reversed. The book then discusses the acquisition of knowledge as an outcome of theory and practice. This discussion focuses on how objectives determine the character of education as it relates to the development of the curriculum as an instrument of fulfilling objectives and national purpose.

In utilizing the imperative for an effective curriculum to suggest the need for effective relationships among nations based on understanding, the system of education must go through the process of reform to reflect changing conditions in the world. The book outlines elements that constitute differences and similarities in different countries to suggest why the educational systems are what they are. The book argues that the system of education is the vehicle of serving national purpose. It concludes that without an effective knowledge of conditions that exist in the world, education cannot translate into understanding. Without understanding as a product of knowledge and knowledge as an outcome of good education, there is inevitable conflict among nations.

To serve the purpose for which it is designed, the educational system must not be allowed to become a haphazard operation, even though it is based on good intentions such as good theory, objectives, and curriculum. Nations, especially those in the Third World, must not blindly duplicate educational system in other nations without making adjustments to suit their own needs. Nations must remember that only an educational system that serves the needs of individual students in a country will serve the needs of the world community.

Finally, the book discusses some problems that all nations encounter in their educational systems. No nation is immune to problems. How nations attempt to resolve these problems provides a fascinating account of the struggle for survival. It shows that these problems are detractors of the educational process and that unless they are resolved education will continue to deteriorate and will have a profoundly adverse effect on national endeavors and relationships among nations.

The last chapter presents summaries of the preceding main features and arguments. It also draws some conclusions and discusses some implications: (1) Nations need other nations to make progress. This need is demonstrated by the kind of relations they have with other nations.

(2) Relationships among nations cannot be assumed, they have to be developed based upon the acquisition of knowledge. (3) Knowledge is a product of good education. (4) Any national leadership that is having problems in developing good relationships with its own people cannot develop good relationships with other nations. Conversely, any nation that is having difficulty in establishing good relationships with other nations cannot establish good relationships with its own people. In that situation, as the Scriptures say, such leadership must reconcile itself with its own people first. (5) Successful relationships between national leadership and the people is a prerequisite of successful relationships with other nations. (6) Successful relationships between national leadership and the people are at their best when they are based on democratic principles.

# *Acknowledgments*

In the process of writing a book that covers critical areas of nations, one must rely on the materials supplied by those who can provide them, as well as, of course, on other sources. For this reason, the author wishes to thank the embassies of the former Soviet Union, Japan, and several countries of Africa in Washington, DC, for sending him the materials he requested and needed to produce this book.

The author also wishes to thank a number of his colleagues at Northern Arizona University for the support and encouragement they have given him. He is also grateful to members of the National Social Science Association, the Association of Third World Studies, and the Comparative and International Studies Society for their encouragement while he was presenting papers at professional conferences from 1993 to 1999. The idea of this book came from those papers.

The author also thanks Betty Russell and George Howington, both in the Center for Excellence in Education at Northern Arizona University, for programming the computer to produce the manuscript more efficiently. He also wishes to extend his special appreciation to the Office of Regents Professors at Northern Arizona University for financial support to enable him to travel to conduct the research he needed to complete the study. He also wishes to thank the staff of Cline Library and Mary Gray in the Faculty Services Office in the Center for Excellence in Education, for various forms of assistance she gave him in the production of the manuscript.

The author also wishes to thank Linda Gregonis, indexer and proofreader, for going through the proofs carefully and doing the index; and Katie Chase, copyeditor at Praeger Publishers. The author wishes to express his special gratitude to Karl Doerry and Joan Fagerburg of the International Studies Office at Northern Arizona University for the support that they gave him in the conduction of the study. Finally, the author wishes to express his special appreciation to the National Archives for giving him permission to include some photographs in this book.

# Introduction

## THE PURPOSE OF THE BOOK

The symbol Y2K to represent the approach of the year 2000 as a new millennium also represents hope and a degree of uncertainty about the future. Among the reasons for this uncertainty is that the new millennium started with events that had a profound effect on relationships among nations. The hijack of an Indian airline the last day of December 1999; the brutal civil war in Russia, caused by separatists in Chechnya; the struggle for secession in Sri Lanka and the assassination attempt on its president, Chandrika Kamaratunga; the violence that broke out in Indonesia killing 250 people; the stabbing of former Beatle George Harrison on December 31—all combine to accentuate the uncertainty that appeared to characterize the beginning of the new millennium. Bomb explosions on Wall Street on February 11, 2000, and in Japan and India on the same day suggest the conclusion that the new millennium was starting with a measure of crisis in the relationships among nations. The activities led by Asama bin Laden, considered the mastermind of international terrorism and believed to be behind the bomb expositions in Nairobi and Dar es Salaam, both in 1998, forced the United States to take extraordinary measures to ensure the security of the nation. These events showed ominous developments that indicated deterioration in relationships among nations.

Amid these disturbing events, however, emerged a hope that people all over the world would gain new knowledge to understand that terrorism and violence among nations are not the answers to problems of conflict among them. New peace talks that were held in Washington, DC, between Syria and Israel raised hopes that peace in the Middle East might now be within reach. Knowledge was crucial and fundamental to the process of understanding that led to negotiations among the warring nations of the Middle East as well as among other nations. The responsibility of developing this knowledge among people of different nations rests squarely on the shoulders of government leaders. In the end they become beneficiaries of an educated, and thus informed, citizenry. This study is a call for nations to make an effort to educate their people as a condition of acquiring knowledge and understanding so as to create peace among them.

When the U.S. Senate voted on October 14, 1999, to reject the Nuclear Test Ban Treaty that President Bill Clinton had negotiated with other nations, there was a strong feeling that the Republican-controlled Senate was acting in exactly the same way as it did in rejecting United States involvement in the founding of the League of Nations under the Versailles Treaty in 1919. When Senate Majority Leader Trent Lott said that the Senate would not rubber stamp decisions of the president as the reason for its rejection, some Americans who remembered their history concluded that he was, in fact, the Henry Cabot Lodge of 1999, and that he relished this analogy. Lott, like Lodge in 1919, did not appear to understand the danger to peace and security of the world posed by the proliferation of nuclear weapons in this age. He was merely motivated by the constitutional provision that the Senate have a say in the manner in which the president conducted foreign policy. Like the action of the Senate in 1919, the rejection of the treaty also posed questions about the kind of relationships the United States would have with other nations.

One must put the Senate rejection of 1999 and Lott's role in it in the context of recent developments among nations. When U.S. President George Bush and Soviet President Mikhail Gorbachev signed the nuclear arms reduction treaty in Moscow on July 31, 1991, they ushered in a new era of relationships between the two superpowers and among members of the world community. These new relationships among nations, unlike those that came in the era of the cold war, were based on genuine efforts to ensure understanding in order to have enduring peace and cooperation that nations needed for development.

The purpose of this book is to discuss the role that education plays in shaping the development of knowledge that nations must utilize in developing relationships among themselves. Out of these relationships nations develop national character that they must have to identify their capacities to play important roles in exerting positive influences in shaping the development of the world itself. This is a mighty challenge and responsibility. Every nation should avail itself of this opportunity. But whether a nation rises up to meet this challenge and utilize the opportunity to do so depends on the goals it sets for itself. Among these goals is how it sets out to secure the education it needs to have the knowledge of other nations crucial to its own development.

A case in point: soon after South Africa gained internationally recognized independence following the elections that were held at the end of April 1994, the new government that came out of those elections, led by Nelson Mandela, recognized that during the previous twenty years South Africa had been ostracized by the world community because of its highly racially discriminatory policy of apartheid. Therefore, among the first things that Mandela's government initiated was to establish diplomatic relations with other nations, beginning with those in Africa. To do this successfully the government also initiated greatly needed reform in its education to make it relevant to world conditions of the time. Mandela could not take chances with delay in this endeavor because it was crucial to how South Africa conducted itself among other nations and the kind of relationships it had with them.

Within a relatively short period of time South Africa was thrust in the middle of a major crisis in Africa. Zaire was going through a period of destructive civil war caused by the dictatorship of Sese Seko Mobuto, who seized power in a military coup in 1965. Mandela and his government undertook to mediate between Mobuto and the rebel leader, Laurent Kabila, in an effort to find a solution to the problem. Although those efforts were futile because of hardened positions taken by both sides in the conflict, the world community came to know the reputation of Mandela as a peace maker. Considering that this was a man who had spent twenty-seven years in political prison for opposing apartheid, Mandela proved to be a remarkable man and statesman. The combination of knowledge and dedication to principle led to this endeavor and accomplishment. This approach makes this book relate the acquisition of knowledge to the development of relationships among nations based on understanding and peace that they need to insure this development.

The approach made in this book is quite different from the conventional approach to what is generally known as international education in some important respects. Instead of discussing how education initiated in nations constitutes a definition of knowledge and understanding among nations, this study attempts an integrated approach in which specific educational features are presented relative to their appropriateness in meeting the needs of students in any country. When education meets the needs of students, it gives them the knowledge they need to respond to the needs of the nation of which they are part. When this happens, that education creates a social environment that places a student in a position to respond to the needs of the world community. It is a misnomer to call education international simply because it is intended to carry elements of relating to other nations. In this book education is considered to generate knowledge needed among nations because it becomes a means of improving relationships among nations.

International education implies that certain features of it are identical, such as the curriculum, instructional strategies, goals, theory, administration, problems, financial support, and the like. The truth of the matter is that there is no such thing. The approach made in this book is to present education as a basis of acquiring knowledge that nations need to utilize in order to have meaningful relationships with other nations. This is the latest trend in considering education as a means of improving diplomatic relations among nations. This perspective enables the author to develop a coherent argument that enables the reader to see and follow the critical nature of the influence of education in the development of relationships among nations

Nations develop education to meet the needs of their students in order to prepare them adequately to meet their needs. The fact that in 1992 the Soviet Union, as it had been known since the Bolshevik Revolution of 1917, went out of existence and was substituted by the federation of independent republics, does not negate the reality that for seven decades the country operated under a socialist system. This book helps put the major developments that took place during that time into the context of their significance to the dramatic events that began to unfold in 1990.

## RATIONALE OF THE BOOK

The development of the world falls into four basic categories: Western democracies, socialist nations, emerging nations, and Third World nations. Because, since the end of World War II, each of these four areas has been facing enormous problems in its education, mainly related to problems they have been having in relationships they have tried to develop with other nations, a question must be asked: Are there some things that each could learn from each other to find solutions to those problems? This is the question the reader is invited to answer. In considering it, the reader needs to consider the causes of the coup attempt in the Soviet Union on August 19–21, 1991, and its implications for the demise of the Soviet Union itself.

There is no evidence to suggest that the dissolution of the Soviet Union and the creation of the association of independent republics have improved conditions of life of their people. One must understand that Mikhail Gorbachev was highly sensitive to conditions imposed on the Soviet Union by the nonaggression treaty that Adolf Hitler and Joseph Stalin signed on September 29, 1939, supposedly to assure the people living in the two countries a peaceful life in keeping with their national character.

But that is not what happened. Over the years Gorbachev did not think that it was right to keep the Soviet Union together under conditions that the people did not approve. His personal character and conscience combined to convince him that it was better to dissolve the country than to keep it together by force.

The general decline of the economy in the world and the rapid increase in population have combined to demand closer relationships among nations. The crisis caused by these factors reached alarming proportions by 1992 and cast a long shadow of doubt on the ability of national leaders to shape the future of their countries using only national resources. Moving away from the conventional approach of discussing the role of education in nations of these four major areas of the world, this study makes an approach to the discussion of how education can be utilized to seek solutions to economic problems in the world. This, therefore, seems an appropriate approach to education intended to improve understanding among nations so they can initiate that cooperation.

## THE ILLUSION OF MILITARY POWER

Indeed, the world of 1991–1992 was experiencing enormous problems that seemed to defy solution. The rapidly increasing population—estimated at 5.3 billion people with an annual growth rate of 1.8 percent and with per capita income of $3,470—has compounded the problems of poverty and declining resources. The inability of nations to find solutions to their own national conflicts caused by unfair distribution of opportunity has accentuated the age-old myth that military power insures national security. This is why national priorities have been influenced by huge military spending that has robbed the people of their legitimate right of access to national resources to insure development and security. The end of the cold war means that national priorities have to be set. That, by the beginning of 1992, this had not been done created an international climate that raised questions about the nature of relationships among nations.

## KNOWLEDGE AS THE ESSENCE OF PROPER BEHAVIOR AMONG NATIONS

An example of the tragedy of misunderstanding is a story told of what happened toward the end of World War II. Sensing that they were losing the war, the Japanese tried to make peace overtures to the Allied forces. They sent a message in Japanese to that effect to President Harry S. Truman. President Truman replied immediately to ask the Japanese to indicate their intention precisely. The Japanese are reported to respond in one word, *Mokusatsu*, which has several meanings depending on the context in which it is used. It can mean "We are considering details." It can also mean "Postpone or delay decision or action." On receiving this reply President Truman and his advisors concluded that the Japanese were not genuinely interested in making peace, and decided to use the atomic bomb on the Japanese cities of Hiroshima and Nagasaki to end the war, causing the first, and hopefully the last, military nuclear holocaust in the world.

A story is also told of a rich American whose wife was visiting the Middle East. She saw an expensive artifact which she wanted to buy. But because of the cost she decided to ask her husband if she could buy it. She quickly sent a telegram to ask him and gave the price of the artifact. He responded immediately to say "No, price is too high." In transmitting the reply to her the telegram company omitted proper punctuation between "No" and "price," so that the reply read "No price is too high." His wife bought the artifact. When she returned home her husband was not pleased, causing severe strain in the marriage. If lack of understanding can occur between people of the same language and culture, what would one expect between those of different cultures and languages?

The fact of the matter is that whether or not national leaders are democratically elected, they institute legislatures as an instrument for carrying out their own political agendas. The sad part of all this is that the people often regard national leaders who take them into war as heroes. This is why President Bush's popularity rose sharply at the conclusion of hostilities in the Persian Gulf in 1991. The people tend to believe anything their national leader says and give him the support he says he needs to carry out a national policy he claims to be in the interest of the people. Any action that may question the policy of such a leader is considered unpatriotic. These are characteristic features found in all national leaders, but they do not contribute positively to national purpose. In January 1992, for instance, the economy of the United States was weakened by a combination of powerful factors that included the aftermath of the war in the Persian Gulf.

The second disturbing aspect of the illusion of military power is that because national leaders are not able to see their own errors, they operate on the assumption that the party with which they are in conflict is always wrong and that they are always right. This is the environment in which President Saddam Hussein convinced his followers to see President George Bush as the ultimate threat to the world of Islam. This is also the same environment that President Bush utilized to convince his fellow Americans to believe that Hussein was the embodiment of Moslem extremism that must be stopped to deny him an opportunity to become another Adolf Hitler. The frequent use of such terms as "the Great Satan" and "the Infidel" to characterize Western leadership, "the brutal dictator" to characterize Hussein, and "the evil empire" to characterize the

Soviet Union contributed nothing to the creation of a climate of real knowledge of the issues that caused conflict between nations and the need to initiate dialogue to resolve problems. Refraining from using extreme language would have enabled the parties to understand and appreciate the concerns of the other. The process of understanding and appreciation requires education. Indeed, the conflict in the Persian Gulf underscores the importance of the thinking that national leaders need education to understand the essence and the art of diplomacy.

Another critical problem that stood in the way of seeking a peaceful resolution to the crisis in the Persian Gulf is the enormous ego that manifested the attitudes and actions of both President Hussein and President Bush. This problem was caused primarily by previous international events whose impact they sought to turn into an advantage. On the one hand, having come out of the six-year war with Iran, Hussein, seeking to fill the regional leadership void left by the death of Anwar Sadat, wanted to assert himself as the undisputed leader of the Arab world. On the other hand, having endured the humiliation of the war in Vietnam and the tragic drama of the hostages held in Iran and Lebanon in 1979, Bush sought to assert his own leadership role in the Western world.

Indeed, the personality of both men left no room for dialogue or accommodation. Instead, they acted in ways that accentuated rhetoric that was partly carried out by the media. This is why, at the conclusion of the war with Iraq in 1991, Bush proudly proclaimed that the Vietnam syndrome was finally over, suggesting that he used the war with Iraq to eliminate the residual effect of the demise the United States had endured in the conflict in Vietnam. President Bush's proudest moment was his claim that the Patriot missiles had elevated the American national spirit to a new level of national pride and self-confidence. He appeared to neglect the importance of developing an ability to reason out things, rather than to utilize military power to seek solutions to international problems. Indeed, it is quite clear that both men needed a new level of education to help them understand that humility and self-restraint are distinct qualities of national leaders and that they do not diminish the power of leadership and the office they hold simply because they seek to understand the concerns of their potential adversary as a condition of dialogue. This suggests that education is the essence of political behavior and action. To neglect its development in favor of building the military is to undercut the very essence of national endeavors.

## THE IMPORTANCE OF KNOWLEDGE IN CONTEMPORARY WORLD SETTING

The situation discussed above is a reality that delegates in San Francisco took into account in their deliberations. But by 1992 too many leaders had already forgotten this basic principle. The world of 1991 showed much that could be related to events of earlier times. The change of leadership in Britain from Margaret Thatcher to John Major, the continuing saga of apartheid in South Africa, the conflict between Mikhail Gorbachev and the Baltic states, the political crisis in East European countries, and the end of the Soviet Union—all were manifestations of conditions that could easily lead to a major global conflict unless nations learn what they must to bring about a lasting peace.

The sad part of the tragedy in the Persian Gulf is that in this kind of environment the real causes of the conflict were not addressed. On the one hand, Hussein, claiming to be the guardian of the Palestinian cause, wanted linkage to the crisis caused by his invasion of Kuwait. On the other hand, Bush, believing that he was the guardian of Western democratic values, rejected the idea of linkage and argued that the invasion was nothing less than naked aggression that must not be allowed to stand. Failure to resolve this difference through dialogue is what caused the war in the Persian Gulf in 1991. Must one assume that differences of opinion on issues of international relationships and human existence could be resolved only by military means and not by applying reason? It would be a sad day for the international community to be forced to accept such thinking. Yet, in 1991 this kind of thinking became the norm of international relationships when the United Nations itself voted to authorize military use to force Iraq out of Kuwait. Then, on January 12, the U.S. Senate voted 52 to 49 and the House of Representatives 250 to 183 to authorize President Bush to use military means to force Iraq out of Kuwait. While this action yielded considerable political fallout, it had its dark side: the lingering and devastating effect that would last for years. Victorious in military action, the United States entered a new phase of economic decline that forced Bush to undertake a mission to Japan in January 1992 in an effort to revive the declining economy.

In examining the role that education must play in helping nations seek an improvement in human condition and relations between them, one must remind oneself of the diagnostic approach that the world community made at the conclusion of the war in 1945. This is the place and time that this study begins. Painful as this exercise was, the delegates to the San Francisco conference concluded that rather than blame the Axis powers for causing the war, all nations must share the responsibility for its outbreak. If they had come to this conclusion earlier, the war would have been avoided in the first place. If nations had come to this realization in 1991, the devastation caused by the war in the Persian Gulf would have been avoided and the billions of dollars used to wage the war could have been directed at the much-needed social services that not all countries have been able to extend to their people.

Neither the U.S. Senate nor the House of Representatives predicted the setting on fire of oil fields in Kuwait and the displacement of the Kurds as outcomes of the war. If the restoration of Kuwait was accomplished at the price of these factors, then one must conclude that the victory that allied coalition forces thought they scored against Hussein must be considered a disaster. This means that using military means to force Iraq out of Kuwait had a much darker side in the form of human cost that could not be measured.

There is another cost to this tragedy: prospects for peace in the Middle East, which Western nations thought would become possible with the defeat of Iraq, have remained as distant as ever. The shuttle diplomacy that Secretary of State James Baker initiated at the conclusion of hostilities did not yield any tangible results. Indeed, Baker's efforts amounted to the days of Henry Kissinger reincarnate: shuttle diplomacy with its weak side. As the presidential campaign got under way in August 1992, President Bush removed Baker from the State Department and appointed him manager of his reelection efforts. The fears that Israel and its Arab neighbors had about the intention of the other even intensified as both sides hardened their respective positions, refusing to see the critical issues they faced from the other's perspective. With Baker out of the negotiations, the crisis in the Middle East took a dramatic turn for the worse.

## CONSEQUENCES OF MILITARY ACTION

There is yet another disturbing aspect of the war in the Persian Gulf that the Western forces had not anticipated. As it progressed and allied forces were reported to be within striking distance of victory, social and economic conditions in the United States began to deteriorate rapidly. In his PBS television program on June 2, 1991, Bill Moyers gave the following facts as an outcome of the war. Nearly a million Americans were lining up for welfare benefits that were not there. The recession was having a devastating impact on education as nearly 54 percent of the programs were being cut. Hospital care and other services were being reduced. The scourge of homelessness was rapidly increasing and the plight of the less fortunate was deteriorating. In New Jersey the Office of Social Services was advising those fifty-five years and older to seek economic and financial help from their children in order to survive.

Many American servicemen returned home from the Gulf to find their families in a state of economic ruin. Some experienced family trauma that they had not anticipated, such as divorce. Even conservative journalist George Will argued in June 1991 that the war with Iraq had left behind "broken homes, broken hopes, and broken hearts" in both Iraq and the United States. Tom Foley, the Speaker of the U.S. House of Representatives, added on June 16 that the preoccupation with the war in the Persian Gulf had created an array of problems at home that the nation was now finding hard to resolve. On August 2, ABC published the results of a poll that indicated that those Americans who had supported going to war with Iraq now questioned the decision to do so by a margin of 54 to 46 percent.

While this was happening, controversy between the president and the Democrats in Congress over the civil rights bill of 1991 was having a paralyzing effect on the political process. Can one conclude that all these adverse effects justified going to war with Iraq over Kuwait? Why was it not possible to utilize human reason to resolve the problem of Iraq's invasion of Kuwait? Yes, the Bush administration argued that it had tried to resolve the problem through dialogue, but the conditions Bush specified for such dialogue undercut the very essence of its universal meaning. This is why on May 16, 1991, Baker returned to the United States to report to President Bush that he had accomplished nothing on his shuttle diplomacy. On May 18, during a television broadcast, Bruce Morton of CBS concluded that the comprehensive peace that the United States had hoped would result from the defeat of Iraq had remained as distant as ever, and suggested that what may be needed to find solutions to the problems of the Middle East was a new strategy—education.

The tragedy in the Middle East also shows that there is always a price to pay for conflict as long as nations refuse to learn about the concerns of other nations and as long as they see issues exclusively from their own point of view. To reach this realization and alter their thought processes, all nations require an education that creates a climate of understanding so that problems can be resolved. The truth of the matter is that conflict exists in human existence only because people do not know what it takes to avoid it. In May 1991 Bush came close to recognizing this reality when he addressed another unexpected fallout of the war with Iraq.

Speaking to the graduating class of the U.S. Air Force Academy on May 24, 1991, President Bush decried what he saw as the proliferation of weapons of massive destruction in the Middle East, and indicated that his administration would do everything in its power to stop it. However, Bush's decision to continue supplying weapons to what he called "our friends in the Middle East" manifested a classic example of the kind of behavior that has always been one of the major causes of conflict between nations. He failed to emphasize the importance of understanding and dialogue as principal pillars that sustain the edifice of lasting international peace.

The sad part of this unfortunate development is that neither Bush nor any other world leader could do anything to stop it. Although Bush outlined his plan to eliminate weapons of massive destruction in the Middle East, he fell short of explaining the need to initiate an international approach to the development of an educational system as a strategy to enable all people to understand the importance of the mutuality of trust through utilization of knowledge. In stating, "We are committed to stopping the proliferation of weapons of massive destruction in the Middle East," Bush neglected to put all relevant aspects into proper perspective. The tragic death of Rajiv Gandhi in May 1991 demonstrates the equally tragic outcome of resorting to violence or military action to resolve human and international problems. Bush must have been frightened by the extent of the destruction he saw during the war with Iraq, and he must have pondered what the future held if nations did nothing to learn to resolve problems through dialogue.

## RELEVANCE OF KNOWLEDGE TO THE HUMAN CONDITION

The knowledge that before the war in 1939 educational opportunity was the privilege of a few individuals, the reality that economic development was not possible without adequate education, the reality that poverty and urban decay were a product of the Industrial Revolution, the knowledge that political and economic power were inherited rights of a few—all these factors combined to create an international climate that, by 1939, made conflict on a world scale inevitable. The balanced and objective approach the delegates to the San Francisco conference made to seek solutions for the world was also evident in other areas of their endeavors. They concluded that the environment of conflict was created because people of the world did not know each other because they were not sufficiently educated to understand the causes of human conflict. That they placed the responsibility for this situation squarely on the shoulders of national leaders substantiates the conclusion that national leaders design policies that, while seeming to serve the interests of their nations, actually serve their own political interests.

However, one must not negate the reality that the delegates to the San Francisco conference took into account in concluding that educational development was the best means of resolving conflict, both international and national. As it lay in ruins, Japan realized in 1945 that before the war it had a fully developed industry which it gambled away in military adventure. Now, it was time to start all over again. In this context it is interesting to note that the delegates to the San Francisco conference saw a definite relationship between the effort to create ideal national conditions and international peace and security. They readily recognized that when people of any nation had the right to education, economic security, political participation, and basic civil liberties that include freedom of speech, self-expression, and association, they provide a stable national environment that eliminates national conflict. This environment translates into the creation of an environment of international peace and security. The delegates to the San Francisco conference emphasized that the journey to this international destination must begin with a single educational step and underscored their belief in the value of education as a relevant factor of the human condition.

In spite of the enthusiasm of the delegates to the San Francisco conference to utilize education to create a brave new world order in which the position of the individual would supersede the political interests of the national leaders, there were enormous problems that they did not anticipate. The rapid increase in population translated into a rapid increase in school enrollment. The poor facilities then in existence combined with poor resources to limit the effectiveness of the new thrust in seeking improvement in education. The new level of enthusiasm among parents to provide their children an opportunity for education as a preparation for the future accentuated the hope among the dispossessed that the route to a better future lay in their pursuit of education. Decline in economic programs also combined with rising inflation and declining national resources to severely impinge on the efforts nations were making individually and collectively to plan a future different from the past.

## USING KNOWLEDGE TO CREATE A BRAVE NEW WORLD

In spite of recognizing these problems, the delegates to the San Francisco conference established an impressive set of objectives to guide their actions. They set 1960 as a target date for all nations to achieve 100 percent literacy. They decreed that every child in every country must be allowed to attend school. They passed a resolution calling on all nations to establish adult literacy programs to combat illiteracy on all fronts. They called on all nations to cooperate in building the economy and national institutions in order to meet the varying dimensions of human need and to serve the educational purpose of their people. That the participants of the San Francisco conference also called on all nations to reform the political systems so that they would become more representative in their operations in order to sustain democracy was a condition demanded by the times. They reminded national leaders that they hold office as a public trust, and that if they violated that trust they must be removed from office. They called on national leaders to observe at all times that sacred democratic principle: governments are instituted with the express consent of the governed. They created Unesco as a global agent to coordinate cultural, educational, and scientific programs throughout the world relative to global endeavors to bring about improvement in the human condition.

## ORGANIZATION OF THE BOOK

Chapter 1 examines the ideals, aspirations, crisis, and strategies that Woodrow Wilson tried to utilize to resolve problems of difference of opinion between himself and Senator Henry Cabot Lodge on the merits of the U.S. involvement in the formation and functions of the League of Nations. This discussion sets the stage for the discussion of the consequences of the Senate's rejection of the terms of the League in Chapter 2. Then in Chapter 3 the study discusses the reaction of the world community to the founding of the United Nations following the end of World War II in 1945, and the agenda it established for action in the future as well as the goals it set to be met by 1960. This time the U.S. Senate readily voted to accept the founding of the United Nations.

Chapter 4 outlines some fundamentals of education to initiate understanding among nations, the problems they encounter, and possible solutions. Chapter 5 discusses the influence of education in acquiring knowledge of other cultures on which to base relationships. Chapter 6 covers the founding of the United Nations and Unesco and their roles in seeking solutions to problems of relationships among nations. Chapter 7 discusses the role of national leadership in designing relationships.

Finally, Chapter 8 presents a summary of the study, reaches conclusions, and discusses implications. This chapter also offers some interpretive insights that are critical to a national approach to education to secure the knowledge needed to understand other nations and structure meaningful relationships with them. The fundamental consideration is the question: What do nations need to do to design educational systems that adequately respond to the needs of their people as a condition of meeting those of nations so that they have meaningful relationships with other nations? Some answers are in this book. In approaching the subject of relationships among nations in the manner that he has done, the author hopes that this book provides some important insights into problems that nations encounter in educational systems as they try to have those relationships.

The world today faces enormous problems that no nation has sufficient resources to solve alone. Economic decline, international terrorism, AIDS, population explosion, trade imbalance, ethnic and cultural conflict, decline of national resources, effect of global warming on agricultural production—all require close cooperation among nations to solve. Without creating good relationships among themselves, nations cannot cooperate in seeking solutions to these problems, and without cooperation they will continue to drift into the mire of conflict.

# The Legacy of Woodrow Wilson

A general association of nations must be formed under specific covenants for the purpose of affording mutual guarantees of political independence and territorial integrity to great and small states alike.

Woodrow Wilson, 1918

## WOODROW WILSON THE MAN

In the twentieth century efforts have been made more than in any other period in human history to insure world peace based on the acquisition of education and understanding. Twice during this century, in 1914 and in 1939, the world came to the brink of self-destruction through war. Among those who made an effort to save the world from this self-destruction was Woodrow Wilson, the 28th president of the United States, who served from 1913 to 1921. To understand Wilson as a world leader who made an effort to promote peace in the world, one needs to understand him as a man.

Woodrow Wilson was born in Staunton, Virginia, on December 28, 1856, the year Booker T. Washington was born. He was the third of four children of Joseph Ruggles and Janet Wilson. The Wilsons named their son Thomas Woodrow Wilson. As a child he was known as Thomas, but he dropped Thomas soon after he was graduated from college and became known simply as Woodrow.[1] His grandfather, James Wilson, was a Scottish-Irish immigrant who had become a well-known newspaper man in Ohio. Wilson's grandmother was born in Carlisle, England, near the border with Scotland.[2]

From the time he was a young boy, Woodrow was introduced by his family to an environment of religious piety and scholarly achievement. From his birth Wilson lived among people who were deeply religious and who believed in Presbyterian doctrine and stressed the importance of education.[3] Before he reached the age of two, Wilson and his family moved to Augusta, Georgia, where his father had been appointed pastor of an influential church. From age four to eight Wilson lived in an environment of civil conflict generated by the issue of slavery. By the time Wilson became aware of the coming civil war he heard in 1861 someone talk with great excitement that Abraham Lincoln had been elected president of the United States and that his election meant that a civil war was inevitable because the North and the South felt very strongly about their respective views of slavery.[4]

During the Civil War Joseph Wilson, a strong supporter and sympathizer of the South, converted his church into a hospital and offered comfort to the Confederate military personnel and gave every assistance he was able to give. Out of this activity Woodrow began to understand what it meant to support a national cause. This realization would later play a major role in his involvement in trying to shape the course of world affairs.

Wilson did not attend school until he was nine years old, partly because he was a frail child. However, his father made sure that he received good basic education while he was still at home. On weekends Joseph took him to a local corn mill or to a cotton gin to learn about industry and manufacturing processes. During the Civil War Joseph also took him to ammunition factories and iron foundries in Augusta to learn about how they operated. He also taught him the art of making exact expression of ideas necessary for understanding the issues that society was facing.[5]

At home the Wilson family read the Bible together every day and gathered to sing hymns on Sunday evenings. In 1870 Wilson's father was appointed professor in the Presbyterian theological seminary in Columbia, South Carolina. Three years later, when Woodrow was seventeen years old, he enrolled in Davidson College in North Carolina. At that time the college, like other educational institutions, suffered from the effects of the Civil War. Students were expected to provide their own water and firewood and perform other chores at the school to keep it running.[6] Because Wilson was not strong physically his health began to deteriorate. This forced him to leave Davidson College after his freshman year without making plans for the future of his education.

Within a few months after he left Davidson College Wilson's health began to improve steadily. In September 1875 he enrolled in the College of New Jersey (later known as Princeton University) in Princeton. This was the beginning of a relationship between Wilson and an institution in which each would shape the future of the other. Wilson took his studies seriously. At the age of nineteen he fully understood what his family expected of him. He participated in public speaking as part of his formal education. As a result he was elected leader of his debating team. He also became interested in reading biographies of famous men or statesmen. In his senior year at the College of New Jersey he was elected editor of a college paper, *The Princetonian*, which addressed some critical issues on campus and in Princeton itself.

In spite of his ability to debate, Wilson declined to compete for the senior debating trophy when he was invited to argue in favor of protective tariff, a controversial national issue at the time. He did not wish to add fuel to an expanding national controversy, even though he had some ideas about the topic. He was a strong believer in free trade to the extent that nothing would persuade him to argue against it. He believed that a protective tariff was against free enterprise and, if implemented, would hurt U.S. ability to compete with other nations whose goods were of poorer quality.[7] But Wilson elected to keep his views to himself at this critical point in time when the controversial issue was being discussed.

In 1879 Wilson graduated from the College of New Jersey, 38th in a class of 106. He planned to pursue a career in public service. In October of the same year Wilson enrolled in the law school of the University of Virginia at Charlottesville. He believed at that time that the study of law would provide him the best road to the career he desired. He took an active part in the university's debating club. But in 1881 he withdrew from the school because of poor health. The following year, he established a law office in Atlanta, Georgia.

But in the fall of 1883 he realized that he was not cut out to be a lawyer and he decided to become a college teacher. For Wilson this was a time of searching and testing. It was a time of reflecting and planning his future as his life seemed to be at a crossroads. He needed a fresh start to give his life direction and purpose. It was a time of assessing the impact of contemporary events in his life, a time of searching for new meaning. He knew that he could not continue to change occupations frequently without losing direction and purpose in life. He also realized that he was getting older and must come to terms with the expectations of his family. But true to American tradition, his family refrained from influencing his decision about a career or his future.

At this time Wilson was trying to develop new relationships with various people he came into contact with. He knew that other people were bound to have a considerable impact on his own life. One such person was his classmate Robert Bridges, who was instrumental in securing an opportunity for him at Princeton. He knew that his success in future endeavors would depend on the support and assistance given by those he had come to know, as well as on his broad appeal to the public. On the basis of this conclusion Wilson wrote a letter on January 30, 1887, to Bridges to say that he was going to give all his time to the study of political science because he had come to the conclusion that national development and relationships between people and nations was about politics.[8]

Wilson appealed to Bridges and other people with whom he corresponded to respond to his suggestion of a strategy as he was planning his future. In this manner he created an environment which he later used to be effective as a leader and decision maker. But in initiating this strategy Wilson remained true to ideals that were part of the leadership that was emerging in Europe during the Industrial Revolution, that a successful national leader was one who was sensitive to the needs of the people.[9] Once he embraced this basic principle, Wilson would never abandon it throughout his life. The letter to Bridges was among the first he wrote to friends and associates in order to make sure that he was on the right track in planning his future.

On July 23, 1889, Wilson again wrote a letter to Bridges, this time to say that he had a very useful discussion with Francis Patton, the revered president of Princeton University, about the possibility of assuming the position of professor of public law there, and that he found Patton knowledgeable about academic issues that a university should address. He asked Bridges to offer any thoughts about the prospects of him accepting the position if it was offered. In this public relations campaign Wilson placed himself in a strong position to exert influence among the people he knew were influential in some of the things he wanted to do. He knew that having the support from individuals like Bridges would strengthen his own position in the future. When Bridges wrote back to support his intent to apply for the position at Princeton, Wilson felt that he was on the right road.[10]

In the letter to Bridges, Wilson went on to say that the interview with Patton focused on future plans at Princeton and the results of fulfilling them. Wilson concluded by saying that he thought he had a favorable impression of both Patton and Princeton, but he needed the response of his friends and associates on the possibility of his accepting the position there before he made the commitment. There is no doubt that Wilson was covering all the bases as he planned his future. There is no doubt also that in Bridges Wilson had found a reliable and dependable friend.

These two letters to Bridges show two qualities about Wilson. The first quality is that although he was quite confident in his ability to plan his own future by himself, he realized that he needed the support and assistance of other people to strengthen his already high degree of purpose in his life. His decision to devote himself to the study of politics as an honorable vocation would later lead to an effective service to his own community, his country, and the international community. He projected himself in a positive way as he decided that politics was going to be his chosen career.

The second quality is that he considered it essential to trust other people in the collective effort that he felt must be made to make political action benefit society. He concluded that the benefit of this form of public service was satisfaction that he was contributing something positive for others. This was the spirit that came out of the Industrial Revolution. Like other national leaders from of this period, Wilson did not see political activity as benefiting himself, but people in society who were unable to do something for themselves to improve their lives. He therefore regarded politics and politicians as an instrument of realizing national goals.

With these qualities Wilson was on his way to becoming a statesman who understood what it meant to serve the needs of humanity in all their dimensions. His secretary of the navy, Josephus Daniels, concluded that "Wilson belonged to a small but superb group of individuals who were bred on disciplined poverty and nourished by qualities of sensitivity and impulses of thoroughbreds and by the pedigree of spiritual values."[11] Daniels went on to add that once Wilson understood the importance of applying these values in his own life, he began in earnest the search for himself, and when he found himself he was destined to set the world on a new level of accomplishment in serving its needs. Daniels concluded that these qualities made Wilson an unusual person who had a mastery of the art of politics as well as a scholar, a genuine social reformer, and a vigorous fighter of human rights.[12]

One must reach the conclusion that if the world saw in Wilson the human spirit that transformed the peripheral or mediocre performance of man into a new scale of human endeavor at its best, it was because Wilson represented the best of human qualities that shaped human character and society into something larger than the basic elements of human essence. Wilson also exhibited something unique and noble from his Presbyterian family members and his Irish-Scottish grandfather, as well as his parents, into a milieu that created in him the legacy of human goodness in all its sublime conditions. Wilson tapped into those resources to find new meaning in his life for the benefit of the world.

Among the pathways that Wilson followed in search of himself was his avid reading of *Aurora*, a newspaper edited by William Duane, an ardent follower of Thomas Jefferson's ideas of the role of the individual in seeking improvement of society. Wilson discovered that in his enthusiasm to embrace the ideas and ideals of Jefferson, Duane was brought before the court to answer charges of violating sedition laws.[13] Woodrow's grandfather, James Wilson, was totally surprised by Duane's arrest because he thought he had come to the United States in 1807 from Ireland to enjoy freedom of the press, but only to find that there were laws in his new land that imposed restrictions on that freedom.

When Duane was appointed military officer in eastern Pennsylvania in the war of 1812, James Wilson was appointed to succeed him as the managing editor of *Aurora*, making it possible for him to understand that the sedition laws in existence were wrong for the United States. When Woodrow's father, Joseph Ruggles Wilson, was born on February 28, 1822, his father James made sure that he was introduced early to the world of letters as soon as he was able to understand that world. From early boyhood, Joseph was an accomplished reader of books. His success in academic effort showed qualities of scholarship that later elevated Woodrow to national prominence as a scholar.

As Joseph grew and gained new experiences, he demonstrated a high level of intellect in his educational pursuit. He entered Jefferson College, a Presbyterian college in Cononsburg, Pennsylvania, when he was 18 years of age, where he studied theology. He graduated as valedictorian of his class in 1844. The next year he taught at Mercer School in Pennsylvania.

For Joseph to teach school was part of the call he had to answer for the ministry. Joseph then spent one year at the College of New Jersey to broaden his educational experiences.[14] This gave him the experience that he needed to be successful as a minister of religion and the influence that he needed to become a successful preacher. This also gave him an opportunity to pass on to his son, Woodrow, the kind of influence that he needed to generate a unique personality that would place him in a position to exercise effective leadership in American society and later in the international community.

## WILSON'S EDUCATIONAL ENDEAVOR AND ACADEMIC SUCCESS

This environment gave Woodrow an opportunity to broaden the base of his search for himself. Besides deciding that he wanted to enter public service, he had not yet concluded his search for a career based on a more clearly defined line of work. He decided that he had the qualities of national leadership that he felt capable of providing assistance needed by both the United States and the international community. His educational endeavor was an integral part of that search. Beginning in 1885 Wilson pursued his education with a single purpose of preparing himself for that leadership role, both at home and in the world. Now that he had defined the purpose of his search for himself, he saw directions of his development very clearly.

In his first wife, Ellen, Wilson had a reliable and dependable ally and support. She was influential on his decisions because she recognized the talents and qualities that he possessed as critical to the future of the country. In the fall of 1885 Wilson began a three-year period as assistant professor of history at Bryn Mawr College, a school for women in Bryn Mawr, Pennsylvania. From there he taught history and political science at Wesleyan University in Middletown, Connecticut. Also in 1885, Wilson enrolled in the graduate school at Johns Hopkins University to study political science. He also published his first book, *Congressional Government: A Study of American Politics*. Educators, lawmakers, and students praised it as a definitive analysis of the federal government and its functions.

Wilson revised the book to suit the dissertation format and presented it as his doctoral thesis in political science. In June 1886 Johns Hopkins conferred the Ph.D. degree on him after he successfully defended it. But Wilson's education was by no means over. He continued to study various topics that formed important components of his study of relationships among nations as a preparation for his future work in promoting peace and understanding among them. Only Wilson, because he had identified his purpose in life, could understand exactly what he was doing. Also only those who were very close to him, like his wife Ellen and Robert Bridges, knew what he was doing, and gave him their full support.[15]

Wilson was committed to making the United States a major player in the arena of relationships among nations. At this time relationships between Russia and Japan were deteriorating rapidly because of their efforts to sustain their own national interests in Korea. In 1889 Wilson published *The State*, a textbook in comparative government. The book was considered Wilson's most important scholarly work. It was also the main reason why the board of trustees at Princeton University invited him in 1890 to join the faculty as professor of jurisprudence and political economy. Wilson was on his way to becoming a national political figure.[16]

As professor Wilson helped make Princeton University a leading institution of higher learning in the country, competing with the existing major universities of the time, such as Harvard, where, since 1869, Charles Eliot was taking pride in its founding in 1636 and was trying to make it a model university in the world. Wilson's own alma mater, Johns Hopkins, made famous by the attendance of John Dewey who received his Ph.D. from there, was also on the rise. Yale, chartered in 1701 as the third oldest university in the country after Harvard and William and Mary (chartered in 1692), was also making claims of being a leading university in the country. Wilson's articulate lectures, his personality, his innovative approach to teaching and scholarship helped transform Princeton into an institution that was greatly admired by other universities. The quality of work that Princeton was offering became the admired example and the envy of other universities in the country.

Wilson knew that since its founding in 1746 by the Presbyterian Church as the College of New Jersey, to train religious ministers, Princeton was becoming an example of excellence in educational achievement,[17] and he was determined to make that achievement even better. When he was invited to be a member of the faculty at Princeton, Wilson understood the need to do nothing less than his best in seeking improvement in the quality of the courses that it offered to enable its students to play an important role in the development of the country. To the faculty of Princeton Wilson became an inspiration and example of a dedicated individual who was determined to make a difference in the work of a national institution.

Wilson was so successful as a professor at Princeton that on June 9, 1902, he was unanimously elected its next president. He had been professor there since 1890, a mere twelve years, which he used to build an unassailable reputation as a scholar and academic leader. In those twelve years Wilson had become the consummate academic professional person, the unquestionable master, with an undisputed understanding of issues that transformed a university into an institution of a rare kind. In his inaugural address on October 25, 1902, Wilson said, "We are not put into this world to sit still, we are put into it to act in a new age. We must lead the world"[18] to its salvation.

Wilson's success as a professor at Princeton University was partly because his education included two trips to Europe in 1896 and 1899. He always had a profound admiration for British people and traditions, especially its leaders over the years. Ray Stannard Baker concluded, "No studies delighted him as keenly as British history and politics. Many of his heroes were English—Burke[19] foremost of all—and his literary admiration centered upon English writers. Wordsworth[20] was the poet he admired most. His devotion to Shelley[21] and Keats[22] reached back to his ardent days as a student."[23] These trips enabled him to learn valuable things that later helped him in seeking solutions to problems of Europe when he assumed the position of national leadership.

Wilson's education, both formal and informal, was intense. For example, in 1892 he wrote his first definitive book on history, *Division and Reunion*, which was edited by Albert Bushnell Hart, professor of history at Harvard University. The book covered developments in the United States from the beginning of Andrew Jackson's administration in 1829 through the Civil War to the end of Reconstruction in 1889. Both Wilson and Hart realized that this was a very difficult period in American history to write about objectively, because there were serious sectional prejudices that stood in the way of unbiased scholarship.[24]

In a letter dated August 11, 1892, written to Horace Scubber, a close friend and associate, after he had completed the manuscript and was in the final stage of revising it, Wilson admitted that while he felt that this book had to be written it presented him formidable problems that he could not easily overcome. He added, "It took every bit of my time; from now till the moment our college term begins I seek a few days of relaxation to finish it, as it took all summer to write it."[25] There is no question that Wilson realized that sweat and toil are the price of success in scholarship. This is why the book was a great success.

## WILSON IS ELECTED PRESIDENT OF PRINCETON UNIVERSITY

Among events that placed Wilson in a position to play a decisive leadership role in both the United States and the world was his election as president of Princeton in 1902. The election came as a total surprise to the university community. No one had expected it, not because Wilson was not qualified, but because he was so successful as a professor that he had given no indication of his interest in the position of president. The man Wilson succeeded as president, Francis L. Patton, had served for fourteen years and wished to retire to spend more time with his family. He felt he had given Princeton University the best fourteen years of his life and that a new face should come into president's office to provide new ideas needed to ensure progress.

Patton was a seasoned professional and a brilliant administrator, a cunning diplomat who made an effort to understand each member of the faculty and his potential contribution to the quality of work that Princeton University was giving to its students and the community. He was thoroughly groomed and well grounded in democratic principles of running a university. Patton also strictly respected and practiced the philosophy of collective governance as an operational principle that gave meaning to Princeton and a sense of belonging among the faculty. He depended on the power of persuasion, rather than coercive action, to enable the faculty to see things the way he did, and blamed himself whenever there was disagreement. For these reasons Patton was a very difficult man to succeed. Was there anyone able to follow in his footsteps?

Wishing to preserve his legacy and protect the image of the university as a national progressive institution and the record of his accomplishment, and unwilling to take chances with the selection of his successor, Patton decided to play a major role in deciding who would succeed him. He kept a well-guarded secret of his choice until the last moment. For many months while everyone was speculating about who would succeed him, Patton had long decided who that would be. He did not discuss his choice with anyone, including members of the board of trustees that included former president of the United States, Grover Cleveland.

Suddenly, in June 1902, Patton announced that he was nominating Woodrow Wilson as the next president of Princeton University. He had not even discussed this with Wilson himself to make sure that he would accept the position if it were offered. At the same time he nominated Wilson, Patton succeeded in persuading John A. Stewart, a member of the board of trustees, to endorse the nomination and close nominations. Although David B. Jones, another board member, tried to raise questions about the procedure, Patton and Stewart succeeded in ending further discussion about the nomination and called for a vote. There were therefore no other nominations. This shows that Patton had considerable influence on how the board of trustees conducted its business.

In this unprecedented action Wilson's nomination and the action of the board of trustees in voting on a single nomination broke two traditions that began with the founding of Princeton University in 1746. The first tradition was that an ordained Presbyterian minister was always appointed president and Wilson was not.[26] He had not even submitted an application for the position. The second tradition was that there should be more than one name in nomination—usually there were three finalists—to allow discussion before a secret ballot was taken. Ray Stannard Baker concluded that in breaking both traditions the board of trustees was accepting Patton's suggestion that Wilson was an exceptional leader who, because of his outstanding ability and qualities, did not need to go through the established formal process and traditions of selection and that both Patton and Stewart had acted on this assumption.[27]

On June 25, 1902, two weeks after the process had been completed and Wilson was declared the next president of Princeton University, G. Bayard Dodd, a close friend of Wilson's, wrote a letter to him to express his support for the process that Patton and Stewart had initiated: "I never saw many men of many minds unite so promptly without debate, without hesitation at the mere mention of a name. When the ballot was taken I thought that there might be one or two blanks. But every man had promptly cast his ballot without consultation and hesitation, and when the vote was announced we all agreed that it was the act of Providence."[28]

Immediately following its decision, the board of trustees appointed a committee of four members, all devoted supporters of Wilson, to inform him officially that he had been elected the next president of Princeton University. The members of this committee were Francis L. Patton himself, the retiring president as chair, Cleveland Dodge, Cyrus H. McCormick, and C. C. Cuyler. The committee found Wilson at home and delivered the stunning news to him. Ray Stannard Baker concluded that Wilson was totally surprised to learn that the board of trustees did not follow the usual procedure of selecting a president.[29]

In the spirit of spontaneity that characterized the action of the board of trustees, Wilson responded in a similar manner. But the question still remained: Was he able to match his capacity with his skills? Patton would no longer be there to guide him and offer assistance in maintaining academic traditions that had made Princeton a great institution. At that point a group of alumni members and students escorted Wilson to the steps of Old Nassau, where he was wildly cheered and was called upon to speak. But he only acknowledged the enthusiasm with which he was being received.

Reaction of the outside world to Wilson's election was equally extensive. In New York and Philadelphia newspapers ran editorials praising Wilson as the next president of Princeton. The *New York Times* of June 11, 1902, ran an editorial in which it said,

The new president is a man of distinction. His political writings have made him already well known to the country and the world as a man capable of clear straightforward thinking upon the problems of government. His education testifies to his fitness for new responsibility. The duty of the college graduate to take part in public affairs is a trite theme of the orator and essayist. President Wilson's influence upon the undergraduate body at Princeton should be a high degree favorable to the working out of that ideal. Under his direction a new life, a higher fame, and a greater usefulness to the youth of the nation, the nation itself await the university.[30]

No one was more humbled by this positive response to his election than Wilson himself. This provided an environment that compelled him to rise above the level of an ordinary college administrator to make a lasting imprint on academic traditions at Princeton University. Wilson's star was rising faster than anyone could have predicted. The editorials about Wilson's election were not limited to newspapers in the North. The *Charlotte Observer* of June 12, 1902, ran an editorial under the title, "A Southerner to Preside Over a Great Northern School," and went on to say "the people of Virginia are proud of the distinguished compliment. Wilson is a Virginian through and through."[31] Edward Ingle, Wilson's close friend who sent him a collection of these editorials remarked in one of his letters, "Homer would envy you."[32]

In a letter dated June 28, 1902, addressed to her cousin, Florence Hoyt, Mrs. Wilson described the enthusiasm that was coming from different directions regarding her husband's election:

The letters and newspapers are both wonderful. As for the professors, students and Princeton people generally, the scenes here are indescribable! It is enough to frighten a man to death to have people love and believe in him so and expect so much. Yet on the other hand it is like going in with the tide. He is only the leader of the Princeton forces, and all this enthusiasm will surely be a strong power impelling the university forward. You know that he was unanimously elected on the first ballot—something unique in college history. One of the trustees told me that those 26 men had never agreed on anything in their lives before, yet in this they were perfectly unanimous. No other name was ever proposed.[33]

With each accolade that he received Wilson edged closer to national prominence.

In December 1906, barely four years after he was elected president of Princeton, Wilson faced a controversy that would determine his place in the history of both Princeton University and the country. He returned from a trip to Europe, where his ideas of a university were considerably sharpened, with insights of a prophet, visions of a poet, and the determination of a crusader to make Princeton University a leading institution in the country. He was not going to allow Charles Eliot[34] the monopoly of a dominating reputation; he wanted to have his place in the sun. He was therefore determined to work hard to place Princeton's reputation as a major national institution on a level where its programs and students were unique in every way.

On his return from Europe Wilson became more convinced than ever before that a university existed for one fundamental objective: to educate students and prepare them to play a major role in shaping the character of society. He concluded that any other purpose was secondary. He ordered the hiring of instructors of high academic qualification and personal qualities that enabled them to do their work well and to admit students with a clear purpose of coming to Princeton University. Wilson placed these conditions because he had seen a tendency among faculty members and some students at Princeton to emphasize social benefits as a more desirable outcome of education and he did not like it. How was he going to bring about change of perception of the proper purpose of education without being confrontational?

In adopting his position Wilson argued in 1906, "When the world is looking to us as men who prefer ideas even to money, are we going to withdraw and say after all we find we were mistaken: we prefer money to ideas?"[35] While Wilson was responding to the tendency to socialize more than to secure solid education at Princeton, he was also addressing the issue that some faculty members and students were promoting, the idea of establishing a graduate school away from the undergraduate establishment.

In extending his position about what he thought Princeton must be, Wilson was acutely sensitive to its implications for the country and the world. This strategy enabled him to see the problems of Princeton in relation to those of the country and the world. In utilizing this strategy

Wilson gained maximum experience that he would later need to confront problems of relationships among nations. Wilson offered three proposals to solve the controversy that was growing at Princeton.

The first proposal was that the curriculum should be reformed to allow maximum accessibility to an academic environment that would bring undergraduate students and graduate students together to share common educational experience. The second proposal was that Princeton should introduce a system of tutorial instruction similar to that he observed in Britain for all students. The system of tutorial instruction would allow both undergraduate students and graduate students to have common instructors who would be sensitive to their educational needs. The third proposal was that freshmen and sophomores should be housed together, juniors and seniors should also be housed together, and unmarried members of the faculty and graduate students should also be housed together.[36]

Wilson concluded that if these three proposals were accepted they would transform Princeton University from offering good educational experience to offering better education for all students, faculty members, and the entire community. They would also make Princeton a national institution of higher learning quite capable of meeting the needs of the entire world. Ray Stannard Baker concluded that while Wilson's interest in addressing problems of Princeton was primarily educational, his major objective was to serve the needs of the nation by providing trained leadership in critical areas of national development.[37] Wilson himself provided the example that was needed to chart a new course toward an endeavor to national greatness.

What one sees from Wilson's initiative is that he did not want to be part of a university that was degenerating into academic mediocrity. Either Princeton would elevate its academic standards to a new level of excellence or he would not be a part of it. Wilson was also quite successful in weathering the storm of controversy that started while Francis L. Patton was still president, when Professor William Magie led a movement for the kind of reform that the faculty had in mind. While Patton was opposed to that reform, Wilson took no part in the controversy. But after 1902 he could not remain uninvolved any more because he was now president. As president Wilson took an active part in seeking solutions to problems.

Wilson's involvement brought him into the middle of the controversy surrounding the idea of separating the undergraduate school from the graduate school. The controversy had been put on the shelf during the last few months of the Patton administration. Now that there was a new president, the faculty wanted it resolved so that students would know how to plan their study program and the faculty would know how to advise them. Wilson had already expressed his views in what appeared to be a compromise solution in form of the three proposals he outlined after his return from Europe in 1906. It was now up to the faculty to respond. But the faculty did not respond immediately because it did not wish to engage in new controversy as the new president was assuming office.

Wilson's willingness to learn new ideas about running a university had the effect of broadening his own educational experiences. Because of the skills he demonstrated in resolving problems Princeton was facing, Wilson was cast in the national spotlight. In an era that was looking for well-educated people to provide effective national leadership, Wilson could not escape the call to service higher than the presidency of Princeton University. For the next four years, Wilson captured the imagination of people who were searching for individuals to exercise national leadership at a critical point in the history of the United States.

Josephus Daniels summed up the world of Woodrow Wilson as he saw it in 1910:

"As professor and president, Wilson had become a prime favorite as a public speaker, often addressing gatherings of business men and public men, as well as educational bodies. His plain-speaking and dissection of evils, clear conception of remedies, and his original and clear-cut way of presenting his real views made him a leading figure among educators who felt the call to serve their country as well as their college. He had been speaking his mind since his graduation. The forum of president of Princeton gave him a national audience. Now the dramatic quality of his utterances, as well as his frank turning the light upon college problems, challenged public attention."[38]

## WILSON IS ELECTED GOVERNOR OF NEW JERSEY

Wilson's term as president of Princeton University extended from 1902 to 1910. In that period he served Princeton successfully and faithfully. Nothing had been done about the three proposals he had made in 1906 to resolve the controversy on graduate school and undergraduate school. These are the circumstance that, in July 1910, James Smith, former Democratic U.S. senator from New Jersey, and George Harvey, editor of the influential *Harper's Weekly*, took into consideration in reaching the conclusion that the Republican party had controlled the office of governor too long and that it was time for change.

In reaching this conclusion Smith and Harvey were aware that since Abraham Lincoln Republicans had always assumed the right to succeed him in any state or national elected office. But in doing so many federal officials were vulnerable to practices that compelled people across the country to question their principles. Josephus Daniels concluded that under the Republican party state officials in New Jersey were hopelessly placed in the hands of big business, especially the public service companies. At the same time the Democratic party had been out of power and there was nothing to stop the Republican party from becoming agents of privilege and corruption.[39] As public confidence was lost the people had two choices: either they would not care any more about participating in elections, or they would vote in new people.[40]

These were the conditions that influenced Smith and Harvey to suggest that it was time for change of party in the governor's office. On September 15, 1910, the Democratic party officially nominated Woodrow Wilson as candidate for governor of New Jersey. Wilson's wife, Ellen[41] was so surprised that she asked him if the two men were joking. Wilson responded by saying that he did not think they were joking.

Grier Hubben, a professor who had become Wilson's opponent on the faculty of Princeton University, was elected to succeed him, creating a new level of controversy on campus. Hubben had come to resent Wilson's popularity and wanted to redirect the programs that were associated with Wilson. Among the things that Hubben wanted to do was build a graduate college quadrangle on the golf links as a memorial tower to Grover Cleveland.[42] The tower can be seen for miles across the countryside. More than any other outward feature of Princeton, it became the mark, the symbol of Princeton University. During the next two months political activity in New Jersey centered on the quadrangle dormitory at Princeton University in an effort to put Wilson in a difficult political situation which he would find hard to explain.

The Republican party thought it had an issue suggesting that if Wilson could not handle and solve the problems at Princeton University, how could he handle and solve the problems of New Jersey? During the next few months that Wilson was at Princeton he was able to influence the direction that development took to the satisfaction of everyone. In the end, the issue that the Republicans thought would put him in a difficult political position turned out to be his advantage. His nomination for governor immediately changed the complexion of politics and put the Republican party in a difficult position, unable to match the caliber of Wilson and his superior knowledge of the issues.

On October 20, 1910, Wilson resigned from the presidency of Princeton University to run for governor of New Jersey. His campaign style convinced not only the voters of New Jersey, but also Americans across the country, that the country needed a new kind of leadership. New Jersey was about to end the monopoly of political power that the Republican party had exercised for many years. As soon as the election was over Wilson embarked on a major program of reform. Among the areas that needed reform were ending election of U.S. senators by the state legislature; having the state legislature pass a bill on primary elections; having county officials take office by election, rather than by appointment; passing legislation to allow cities to elect city officials.

During the next two years New Jersey experienced true democracy which it had not experienced in the many years of Republican monopoly of political power. Wilson did such a superb job that the Democratic party had other ideas about his leadership in a larger field. No one in recent political history of the United States was rising so rapidly. From this point on things were done differently from how they were done in the past. The system of patronage had come to an end. The people of New Jersey now began to feel that they belonged to a system that cared about them, and that they had a sense of belonging that increased their confidence in political activity.

What did Wilson have that was promoting his star to rise so fast? His nomination for governor shows a remarkable speed with which his political fortunes were rising, not only in New Jersey, but also in the country as a whole. In addition to winning the governor's race, Democrats also won the legislature. Wilson was the kind of governor that New Jersey and any other state, for that matter, needed to carry out reform. Josephus Daniels described the qualities that made Wilson rare in the politics of New Jersey, saying that his matchless campaign style, his honesty in dealing with issues, his ability to communicate his message to the people, his mastery of the problems were among the qualities that made Wilson unique.[43]

## WILSON IS ELECTED PRESIDENT OF THE UNITED STATES

Wilson was in the governor's office barely two years when the Democratic party thought he should be nominated for president of the United States in the elections of 1912. The reform that he had initiated so far brought him into the national spotlight at an opportune moment. In 1911, while Wilson was trying to settle in the governor's office and focus on his new responsibilities, conditions made him realize that he must answer a call for higher national service. In that year the progressive wing of the Democratic party was seeking a suitable candidate for president of the United States to replace William Jennings Bryan, who had lost to William McKinley in 1886 and to William Howard Taft in 1900 and 1908.

In 1912, not wishing to be regarded as a perpetual loser, Bryan supported the candidacy of Woodrow Wilson in the presidential elections. (Wilson rewarded Bryan by appointing him secretary of state.) Wilson had clearly become a candidate for president. He began to speak on national and international issues in a way that demonstrated advanced knowledge of the issues in a way no other candidate would match. Immediately he attracted the attention of the Democratic party and the general population of the country. Wherever he went he appealed to the people by the poignancy of his speeches, his knowledge of issues, and the manner of his deliverance of his message. His professional sharpness and articulation became the hallmark of a polished and dignified individual. Wilson was on the move.

Wilson was governor of New Jersey barely two years when dramatic events were taking place. Although William Jennings Bryan was considered an orator, [44] he did not match the level at which Wilson demonstrated oratory performance. Wilson and Grover Cleveland were the only Democrats to serve as president of the United States early in the twentieth century.[45] When the Democratic National Convention met in Baltimore on June 20, 1912, Wilson was not assured of the nomination because Champ Clark, a powerful speaker of the House of Representatives in Missouri, was a leading candidate and he presented a formidable challenge to Wilson. But when Bryan rose to say that he would not support Clark, he succeded in persuading delegates to support Wilson. On the 46th ballot Wilson received the nomination of the convention for president of the United States.

Wilson's nomination meant almost certain election because the Republicans were badly divided between William Howard Taft and Theodore Roosevelt. The main wing of the Republican party supported Taft while the progressive wing supported Roosevelt, who had succeeded William McKinley who was assassinated in 1901 and served until 1908 when Taft was elected. Josephus Daniels concluded that to see how Wilson was destined to win the presidential election of 1912 one must understand why Benjamin Harrison lost to Grover Cleveland in 1892. He suggested that because Republicans had been in office too long, Harrison did not offer Americans anything new; he took it for granted that since he had won the election of 1885 over Cleveland, he would win again in 1892.

Harrison's complacency is why Cleveland launched a vigorous campaign against him, offering new ideas exciting to American voters as the twentieth century was about to begin. Harrison's administration was therefore not very popular. While Harrison himself was one of the notable lawyers who had served with considerable ability as magistrate, he had a reputation of being cold as a politician.[46] He lacked ability to pay attention to detail and lacked vision to inject excitement in his approach to the problems that his administration had created or had not been able to solve. The economy was doing as well as it should have. But he failed to make plans to accommodate a demographic shift from rural areas to urban areas. He did not create facilities for education to meet the needs of the growing student population. Cleveland addressed all these issues and invited educators such as John Dewey, Charles Eliot, and William Harper to come forward and offer their ideas of what to do to plan for expansion in education. The election of 1892 was very different from that of 1885.

By the beginning of the campaign of 1912, Harrison's reputation as a cold individual, even though he was not running for the office of president, combined with the general reputation among voters that Republicans had lost the vision of Abraham Lincoln to offer an effective leadership that the country needed as it was entering the twentieth century. The split within the Republican party between William Howard Taft and Theodore Roosevelt further eroded the confidence of Americans in the Republican party in general. The frequent attacks of each other made Roosevelt and Taft look like candidates who had no agenda to offer to the country. Taft himself and his administration lacked popular appeal at a time of great expectations. In this kind of political environment both Taft and Roosevelt were steadily losing the support of people who had helped the Republicans win the elections of 1904 and 1908.

While this was happening Wilson and his running mate, Thomas R. Marshall, who had successfully served as governor of Indiana from 1909 to 1912, ran an effective campaign addressing issues that were of interest to voters: the economy, problems of urban development, educational facilities, and immigration. Although U.S. relationships with other nations was not an issue, Wilson and Marshall addressed it to enable Americans to understand that the United States must relate to other nations because it was part of the human family. They argued that the action that Roosevelt took in 1904 to mediate in the war between Russia and Japan was necessary to ensure that U.S. interests in the Pacific were protected.

However, during the campaign, neither Taft nor Roosevelt claimed credit for the construction of the Panama Canal because they were busy attacking each other and so denied Americans an opportunity to evaluate their candidacy in a manner that would have offered them an option. It turned out that Wilson and Marshall were outstanding candidates; if they were not, one wonders, what kind of national leadership would the country have for this critical period? Perhaps those who hold public office need to know that the interests of the country are far more important than their exchange of bitterness and quarrels.

One sees this practice during the season of primary elections when negative campaigning is clouded with slinging mud. When Roosevelt later admitted that he was implicated in the revolution that created Panama as an independent country from Colombia on November 3, 1903, so he could manipulate its new government to build the canal, the relationship between Panama and the United States deteriorated and the United States as a nation of constructive influence around the world was seriously hurt. Members of the Wilson administration were not oblivious to this historical fact. That is why there was need to develop a new approach to U.S. relationships with other nations. This is also why a new treaty was signed in 1978 between Panama and the United States, providing for gradual turnover of control of the canal to Panama by the end of 1999. But on December 20, 1989, U.S. Marines invaded Panama and arrested its leader, General Manuel Antonio Noriega, and brought him to the United States to stand trial for dealing in illegal drugs. He was convicted and at the time of writing this book, was in prison in Florida.

Perhaps one reason why Roosevelt and Taft did not claim credit for building the Panama Canal is that it was not opened until 1920. Wilson and Marshall ran a clean campaign focusing on issues important to the country and the world. A few days following their nomination, members of the Democratic National Committee and the candidates met at Sea Girt, New Jersey, to discuss the conduct of the campaign to make sure that it would go well. The committee found that the candidates had already outlined principles of decency in every aspect. There was some discussion about W. F. McCambs, who had been chairman of Wilson's prenomination committee. McCambs was considered in some circles of the Democratic party to be somewhat too zealous and aggressive in his pursuit of the political philosophy of the Democrats. After the discussion it was decided that McCambs would remain chairman of the campaign committee.[47]

Indeed, McCambs did so well in managing the campaign that he is credited with the Wilson-Marshall victory. Because McCambs suffered poor health immediately following the election, he requested Wilson not to consider him for inclusion in his administration. Wilson knew that in McCambs he had an efficient person who would have made a substantial contribution to the quality of service his administration was going to offer to the country and the world. As the election campaign progressed U.S. Senator Robert La Follette, Republican from Wisconsin, responded to Roosevelt's charge that in nominating Taft the Republican party was stealing the election by saying that no one had been ready to steal the election more than Roosevelt himself.

Instead of easing the tension that was dividing the Republican party into two opposing camps, La Follette's remarks did more damage, making both Roosevelt and Taft more vulnerable to defeat. On October 14, barely a month before the election, the entire country was gripped by a moment of tenseness. As he was recognizing the cheering crowd in front of a hotel in Milwaukee, Roosevelt was shot by John Shrank of New York. Although he was badly wounded, Roosevelt insisted on being driven to the auditorium where he spoke for an hour and half, saying that he was as tough as bull moose.

From that moment Roosevelt carried the nickname of Bull Moose. In showing respect for their opponent Wilson and Marshall canceled their scheduled appearances until Roosevelt was ready to resume his campaign after treatment and recovery. They did not want to take advantage of the condition of a stricken opponent who could not respond. Taft had long ceased to be a viable opponent. However, the assassination attempt helped neither Roosevelt nor Taft. Voters saw both men as being motivated by personal interests, rather than those of the Republican party and the country. When election results were known, Wilson and Marshall received 6.3 million popular votes, Roosevelt 4.1 million, and Taft 3.4 million. This translated into 435 electoral votes for Wilson, 81 for Roosevelt, and 15 for Taft. The presidential election of 1912 was therefore decided on that basis.

As soon as the election was over Wilson and Marshall went to work. They developed an agenda for action that covered essential components of relationships between the United States and other nations based on six principles:[48]

1. introducing a tariff system that did not exclude the United States from its proper role in the commerce and trade among nations by turning the U.S. government into the hands of special interest groups;

2. developing a banking and currency system that was based upon the necessity of the U.S. government to sell bonds in order to facilitate trade with other nations;

3. developing a national industrial system which placed no restrictions on labor and human freedom to engage in free enterprise to promote trade and commerce;

4. developing adequate agricultural policy and industrial policy to promote production of sufficient food to feed the growing population and products to trade with other nations;

5. developing adequate water supply to expanding cities, preserving national forests, and protecting ecological balance and the environment;

6. developing a system in which the government could respond to the needs of people in an emergency.[49]

## WORLD WAR I AND WILSON'S INITIATIVE FOR LASTING PEACE

At his inauguration on March 4, 1913,[50] Wilson said that the United States must remain alert and vigilant to events elsewhere in the world that might have serious impact on its relationships with other nations. He also said that the future of the United States in the industrial age depended on its relationships with other nations. It did not take long for events to prove that Wilson was right in his prediction. On May 7, 1915, a German submarine torpedoed the British ocean liner the *Lusitania*, killing 1,198 passengers including 128 Americans.

Naturally, this tragedy aroused the anger of people in the United States, who demanded immediate retaliation. Wilson concluded that such action would bring the United States into the war, which had been raging in Europe since June 1914. He resisted the pressure to take a rash action in response to the tragedy. Germany argued that while it regretted the sinking of the ocean liner, it was caused by conditions of war.

When, on February 1, 1917, Germany announced that it would intensify its submarine warfare, saying that it would sink any ocean liner of any nation including from the United States, Secretary of State William Jennings Bryan resigned in protest of Wilson's refusal to retaliate, saying in a letter to the president, "To remain a member of the Cabinet would be as unfair to you as it would be to the cause which is nearest to my heart, the prevention of war."[51] Wilson responded by saying that he accepted Bryan's resignation only because he insisted and that there was no hard feeling between them. But Wilson informed Germany that the United States would not tolerate any more action that might put its interests in jeopardy. He then persuaded Germany to refrain from any action that was bound to have serious implication on its relationships with the United States. Realizing the futility of his efforts, Wilson declared war on Germany on April 6, 1917.

Although Germany signed the armistice on November 11, 1918, bringing the war to an end, Wilson announced his famous Fourteen Points on January 8 as a basis of peace. While thirty-two allied nations participated in the negotiations for the peace treaty, Wilson, David Lloyd George of Britain, Georges Clemenceau of France, and Vittorio Orlando of Italy were known as the "Big Four" of the conference. But of these Wilson took the center stage as the principal architect of the conference. As he had done in the past, Wilson saw the world far beyond the peace treaty. He envisaged the world bound by a common value system similar to that the Treaty of Westphalia created in Europe in 1648 following the end of the Thirty Years War. He believed that for the good of mankind and themselves, nations of Europe would prefer to eliminate hostility toward each other to embrace a lasting peace.

Because Wilson considered the Treaty of Versailles[52] critical to the security of the world, he carefully considered the terms he believed should be part of it to end all wars in the future and so make it safe for democracy based on his belief "in pacific settlement of international disputes."[53] Wilson also believed that the security of the United States depended, to a large extent, on the security of the world. For this reason the United States must play a major role to ensure success of the Versailles Peace Conference. This is why he went to Versailles having thoroughly prepared to play that role. He was convinced that if the United States failed to play that role the world would fail to reach a lasting peace and war would break out in the future with severe consequences, not only for itself, but also for the United States.

Wilson's proposals for the Versailles Peace Conference were based on his Fourteen Points, which were an expansion of the six principles he developed at the beginning of his administration in 1913. As one reads them, one is reminded of his unwavering commitment to maintaining peace among nations. Wilson presented these points on January 8, 1918, during an address to Congress. The following is a presentation of these points. He called on all nations to observe them in the interest of peace:

1. Open agreements openly arrived at with no secret agreements in the future.[54]
2. Freedom of the seas outside territorial waters, both in war and in peace,[55] except in case of international action to enforce international treaties.
3. Removal of all economic barriers and establishment of equal trade conditions among nations.
4. Reduction of national armaments to the lowest point consistent with domestic safety.
5. Free, open-minded, and absolutely impartial adjustment of all colonial claims.
6. Evacuation of German troops from all Russian territory, an opportunity for Russia independently to determine its own political development and national policy, and a welcome for Russia into the society of free nations.
7. Evacuation of German troops from Belgium and the rebuilding of that nation.
8. Evacuation of German troops from all French territory and return of Alsace-Lorraine to France.
9. Readjustment of Italian frontiers along the clearly recognizable lines of nationality.
10. Limited self-government for the people of Austria-Hungary.
11. Evacuation of German troops from Romania, Serbia, and Montenegro, and independence guaranteed for the Balkan countries.
12. Independence for Turkey, but an opportunity to develop self-government for other nationalities under Turkish rule, and guarantees that the Dardanelles be permanently opened as a free passage to ships of all nations.
13. Independence for Poland.
14. A general association of nations must be formed under specific covenants for the purpose of affording mutual guarantees of political independence and territorial integrity to great and small states alike.[56]

One must make two observations about the Fourteen Points. The first is that in all his thinking and articulation of the terms of the conference at Versailles, Wilson thought in terms of the need to improve relationships among nations as a condition of lasting peace in the world. The security of the world became a stage on which he played out the drama of seeking better relationships among nations for their mutual benefit. He saw freedom of trade, free access to international waters, navigation uninterrupted by any hostility between nations as important conditions of peace in the world. The second observation is that Wilson promoted independence of countries that were still under domination by other nations as necessary to ensure peace.

## OPPOSITION TO THE VERSAILLES PEACE TREATY

As Wilson was succeeding at Versailles in promoting peace among nations, opposition was simmering back home about U.S. involvement in affairs in Europe. On March 26, 1919, Charles Evans Hughes[57] expressed opposition to U.S. involvement in Europe: "It is not the part of Wilson to create expectation on the part of the people of the world which the covenant cannot satisfy."[58] Hughes was expressing opposition to the formation of the League of Nations on practical reasons, he did not think that Wilson had the means to deliver what he was promising in the Fourteen Points because they were based on ideal beliefs that the League would be unable to honor. Wilson soon found out that opposition to U.S. involvement in the formation of the League was led by a conservative Republican U.S. senator from Connecticut, Henry Cabot Lodge.

By the time Wilson arrived at Versailles on December 13, 1918, he received overwhelming acclaim and adulation to such extent that "no such angel of peace had appeared since Christ preached the Sermon on the Mount because he had an opportunity to create a new world."[59] But when he returned home he found that Lodge was busy mobilizing forces of opposition to U.S. involvement in the formation of the League, an organization Wilson knew would ensure the security of the world including the United States. Lodge was opposed to the League for an entirely different reason from Charles Evans Hughes. Lodge felt that the United States had no reason to be involved in European affairs. When the U.S. Senate voted on March 9, 1920, to reject U.S. involvement in the formation of the League, Lodge's hand could be seen through the pages.

On July 10, 1919, Wilson went before the Senate to present the League of Nations as an organization that was intended to ensure the interests of the entire world. But the senators saw him as a U.S. leader who had lost touch with reality.[60] When Wilson saw the unwillingness of the Senate to even reconsider amendments to the charter of the League, he decided to speak directly to the people. On September 26, 1919, while he was campaigning for the League Wilson suffered a stroke and eventually died on February 3, 1924. He had been reelected on November 7, 1916. His death left uncompleted the work that had been part of his life.

## SUMMARY AND CONCLUSION

This chapter was intended to give an account of Woodrow Wilson as a person, professor of political science and history and president of

Princeton University, governor of New Jersey, and president of the United States. The purpose of this account was to lay the background that was important to his involvement in the formation of the League of Nations. No national leader in the history of the United States rose to national and international prominence faster than Wilson. This rise was not an accident of events, it was due to Wilson's clear perception of both himself and the world. He devoted his life to the creation of an organization that he believed would ensure peace and security of the world. He believed that without lasting peace, security of the world would always be threatened. The chapter began with a discussion of Wilson the man to establish a basis of understanding of who he was as a leader of a major university, the country, and the troubled world.

Wilson's legacy did not end with his death in 1924 (ten months before the death of a major political nemesis, Henry Cabot Lodge), it has lived to this day in form of the creation and maintenance of the United Nations. In spite of the U.S. Senate's refusal to ratify the League, today the United States plays a major role in international organizations that are designed to ensure peace and security of the world. Since the founding of the United Nations in 1945 the United States has been involved in events that are meant to ensure understanding and cooperation among nations. The crisis that developed between NATO and Yugoslavia in 1999 demonstrates this conclusion.

## NOTES

1. Josephus Daniels, *The Life of Woodrow Wilson, 1856–1924* (New York: Will H. Johnson, 1924), p. 50. Daniels served as Wilson's secretary of the navy from 1913 to 1921. He therefore came to know Wilson well.

2. Thomas Knock, *To End All Wars: Woodrow Wilson and the Quest for a New World Order* (New York: Oxford University Press, 1992), p. 15.

3. Ibid., p. 17.

4. Ibid., p. 18.

5. Gary Grayson, *Woodrow Wilson: An Intimate Memoir* (New York: Holt, Rinehart, and Winston, 1960), p. 17.

6. Ibid., p. 18.

7. Ibid., p. 23.

8. Woodrow Wilson to Robert Bridges, January 30, 1887, in Ray Stannard Baker, *Woodrow Wilson: Life and Letters* (New York: Doubleday, 1927), p. 2.

9. For a detailed discussion of what British national leaders of this Period did to serve the needs of their people, see Dickson A. Mungazi, *The Last British Liberals in Africa: Michael Blundell and Garfield Todd* (Westport, CT: Praeger, 1999).

10. Wilson to Bridges, in Baker, *Woodrow Wilson: Life and Letters*, p. 4.

11. Daniels, *The Life of Woodrow Wilson*, p. 28.

12. Ibid., p. 29.

13. Ibid., p. 30.

14. Ibid., p. 31.

15. Arthur Link, *Wilson the Diplomatist: A Look at his Major Foreign Policies* (Chicago: Quadrangle Books, 1957), p. 3.

16. Ibid., p. 7.

17. Dickson A. Mungazi, *The Evolution of Educational Theory in the United States* (Westport, CT: Praeger Publishers, p. 55.

18. Baker, *Woodrow Wilson: Life and Letters*, p. 129.

19. Edmund Burke (1729–1797), a social critic and reformer of major proportions is credited with a widely quoted statement, "For evil to continue all it requires is for good people to do nothing."

20. William Wordsworth (1770–1850) was a leading British poet of the Romantic Period of the eighteenth century.

21. Percy Bysshe Shelley (1792–1822) was another British poet of the Romantic Period.

22. John Keats (1795–1821) was also a leading poet of the Romantic Period. Among his famous poems is "A Thing of Beauty Is a Joy Forever."

23. Baker, *Woodrow Wilson: Life and Letters*, p. 75.

24. Ibid., p. 133.

25. Ibid., p. 124.

26. The author recalls that the practice of appointing ordained Methodist ministers as presidents of the many Methodist colleges and universities was quite widespread until recently. In this regard the Presbyterian Church and the Methodist Church had something in common.

27. Baker, *Woodrow Wilson: Life and Letters*, p. 129.

28. G. Bayard Dodd to Wilson, June 25, 1902, quoted in ibid., p. 130.

29. Ibid., p. 131.

30. *New York Times*, June 11, 1902, quoted in ibid., p. 131.

31. *Charlotte Observer*, June 12, 1902, quoted in ibid., p. 132.

32. Ibid.

33. Mrs. Wilson to Florence Hoyt, June 28, 1902, quoted in ibid., p. 132.

34. Charles Eliot (1834–1926) was a powerful and influential president of Harvard University from 1869 to 1908. His influence was felt beyond the corridors of Harvard. For example, in 1892 the National Education Association named him chairman of the famous Committee of Ten to determine the curriculum of secondary schools in the United States. The result was the release of the report that contained the Seven Cardinal Principles of Secondary Education.

35. Daniels, *The Life of Woodrow Wilson*, p. 80.

36. Baker, *Woodrow Wilson: Life and Letters*, p. 215.

37. Ibid., p. 216.

38. Daniels, *The Life of Woodrow Wilson*, p. 74.

39. Ibid., p. 96.

40. In 1982 a member of the Reagan administration, Ray Donavon from New Jersey, was implicated in a corruption scandal that forced his resignation in the same way the Republicans faced a similar situation during the time of Wilson. Although Donavon was found not guilty, he could not go back to his cabinet position. In his anguish Donavon asked a rhetorical question, "Which office do I now go to have my reputation restored?" When a state has had a reputation

of corruption for a long time, it is fairly easy to understand how people can lose confidence in public officials. Donavon was a victim of history.

41. Wilson's first wife, Ellen Louisie Axson, the daughter of a Presbyterian minister, was born on May 15, 1860. She and Wilson were married on June 24, 1885. Ellen died on August 6, 1914. His second wife, Mrs. Edith Bolling Galt, the widow of a Washington jeweler, was born on October 15, 1872. She and Wilson were married on December 18, 1915. She died on December 28, 1961, thirty-seven years after Wilson.

42. Grover Cleveland (1837–1908) was elected to his first term as 22nd president of the United States in 1884 and in 1892 as 24th president. He was on the board of trustees at Princeton University when Wilson was professor and later president. New Jersey was his home state.

43. Daniels, *The Life of Woodrow Wilson*, p. 100.

44. Bryan wrote three books that were considered great: *The First Battle: The Story of the Campaign of 1896* (1898), *The New Declaration of Independence, 1776–1900* (1900), and *A Tale of Two Conventions* (1912).

45. Indeed, since 1869, when Republican Ulysses S. Grant was elected president. No other Democrat was elected until Grover Cleveland in 1885 and 1892. After Wilson no other Democrat was elected until 1832 when Franklin Roosevelt was elected.

46. Daniels, *The Life of Woodrow Wilson*, p. 115.

47. Ibid., p. 117.

48. When the peace conference was held at Versailles at the end of the war in 1919, Wilson expanded these six principles into the famous Fourteen Points as the basis of peace in the world. The Fourteen Points are discussed later in this chapter.

49. Daniels, *The Life of Woodrow Wilson*, p. 129.

50. Franklin D. Roosevelt was the last president to be inaugurated on March 4, 1933, twenty years after Wilson. Under Amendment 20 to the Constitution proposed on March 3, 1932, and ratified on February 3, 1933, all future inaugurations would be held in January.

51. Daniels, *The Life of Woodrow Wilson*, p. 112.

52. When this author visited Versailles Palace in August 1971, he was fascinated to see the room in which the conference was held, the large desk on which this treaty was signed and the chairs on which the Big Four sat, exactly as they were in 1920.

53. Daniels, *The Life of Woodrow Wilson*, p. 273.

54. Wilson was among thinkers who rejected the notion of the balance of power, a practice of secret treaties that had contributed to war in the past and to World War II in 1939. He subscribed to a new thinking of collective security, which required agreement openly made in the interest of nations.

55. Clearly Wilson was thinking about the sinking of the *Lusitania* by German submarines on May 7, 1915.

56. Daniels, *The Life of Woodrow Wilson*, p. 291.

57. Charles Evans Hughes (1862–1948) served as chief justice of the U.S. Supreme Court from 1930 to 1941. He is considered one of the greatest jurists since John Marshall (1755–1835) who served from 1801 to 1835. Among the cases that the Hughes court decided was the *Lloyd Gaines* case of 1938 in which it ordered

the University of Missouri to admit Lloyd Gaines, an African American, into its law school, setting a precedence that culminated in the *Brown* decision of 1954. For details, see, for example, Mungazi, *The Evolution of Educational Theory in the United States*, pp. 125–152.

58. Charles Evans Hughes, Address to Anti-League Club (New York, March 26, 1919) quoted in William A. Widenor, *Henry Cabot Lodge and the Search for an American Foreign Policy* (Berkeley: University of California Press, 1980), p. 266.

59. Gene Smith, *When the Cheering Stopped: The Last Years of Woodrow Wilson* (New York: Time, 1964), p. 43.

60. Townsend Hoopes and Douglas Brinkley, *FDR and the Creation of the UN* (New Haven, CT: Yale University Press, 1997), p. 4.

# Consequences of U.S. Senate Rejection of the League of Nations

A Jew cannot be a citizen of the Reich. He cannot exercise the right
to vote, he cannot occupy public office.
                                        Article 4, Nuremburg Laws, 1935

## THE LODGE FACTOR

When Charles Evans Hughes expressed reservations about the U.S. involvement on the formation and operations of the League of Nations,
saying in March 1919 that Wilson was raising expectations among Americans that could not be fulfilled, he provided ammunition to some members of the U.S. Senate who were already waging a struggle against it.
Leading this fight was conservative U.S Republican Senator from Connecticut, Henry Cabot Lodge. William C. Widenor, Lodge's political biographer, concluded that Lodge himself knew that he was not a popular
politician, and his sense of values and virtue were readily recognized as
liabilities to the Republican party because they were rather extreme. Yet,
in spite of this awareness he exerted tremendous influence on the Senate's rejection of the U.S. involvement in the formation of the League of
Nations, to which Wilson devoted so much time and energy in developing as an organization intended to ensure peace and security of the
world. Widenor concluded that Lodge had neither the understanding
nor the desire to know the nature of the organization that Wilson was
trying to create.[1] His opposition was based purely on political ideology.

Lodge was also chairman of the Senate Foreign Relations Committee in a Congress that was controlled by Republicans.[2] Therefore, he exercised considerable power and influence in that position. Lodge also had two close friends who shared his negative views about the League of Nations and an intense dislike of Wilson. Both were Republicans: Senator William E. Borah from Idaho, and former President Theodore Roosevelt. When Roosevelt died unexpectedly of a blood clot in the heart on January 6, 1919, just as the Versailles conference was getting ready to start, Lodge and Borah felt that they had lost a strong ally for their cause. They had to reorganize their strategy.

It has been speculated that as a thoroughly partisan Republican who saw issues from a partisan perspective, Lodge would have supported the formation of the League of Nations if a Republican president had proposed or initiated it in exactly the same way as Wilson did. It is a well-known fact that Lodge intensely disliked Wilson and his entire program because he was a Democrat. Differences between Wilson and Lodge about the origins of the war in Europe and its implications for involvement by the United States easily led to established differences in political and philosophical arguments about how the United States should respond. Wilson argued that the involvement of the United States in helping to create the League of Nations would minimize the application of the old practice of the balance of power.

Lodge argued that European nations would use the League to expect the United States to ensure their security. This would cost American taxpayers large sums of money, putting severe strain on the economy.[3] Lodge concluded that the best way for the United States to respond to the end of the war in Europe was to do nothing about the League and let European nations deal with their own problems of how to prevent other wars in future. Wilson argued that any war in Europe was bound to affect the United States one way or another. For example, the sinking of the *Lusitania* in May 1915 affected the United States in a way that it could not ignore. Wilson concluded that it was better to take action to prevent a crisis before it occurred than to react to it.

While Wilson was willing to renegotiate clauses of the League of Nations to make it acceptable to Lodge and the U.S. Senate, Lodge himself was not willing to reconsider his opposition to it on any terms to reach a possible compromise. It was therefore evident to Wilson that no matter what he did to make the terms of the League acceptable, Lodge would still campaign against it on philosophical and political grounds. Therefore Wilson, unwilling to give up his vision of the world transformed by understanding and cooperation among nations, decided to fight for his beliefs. But in doing so he did not quite know how formidable an adversary Lodge was. As a matter of strategy, Wilson and the Democrats decided to run against Lodge in 1920 while Wilson himself was campaigning directly among the American people for approval of the League. Lodge was elected to the House of Representatives in 1886 and to the U.S. Senate in 1893. He remained there until his death in November 1924, ten months after Wilson's death.

There was no application of diplomacy between Lodge and Wilson as direct confrontation became the only form of relating they had with each other. To strengthen his opposition to U.S. involvement in the League, Lodge posed three questions based on his political philosophy that he believed had relevance to the kind of policy he thought the United States should pursue: (1) What had started the war in the first place? (2) What caused the U.S entry into the war? (3) What was the purpose for which the United States fought in the war?[4]

Lodge did not accept the argument advanced by the British that the war was caused by German aggression, nor that advanced by the French that it was caused by Germany's deliberate act of disturbing what was known as "the Concert of Europe," an attempt to create conditions of peace based on mutual respect, understanding, and cooperation. Lodge also refused to accept Wilson's argument that the war was a result of social and political behavior in Germany that was seeking control of Europe in the wake of the Industrial Revolution.[5]

Understanding the character of U.S. democracy and wishing to operate under its principles, Wilson recognized Lodge's opposition to U.S. involvement in the League of Nations as part of the democratic process. But he could not accept that opposition as part of the U.S. policy. He also thought that Lodge's opposition was too negative to derive any meaningful elements for inclusion into the official policy, because it was nothing more than an expression of political opinion at a time when nations were being called upon to cooperate in building the structure of relationships among them for the benefit of all. One can see that these developments were leading to the conclusion that the two men were poised for a major unprecedented conflict of personalities and political ideology, a struggle of wills, a duel of principles in an effort to define what policy the United States should design and pursue to suit the needs of a rapidly changing world.

It was not possible to avoid this conflict as the battle line was already drawn and the combatants stood on opposite sides to begin the duel that was destined to shape the future of U.S. politics itself more than it would shape the future of the nation's foreign policy. There were no recognized official umpires, only cheerleaders: Republicans urging Lodge to brace himself for the fight he and they believed in, and Democrats supporting Wilson and reminding him that he had a mission to fulfill, a mission that would one day benefit Lodge's children and grandchildren. Widenor concluded that Theodore Roosevelt compared Wilson's policy and leadership to recognizing the causes of the Civil War all over.[6]

Robert Endicott Asgood concluded that no matter how much they might have tried to bridge their differences, Wilson and Lodge were too far apart in their respective views to be successful.[7] Asgood went on to add that the differences between Wilson and Lodge were fundamental to their individual perceptions, made what they were by their individual character and elements of their personalities cast in Republican and Democratic molds.[8] Therefore the two men realized that only the American people could decide the issues through the election process. But both men also realized that the election process took place only at designated times and that problems of relationships among nations did not wait until after an election.

## LODGE'S OPPOSITION TO THE FOURTEEN POINTS

In order to give substance to his opposition to U.S. involvement in the formation of the League of Nations, Lodge based it on the Fourteen Points. In the first place he expressed his views in a letter to Theodore Roosevelt that Wilson had the United States involved in the war on a totally partisan basis and that unlike any other government, his administration was arbitrary in its action. But, according to the Constitution, only the Congress can declare war based on the reasons that the president outlines. Lodge also concluded that members of Wilson's administration simply became a group of cheerleaders who were supporting an unpopular war in Europe.[9] Although this section of the book focuses on Lodge's opposition to the Fourteen Points in general, it also addresses the implications of two of the points—that agreements between nations must be arrived at in an open forum, and that nations must adjust their claims for territory and colonies to reflect the desire for independence among the colonized people.

Lodge regarded Wilson's conduct in the war as an arbitrary action which he must have known the U.S. Senate would not support. Therefore, Lodge concluded that the Fourteen Points, on which Wilson based the thrust for the reconstruction of Europe after the war, were equally unacceptable. Democrats were worried by Lodge making generalized accusations that did not fit the character and conduct of Wilson at all, because they knew that since his days at Princeton University he demonstrated tremendous respect for democratic behavior. Lodge was encouraged by Senator William Stone, Democrat from Missouri, who was among the first members of Congress to express opinion against U.S. involvement in the war in Europe. Lodge concluded that if this prominent Democrat opposed U.S entry into the war, then Wilson's involvement in the Versailles Peace Conference had no basis.

As Lodge began to focus on possible implications of the Fourteen Points, he wondered how they would be implemented to sustain U.S. interests in Europe. Since he did not see how this could be done, his conclusion was that because Wilson failed to explain how, he did not see their value, either for European nations or the United States. Lodge further argued that if Wilson failed to respond to the sinking of the *Lusitania*, how was he going to use the Fourteen Points to respond to situations that were just as serious in the future? How was he going to coordinate the implementation of the points in varying political environments that existed in Europe? He concluded that because, in his view, the Fourteen Points did not constitute terms of U.S. involvement in events in Europe, they were of no consequence to the interests of the United States or the League of Nations itself.

When Wilson released the Fourteen Points during a speech to Congress on January 8, 1918, the war was still going on. Lodge wondered how Wilson could spell out the peace terms of a war that was not yet over. In all his opposition to the U.S. entry into the League of Nations, Lodge did not have an understanding or vision of the future that Wilson, as a world leader, was able to project. Only a leader like Wilson was able to develop a national policy that was consistent with the needs of the world in the future. No matter how strongly Lodge believed that his opposition to the League of Nations was in the best interest of the United States, he was not in Wilson's position to understand the need to define the elements of a new approach to relationships among nations.

There is no question that Wilson understood the importance of embracing a new thinking about an emerging concept known as collective security, as opposed to the old practice of the balance of power that was recognized as a major cause of the war. Lodge was not even willing to listen to an argument in favor of the principle of collective security as a new element of maintaining peace in the world. Wilson concluded that in this regard Lodge was hurting the future interests of the United States and the world community.

However, it is important to focus on Lodge's opposition to the League of Nations based on his reaction to the Fourteen Points. He concluded that the idea of reaching agreements among nations based on the Fourteen Points was unworkable because their implementation would not result in treaties that would serve the interests of the parties involved; rather, they would create conditions that enabled them to place their confidence in their terms of reference. In that situation nations, including the United States, must depend on other conditions of the treaties that would emerge, such as confidentiality and trust to honor them in matters that related to national security. In those situations public scrutiny that must be part of the democratic process would be eliminated and governments would have to implement terms of agreements with other nations in secrecy.

Laurence W. Martin argues that to expose the special circumstance of a treaty to public debate while negotiations are still going on, which in a free society must be done, would hurt the interests that the treaty is trying to serve. Lodge took this to argue that Wilson's first point, demanding that negotiations between nations must be done in public would hurt the parties concerned.[10] Wilson responded by arguing that living in a democracy as he did, Lodge should have been aware that any government that operates in secrecy on any issues of national interest often has something to hide. His position was that it was better to take the kind of risks Lodge was discussing in doing things in public than doing them in secrecy because any secrecy does not serve the interests of the people.[11]

Lodge also took issue with Wilson's second point, stating that nations must honor freedom of the seas outside territorial waters in peace and time of war. He wanted to know what nations would do if the principle was violated just as Germany sank the *Lusitania* in international waters. Lodge saw the implications of greater conflict because this would be difficult to implement. He argued that Wilson's third point that European nations must make adjustment to their claim for territory and colonies was vague and so difficult to implement. Lodge argued that the rest of the points that Wilson presented were subject to the outcome of deliberations at the peace conference and so there was no need to address them in his peace package.

It is quite possible that Lodge might not have been aware that Wilson was trying to remove conditions that had caused war in the past. Since the conclusion of the Franco-Prussian war in 1871, from which modern Germany was created, European nations began to enter into secret military alliances and treaties that, in effect, caused wars. Otto von Bismarck always suspected that French desire to regain Alsace-Lorraine[12] might threaten the fragile peace in Europe. He therefore entered into secret alliance with Austria-Hungary, whose support he felt was crucial to the security of Germany. This secret alliance was one cause of the war of 1914. In 1882 Germany, Austria-Hungary, and Italy signed a secret treaty known as the triple alliance.[13] Like other secret treaties of the time, this alliance did not contribute to peace and security in Europe.

While partners of the triple alliance formed a powerful relationship that seemed to ensure their security, Austria-Hungary and Italy were not friendly to each other at all, they merely entered into a secret alliance that was intended to play the power game of political influence to sustain their own positions. The desire to initiate honorable relationships based on understanding and cooperation was not their primary motivation. Where would such a practice lead Europe? Wilson saw this as a serious threat to peace and security among the nations of Europe. Members of the triple alliance also quarreled among themselves over territory that Italy thought it should have. They also competed among themselves for the control of the Adriatic Sea.

While this was happening, Germany and Austria-Hungary did not know that by the time the war broke out in 1914 Italy had entered into secret alliance with France to form a dual alliance. As a result Italy remained neutral for a short time and then declared war on Austria-Hungary, making Germany's position far more vulnerable. This is the problem that Wilson saw to state among the Fourteen Points that agreements among nations must be reached openly.[14] Without holding a national position that placed him in a situation to understand these problems, Lodge simply did not know that what was happening in Europe was of critical importance to the United States and that it was in its best interest to influence the direction events were taking after the war.

Wilson also opposed secret alliances because they were the cause of conflict among nations, but Lodge did not seem to understand this in his campaign to stop the United States from becoming involved in the events in Europe and the formation of the League of Nations. After the formation of the triple alliance, nations of Europe found themselves at a disadvantage. In the case of conflict among them, Britain, France, and Russia would have to act separately, whereas members of the triple alliance would react together. In 1894, sensing that they were vulnerable to combined military action, France signed a secret treaty with Russia.[15]

This action means that only Britain remained isolated. It feared that Germany would begin to make demands on itself for concessions. In 1904 Britain and France reached an *entente cordiale* (cordial understanding). By the terms of that agreement the two nations became defense partners. When, in 1907, France succeeded in bringing Britain and Russia into a defense agreement with it, a triple *entente* was formed. By 1912 major countries of Europe had been divided into various secret alliances that did not contribute to peace and security in Europe. For the next two years relationships among European nations became seriously strained as the political environment they created became a tinder box ready to explode in hostility and conflict any time.[16]

Now that Europe was divided dangerously into secret alliances, each group opposed a number of other nations to strengthen its own alliance. In this environment any conflict between two nations would quickly involve all nations. This is what led to the outbreak of World War I. An example of dispute that had serious implications for Europe as a whole was the conflict that brought France and Germany close to war several times from 1905 and 1912 over control of Morocco, "the pearl of North Africa." At the same time Austria-Hungary had occupied former Turkish provinces of Bosnia and Hercegovina since 1878 and formally annexed them in 1908. Russia promised Austria-Hungary in advance that it would not oppose the annexation. In return Austria-Hungary agreed to give Russian warships permission to pass freely through the straits of Constantinople. But Russia could not get other major nations to approve its plan to open the straits to benefit its own trade. It therefore tried to save face by suggesting an international conference to resolve the situation that Austria-Hungary had created. When Austria-Hungary refused to attend the conference, a major conflict began to unfold on a European scale.

These were the facts that Lodge did not understand in opposing Wilson's Fourteen Points, with reference to his fifth point that nations should make adjustment to their territorial and colonial claims. After the fall of the Turkish empire the territory that it used to control became a subject of claim by European nations in their search for new territory to expand their trade. There was no ready agreement as to how this territory could be divided among competing nations. From 1875 to 1884, European nations went through what was known as the scramble for Africa, an intense competition for territory to secure raw materials that were needed during the Industrial Revolution.[17]

Realizing that European nations were about to go to war over territorial claims in Africa, Otto von Bismarck played the role of diplomat in convening a conference in Berlin from December 1884 to February 1885 because Germany, having come out of the Franco-Prussian war in 1871, was not ready to engage in a new war over raw materials in Africa. The conference set out conditions for the colonization of Africa, but those conditions created new conflict. Wilson was acutely sensitive to this situation, making it necessary to add it in his Fourteen Points. Lodge did not appear to understand the importance of this point. Indeed, each of the Fourteen Points addressed a situation that Wilson knew was likely to cause conflict in the future if it was not resolved.[18]

There were other implications of the practice of secret alliances that Wilson was fully aware of but which Lodge does not appear to understand. On March 13, 1912, Bulgaria and Serbia made a secret treaty dividing the territory they planned to acquire as a result of the victory they hoped to score in a war which they planned to provoke with the Turkish empire. By this agreement Serbia was to secure the greater part of Albania and Bulgaria the rest. This secret treaty created an explosive situation in the Balkans as a region. On October 8, 1912, Bulgaria and Serbia then coerced Montenegro to provoke a war with Turkey. Five days later, on October 13, full-scale war broke out between Bulgaria, Serbia, and Montenegro on the one side and Turkey on the other side. But the war was not limited to these four countries, the entire Balkan region was thrown into chaos simply because Bulgaria and Serbia had entered into a secret treaty for the sole purpose of provoking war.[19]

Although two conferences were held in London in 1914 to try to settle the dispute between these four countries, no adequate solution was found about the causes that had led to the war. As a result tension continued to rise in the whole region. In June 1914 Serbia learned that Archduke Francis Ferdinand, heir to the Austria-Hungarian throne and nephew of the Emperor Francis Joseph, planned to visit neighboring Bosnia that month. Members of the secret alliance planned to assassinate him. A Serbian nationalist, Gavrilo Princip, positioned himself to carry out the gutsy plot. On June 28, 1914, Ferdinand and his wife drove through the streets of Sarajevo and a Serbian nationalist threw a bomb at their car, but they were not hurt. The archduke decided to continue the ride. This allowed Princip to fire the fatal shot at the archduke.

Unaware that Serbia and Germany had signed a secret treaty, Austria-Hungary issued an ultimatum to Serbia that same day. But Serbia, knowing that Germany would come to its aid, responded by declaring war on Austria-Hungary. When Germany came to aid Serbia, Russia came to aid Austria-Hungary, and Europe was on fire as World War I started. Germany's use of submarines resulted in the sinking of the *Lusitania*, killing 128 Americans. When Germany refused to observe U.S. neutrality, the United States was left with no choice but to enter the war on August 6, 1917.

In November of the same year dramatic events began to occur in Russia. Czar Nicholas II, who had ascended the Russian throne in 1894, was losing the control he thought he had over his country. As a result of the war, the position of the serfs was rapidly deteriorating and massive starvation became the lot of the people. Riots and demonstrations led to a revolution. When V. I. Lenin returned in a secret train to direct it, few people knew that he had been persuaded by Germany to return to Russia to bring the revolution to a successful conclusion so that Russia could pull out of the war. That is exactly what he did.[20] This secret agreement between Lenin and the Bolsheviks and Germany became the basis of a secret treaty that Stalin and Hitler used to sign a nonaggression pact in 1936, creating bigger problems for Europe.

Lodge's opposition to the formation of the League of Nations was also based on what he saw as the irrelevancy of Wilson's last point that a general association of nations should be formed under specific covenants for the purpose of affording mutual guarantees of political independence and territorial integrity to large and small nations alike. Because Wilson presented his Fourteen Points nearly a year before the parties in the war agreed to an armistice on November 11, 1918, Lodge thought that Wilson was putting the cart before the horse. He therefore concluded that Wilson's action in doing this was tantamount to restoring Germany to its antebellum status, giving it a breathing space in which it could renew the war.[21] Lodge was not aware that Wilson was preparing for the peace conference in advance.

Lodge also concluded that once the United States entered the war under these conditions, without clear indication of victory on the part of the allies, he thought that Wilson and those who supported his policy would be guilty of a criminal act because a treaty without victory would constitute victory for Germany. What Lodge wanted to hear from Wilson was a statement of his intention to pursue the war until victory was achieved before he made any proposals for peace terms. Wilson argued that preparation for the U.S. participation in the peace conference took a lot of time to put the peace package together. Of course, Wilson presented his peace proposals after the war ended.

Several times prior to November 1919 and fearing that he might not have the vote to sustain Senate rejection of the Wilson initiative, Lodge introduced a number of amendments to delay the final vote. However, on November 19, the Senate rejected by the vote of 39 to 35 Lodge's latest amendment to delay the final vote. Following hours of debate the Senate took the final vote on the original motion on the treaty; 41 senators voted to ratify it and 51 senators voted to reject it.[22] Therefore, Wilson's initiative was rejected. This meant that the United States would not be involved in the formation and functions of the League of Nations. The efforts that Wilson had put into forming an organization he believed would bring peace and security to the world went for naught.

On that same day, John Maynard Keynes, a leading economist of the early twentieth century and member of the British delegation to the Versailles conference, resigned to write a book about the economic implications of the reparations that Germany was asked by the treaty to pay in war damages. Keynes also severely criticized the "Big Four," who played a major role in the conference deliberations, for their lack of understanding that the reparations would have dire economic consequences for the entire world because they would cause a rapid decline of the German economy to the extent that the economy of the entire world, including that of the United States, even though it did not participate in the League of Nations, would collapse.

## CONSEQUENCES OF U.S. SENATE REJECTION OF THE LEAGUE

To Wilson there was no doubt that the practice of secret alliances played a major role in creating causes of the war. Townsend Hoopes and Douglas Brinkley conclude that in 1920 alone Franklin D. Roosevelt, then a rising star within the Democratic party, made more than eight hundred speeches in support of the League of Nations.[23] Roosevelt based that support, not on the idealism of Woodrow Wilson, but on practical reasons. But as it became evident that the Senate was not likely to ratify it, Roosevelt began to lose hope. But to Lodge the Fourteen Points had no real impact in influencing U.S. policy toward Europe. The effects of the failure of the League of Nations began to be felt as soon as it was known that it would not function as it was designed and as soon as it was known that the U.S. Senate indicated its intent not to ratify it. Therefore Germany did not feel obligated to honor the peace terms specified by the Versailles Peace Conference. It is important to review briefly what these terms were in relation to Germany's responsibility.

The four outstanding provisions of the treaty included revised national boundaries, reparations, a disarmed Germany, and the formation of the League of Nations. Under these peace terms Germany lost the provinces of Alsace-Lorraine, much of Schleswig, Eupen and Malmédy, Silesia, Posen, and West Prussia. The map of Europe had to be redrawn (see Map 1). While the Versailles Peace Conference did not specify the amount that Germany was expected to pay in reparations, a commission the League appointed in 1921 determined that it should pay 132 billion gold deutsche marks or about $33 billion. But efforts to collect the payment failed because there was no enforcing agent. Efforts made in 1924 and 1929 also failed. At that time the world was in a depression and it was not possible for Germany to make the payments.[24]

## THE RISE OF HITLER AND THE NAZI PARTY

Consequences of the failure of the League of Nations started with the political and economic insatiability in Germany itself, caused by its insatiable hunger for land and power. In 1919 the people of Germany directed the national assembly, which met at Weimar, to draw up a republican constitution. The resulting new government provided for a president elected directly by the people and a ministry responsible to the lower house (the Reichstag). But the Weimar Republic, as it became known, was attacked by three opposition groups within Germany. The monarchists wanted to restore the German empire and reestablish the colonies it had lost in 1915 as a result of the war.[25] The Communists wanted a Communist dictatorship like the Bolsheviks were doing in Russia. The National Socialists (Nazis) demanded their own dictatorship and rearming of Germany for purposes of ruling the entire world. Without an international organization to influence postwar development, Germany was walking a slippery road to anarchy.

Although Friedrich Ebert was elected the first president of the Weimar Republic, to be followed in 1925 by Field Marshall Paul von Hindenburg,[26] who favored the old monarchy, Germany suffered from a severe inflation related to its preparation to pay reparations and as the parties continued to struggle for power. They showed no concern for the welfare of the people or the future of the country as a small group of men started the Nazi party in Munich in 1919. Adolf Hitler joined it in that year and quickly rose to the top position of its leadership. He immediately showed his disrespect for the Treaty of Versailles, especially the provision limiting the German armed forces to 100,000 men. The Nazi party also tore

Map 1. Europe After World War I

the treaty itself to pieces. Germany was on its way to dictatorship by the Nazis under Hitler's leadership. Could the Weimar Republic survive without support from the League of Nations? Because the League could not fulfill its functions without the membership and support of the United States, the Nazi party did not care what the League did. Without the involvement of the United States, the League was crippled from the start, giving the Nazis a blank check to do what they elected to do.[27] Four years later, in October 1929, the prediction that John Maynard Keynes had made in 1919, even though Germany had not paid much of the reparations, came true with the collapse of Wall Street. The world was in an unprecedented economic depression.

Other events relative to activity in Germany quickly began to show that the absence of the United States from involvement in the functions of the League of Nations led to major crises in relationships among nations. In January 1932, when Paul von Hindenburg was elected president, the Nazi party was rapidly building itself as a political machine to control the destiny of Germany and its people. Feeling the pressure to come to terms with the Nazi party, von Hindenburg invited Adolf Hitler to serve as chancellor, a position, according to the constitutional provision of the Weimar Republic, similar to that of prime minister. At first Hitler responded to the invitation by saying that he and his party would not accept positions in the government unless they took control entirely. Von Hindenburg relented and that was all the Nazi party needed to assume dictatorial power in Germany. When von Hindenburg died in August 1934, Hitler abolished the title of president and created for himself a new title, *fuehrer* (leader). He had a definite purpose in assuming this title: to demand that every one take an oath of allegiance to him personally.

## THE NUREMBERG LAWS

On September 15, 1935, the Nazi party introduced what were known as the Nuremberg Laws to deprive Jews of their German citizenship. The prejudice that von Hindenburg first expressed against them at the end of World War I now took ominous and powerful dimensions. As non-citizens Jews were not allowed to marry non-Jews or to hold positions in the civil service or any branch of the government, or to practice law or medicine, or to work as journalists, actors, teachers, or farmers. In short, Jews were denied an opportunity to earn a living. Article 4 of the Nuremberg Laws clearly stated, "A Jew cannot be a citizen of the Reich. He cannot exercise the right to vote, he cannot occupy public office."[28] Louis L. Snyder concluded that within a year after the promulgation of these laws at least 50 percent of the Jews were unemployed.[29]

If the U.S. Senate had ratified the League of Nations it would have been possible to warn Germany that the Nuremberg Laws were clearly in violation of human rights and, if implemented, would result in severe consequences for Germany itself. Or an appropriate agent of the League would have raised a red flag to suggest to the Nazi party that these laws were unacceptable to the international community because they were an assault to human dignity.

The Nuremberg Laws defined a Jew as any of the following: (1) an individual who was descended from two full-Jewish grandparents,[30] or (2) if he was a member of the Jewish religious community, or joined a

Jewish community, or (3) he was married or planned to marry a person of Jewish faith, or (4) he was the issue from a marriage with a Jew, or (5) he was the issue of an extramarital relationship with a Jew.[31] The Nuremberg Laws prohibited Jews from having any contact with non-Jews. Marriages that had already taken place were annulled. Business relations that had been put in place were made invalid. Jews were not allowed to display national colors, and severe penalty was meted out on those who violated these laws.

From the time that the international community knew that the United States was not going to be involved in the formation and functions of the League of Nations, some nations adopted an aggressive attitude and policy in developing relationships with other nations. For example, in 1931 Japan began to plan a military invasion of Manchuria to remove Chinese influence and establish its own influence by bringing the Manchu dynasty to an end. The League of Nations responded to the Japanese invasion of Manchuria by imposing economic sanctions. But without the involvement of the United States, the sanctions were totally ineffective. In 1937, feeling no ill-effect of economic sanctions, Japan invaded China, paving way for a major conflict that rapidly engulfed the world in September 1939.

In 1936 and 1937 Japan signed anti-Communist treaties with Nazi Germany and Fascist Italy making them the Axis powers. It is not clear what brought them together, perhaps their common dislike of democratic values and their blatant violation of human rights, as well as the fact that they were trying to weaken further the U.S. position in its efforts to promote fundamental concern for the welfare of people in all countries. In 1937, feeling that it was secure in the secret treaties it had signed, Japan bombed and sank a U.S. gunboat, the *Ponay*, in the Yangtze River. Although Japan apologized to the United States and agreed to pay $2 million in damages, relationships between Japan and the United States were damaged beyond repair. From this point on it was a question of time before the two nations went to war.

When, on December 7, 1941 (a day that President Franklin D. Roosevelt said would live in infamy), Japan launched a surprise attack on Pearl Harbor, the United States was left with no choice but to enter the war, which finally ended with the use of the atomic bomb over Hiroshima and Nagasaki in August 1945. In 1935 Joseph Stalin tried unsuccessfully to negotiate a treaty with France and Britain in order to ensure Russia's defense against Hitler, who, in 1936 would reach a secret agreement with Francisco Franco of Spain.

When Franco launched a revolution in Spain, Hitler immediately came to his assistance, making it possible to establish a dictatorship that lasted nearly fifty years. In the same year, 1935, Benito Mussolini, seeing that the League of Nations was unlikely to intervene, just as it had failed to intervene when Japan invaded Manchuria, ordered his troops to launch an invasion of Ethiopia. Although Ethiopian forces fought gallantly, they were no match for the Italian forces. Mussolini proclaimed Victor Emmanuel III emperor of Ethiopia and occupied it until its forces were expelled in 1943 as a condition of World War II.[32] Although the League of Nations applied economic sanctions against Italy, the measures were not strong enough to force Italy out of Ethiopia until that time.

## HITLER'S INCREASING DEMANDS AND THE ROAD TO WAR

In 1933, as soon as he felt that he had secured the power that he wanted, Adolf Hitler began to formulate and implement a policy to provoke other nations and to destabilize relationships among them in order to expand his acquisition of territory. Although Germany was admitted into the League in 1926, Hitler withdrew from the organization as soon as he assumed total power in 1933. Immediately he designed the first stage of his strategy to conquer and rule the world.[33] It was a question of time that when the Nazi party started burning books, they would much sooner than later start burning people. A combination of two major factors influenced Hitler to make this initiative. The first factor was obviously the refusal of the U.S. Senate to ratify the League of Nations and Wilson's initiative for peace in the world. President Wilson knew that the absence of the United States from activities of the League would sooner or later make it ineffective in trying to discharge its responsibility to the international community.

The second factor is that Hitler saw himself as the savior of Germany and its people. As a result of this belief he demanded that all German people place their absolute faith in him. In carrying out his action he became an absolute dictator. He never sought the support of the people through the electoral process, nor did he pursue diplomatic ways of seeking solutions to the problems he was creating among nations because of his desire to conquer and rule the world.[34] The thinking that a national leader must seek to conduct the business of the nation in accordance with accepted diplomatic behavior did not form a frame of reference in either his thought processes or actions. Nothing would stand in the way of his desire to be the *fuehrer* of the entire world. This is why he saw Stalin, Mussolini, and Franco, men with whom he signed secret treaties, as nothing more than surrogates or subordinates who were paving the way for his grand entry into the arena of new geopolitics in which he would rule supreme.[35]

The world began to see Hitler's aberrant behavior in the formation of the National Social German Workers party (Nazis) in 1919. Nazi party members shared a belief in the supremacy of the German people, an

Aryan race. The Nazi party also worked to strengthen German military forces in order to bring the entire world under German control. When Hitler was appointed chancellor on January 30, 1933, he began to behave by the basic belief in German superiority. He then began to make demands for territory and provoke Britain, France, and Russia into confrontational politics.[36] In 1936 he sent his troops to occupy the Rhineland. In 1938 he seized Austria and annexed it to Germany.

On September 12, 1938, Hitler announced that he wanted self-determination for all the Sudeten Germans in Czechoslovakia, claiming that they were persecuted by the Czechs. Hitler claiming that Germans were being persecuted? One might as well believe the hyena saying that he would ensure the safety of a lamb that he is baby-sitting. The real reason was that he wanted to use this territory as part of his strategy to advance his territorial expansion schemes. He then annexed the Sudetenland to Germany. This was done under the terms of the so-called Munich agreement, which was signed on September 29, 1938, by Neville Chamberlain of Britain, Edouard Daladier of France, Mussolini of Italy, and Hitler himself.[37] The agreement stated: "The Czechoslovak Government, within a period of four weeks from the date of this agreement, will release from its military and police forces any Sudeten Germans who may wish to be released, and the Czechoslovak Government will, within the same period, release Sudeten German prisoners who are serving terms of imprisonment for political offenses."[38]

Those who see the Munich agreement as an appeasement of Hitler refer to this provision of it to make their case. But what Hitler wanted to do is have more men to increase the strength of his military forces and more land to expand his operational base. Given the climate of weak relationships that existed among nations of Europe at the time, it would have been difficult to restrain Hitler from carrying out his schemes without the role of the United States. He also was greatly encouraged by the action that President Herbert Hoover took in suspending all reparation payments to control the depression. He also regarded the Lausanne agreement of 1932 to cut the German debt to almost nothing as a good response to his refusal for Germany to pay reparations.

By the end of August 1939 Hitler held all the cards, and now without an international organization to restrain his policy and behavior, there was nothing that any nation could do to stop him from launching his plan to conquer and rule the entire world. The failure of the League of Nations also gave him a blank check, all he could do now was to write in the amount he wanted. Although Hitler promised during the deliberations at the Munich conference in September 1938 that he would make no other territorial demands, his behavior quickly proved that he had no intention of honoring any agreement he reached with any other national leader except on his own terms. In March 1939 Hitler seized the rest of Czechoslovakia with no regard for the reaction from France and Britain. He and Stalin signed a nonaggression pact dividing Eastern Europe between them. What Stalin did not know was that Hitler wanted to use this pact as a strategy to launch an attack on Russia itself as part of his plan to expand his operational territory to sustain his objectives.

For Hitler the world was what is was by act of his will, not by the collective action of nations based upon bilateral agreements that had to be honored by every nation that was part of it. He considered himself outside the control of any international organization or law. He also regarded himself as the only leader the world ever needed. His word became law that was intended to affect every nation and its people. He played God by deciding who would live and who would die. He decided who was human and who was not. He decided how much each person was worth. He decided to create and recreate the world according to his own rules.

According to Hitler the world in turn must not be inhabited by those he considered less than human or by those he regarded as incapable of making a contribution to the structure of the power he wanted to exercise. He believed that the Third Reich was destined to rule the world for at least a thousand years. Because he believed what he thought he was, many human beings, including those in Germany, did not fit his definition of human beings or measured to be so by the scale he designed for that purpose.

It would be difficult to refute the conclusion that the combination of these factors formed the framework of Hitler's mind that, on September 1, 1939, he relied upon to order his military forces to invade Poland, triggering the outbreak of World War II. He made a fateful decision to what he was going to do to correct what he thought was the injustice of the Versailles Peace Treaty. But events soon proved that he went too far in his reaction, the kind of reaction only Hitler was capable of. He demanded the German people to give him their total loyalty and unconditional support, promising them what he thought he would give them in return: the entire world under German (meaning his own) control.[39]

The German crowds cheered him as their folk hero, totally unaware that he was corrupted by the dictatorial power that he possessed and launched a campaign to convert his search for power and influence for Germany into a search for personal power and glory. In the end what he considered to be the wrongs of Versailles fell into the background as he pursued the fulfillment of a purely personal agenda. He substituted the dictatorship of the Nazi party for his own dictatorship.[40] But on April 30, 1945, when he realized that Germany was losing the war, he took the easy way out by committing suicide and left behind the carnage he had created for others to clean up.

Beginning in 1934, when he was building the Nazi machine of terror,

Hitler was already busy depriving Jews of their citizenship rights. He ordered the operations of their livelihood closed or destroyed and began a campaign of terror against them. While some national leaders were doing everything in their power to promote understanding through educational development, Hitler was doing everything possible to discourage it, even among his own people whom he depended upon to carry out his schemes of destruction. In that campaign he was quite candid in expressing his disgust for education: "Universal educational is the most corroding and disintegrating poison that liberalism has ever invented for its own destruction."[41]

No matter how a national leader sees his nation, failure to recognize the importance of education for his people leads to national disaster. Alfred North Whitehead, a British mathematician and philosopher, warned of the consequences of failing to promote education for the common good of all nations:

In the conditions of modern life the rule is absolute, the race which does not value trained intelligence is doomed. Not all heroism, not all social charm, not all wit, not all victories on land or at sea can move back the finger of fate. Today we maintain ourselves. Tomorrow science will have moved toward yet one more step and there will be no appeal from the judgment which will then be pronounced on the uneducated.[42]

This sounds like Whitehead was talking directly to Hitler. One wonders how Senator Lodge would have responded to the developments of the behavior of Hitler and his Nazi party. Conditions in Europe at the end of World War I in 1918 and the beginning of World War II in 1939 certainly demanded the involvement of the United States. If Lodge had not led a campaign against U.S. involvement, it would have been possible for the United States to play a constructive role in stopping the carnage that Hitler and the Nazi party caused to create the conditions of World War II and the holocaust. No national leader who perpetrates this level of horror against his people, can find peace of mind. There is always a price to pay.

One must understand Hitler's behavior in the context of a disturbing phenomenon that emerged at the end of World War I in the rise of dictatorships. Given the social, economic, and political factors that resulted from the Industrial Revolution during the beginning of the twentieth century, individuals such as Lenin, Stalin, and Mussolini paved way for the emergence of more ruthless dictators that included Hitler himself. In Italy Mussolini founded the Fascist party in 1919 and imposed on the Italian people an equally oppressive dictatorship as *Il Duce*. In 1936 Franco led a revolution that overthrew the existing Spanish monarch and the civilian government and replaced it with his own dictatorship. This pattern was set for the future, even after the end of World War II in 1945 throughout the world.[43]

## SUMMARY AND CONCLUSION

This chapter has addressed consequences of the U.S. Senate's refusal to ratify the U.S. role in founding of the League of Nations. That refusal was led by a U.S. conservative Republican senator from Connecticut, Henry Cabot Lodge. Born in 1850 and a student of history, Lodge brought to the American political scene an interpretation of history that was incompatible with that of Woodrow Wilson, also a student of history and political science and president of the United States. One fundamental difference of political philosophy between Lodge and Wilson is the way they saw war and peace in the contemporary world and the role of the United States in it. Lodge held the view in 1919 that by instinct or conviction the United States had a duty to defend itself from foreign attack.

Lodge also argued, beginning in 1884, that the United States should not be involved in European affairs. Using his conviction that since Germany was created out of the Franco-Prussian war of 1870 it showed, by 1914, tendencies to define and pursue national policy that was intended to serve its national interests only in the context of the political environment that existed in Europe, and that the United States should remain neutral. He further argued that in the pursuit of its own national interests in the world, the United States must be careful to separate its own national interests from those that nations in Europe were pursuing.[44] Lodge concluded that if the United States was guided by this principle it was more likely to stay out of involvement in the affairs of nations in Europe.

Wilson's views were radically different from Lodge's. He argued that the United States could maintain its own in the face of conflicting positions taken by adversaries in Europe in the short run, but in the long run it would soon realize that the pursuit of its national interests would not be separated from the pursuit of national interests by nations in Europe.[45] He argued further that nations of Europe were motivated by the same ideals that they and the United States shared in common: economic development, desire to maintain social progress, and the need to strengthen democracy as a means of securing peace and cooperation. The United States could influence change in the environment from which nations of Europe could end the dangerous game of secret alliances and treaties that they were playing.

Wilson also argued that the maintenance of peace based on principles of fairness and common values, such as justice, integrity, and honesty in dealing with each other, must be developed on a world basis to have real meaning for all people. This is why Wilson argued in 1915, "The peace of the world can only be maintained by the force which United Nations are willing to put behind the peace and order of the world."[46]

In 1915, sensing that his opposition to the to U.S. involvement in the formation of the League of Nations might hurt the Republican party in the elections of 1916, especially when he became aware that Wilson might be reelected, Lodge appeared to have softened his opposition somewhat. He began to argue that the best the United States could do was mediate in the hostilities instead of being involved in the war. On December 10, 1915, Lodge rose to the floor of the Senate to discuss the effect of what appeared to be the opening salvo in the reelection campaign, a speech made by Senator Hoke Smith, Democrat of Georgia, who detailed the accomplishments of the Wilson administration from 1912 to that point.[47]

The differences between Wilson and Lodge were never resolved. That is why the Senate finally voted not to ratify the formation of the League with U.S. involvement. But the consequences of that decision were extremely severe for both Europe and the United States. Among other things, the birth of the Nazi party in Germany and the Fascist party in Italy in 1919, the invasion of Manchuria by Japan in 1931, the invasion of Ethiopia by Italy in 1935, the outbreak of the civil war in Spain in 1936, the sinking of the *Ponay* in the Yangtze River by Japan in 1937, a series of secret treaties signed in Europe beginning in 1931, and the surprise attack of Pearl Harbor by Japan in 1941—all happened because the U.S. Senate refused to ratify U.S involvement in the formation of the League of Nations. At the end of World War II the U.S. Senate had learned its lesson.

On August 25, 1999, the History Channel reported a postscript to the tragedy of history when it said that beginning in 1970 a generation of Germans born after the Nazi era had a fascination with Nazi memorabilia. For example, Hitler's signature was selling for $5,000 and Eva Braun's lock of hair was selling for $300.[48] Memorabilia of Joseph Goebbels, Hermann Goering, and other members of the Nazi party were also selling for thousands of dollars. This disturbing phenomenon shows that Germans born after the war never came to appreciate the tragedy that the Nazi party caused both the world and their own country. Perhaps it was the failure of their educational system to remind them of the horrors that are part of the history of their country. If anything needs to be done it is restructuring that education to reflect the reality of history.

## NOTES

1. William C. Widenor, *Henry Cabot Lodge and the Search for an American Foreign Policy* (Berkeley: University of California Press, 1980), p. 269.

2. One needs to understand that since Abraham Lincoln, Congress was con-

trolled by Republicans until Franklin D. Roosevelt reversed that trend in the elections of 1932. Up to that time a person who had political ambitions ran as a Republican and invoked Lincoln's memory to win votes.

3. Widenor, *Henry Cabot Lodge*, p. 271.

4. Henry Cabot Lodge to Henry White, February 1, 1920, in ibid., p. 271. The reason Lodge posed three questions was to show that the United States was not involved in the causes of the war and that it should not be part of a peace plan that was part of the war.

5. Widenor, *Henry Cabot Lodge* p. 273.

6. Ibid., p. 275.

7. Robert Endicott Asgood, *Ideals and Self-Interest in American Foreign Policy* (Chicago: University of Chicago Press, 1971), p. 263.

8. Ibid., p. 273.

9. Henry Cabot Lodge to Theodore Roosevelt, April 23, 1917, in Widenor, *Henry Cabot Lodge*, p. 279.

10. Laurence W. Martin, *Peace Without Victory: Woodrow Wilson and British Liberals* (New Haven, CT: Yale University Press, 1932), p. 51.

11. Ibid., p. 53.

12. Alsace-Lorraine, located in the northeast corner of France, had a history of causing dispute between Germany and France beginning in A.D 400. Following the end of the Franco-Prussian War in 1871, the people of this province were given an opportunity to decide through a plebiscite to be part of Germany or of France. Those who chose to be part of France were allowed to repatriate to France because the province became part of Germany. At the Versailles Peace Conference Alsace-Lorraine was reassigned to France, making the Nazis angry and they vowed to take it back and more.

13. Gordon Craig, *Germany, 1866–1945* (New York: Oxford University Press, 1978), p. 31.

14. Ibid., p. 33.

15. David Straightforward, *Wilsonian Idealism in America* (Ithaca, NY: Cornell University Press, 1884), p. 30.

16. Ibid., p. 40.

17. For a detailed discussion of this subject, see for example, Dickson A. Mungazi, *The Mind of Black Africa* (Westport, CT: Praeger Publishers, 1996).

18. Fenier Smith, *The Great Departure: The United States and World War I* (New York: Cambridge University Press, 1964), p. 10.

19. Arthur S. Link, *Wilson the Diplomatist* (Chicago: Quadrangle Books, 1957), p. 137.

20. Peter Jennings, "The Twentieth Century: America's Time," The History Channel, August 21, 1999.

21. Widenor, *Henry Cabot Lodge*, p. 275.

22. U.S. *Congressional Record: First Session of the sixty-sixth Congress of the United States* (Washington DC: Government Printer, November 19, 1919), p. 8571.

23. Townsend Hoopes and Douglas Brinkley, *FDR and the Creation of the UN* (New Haven, CT: Yale University Press, 1997), p. 9.

24. Ibid., p. 270.

25. Germany had several colonies in Africa which it lost in 1915: Southwest Africa (Namibia), Tanganyika (Tanzania), the Cameroons, Rwanda, and Burundi.

At the Versailles Peace Conference there was considerable discussion of what to do with these colonies. Some delegates suggested they be distributed among the Allies as part of the spoils of war. But Wilson came up with a suggestion that was finally included into the charter of the League of Nations' Article 22: "For those colonies which are inhabited by people not yet able to stand by themselves under the strenuous condition of the modern world there should be applied the principle that the well-being and development of such people form a sacred trust of civilization."

26. Von Hindenburg became a national hero when he designed a military strategy for defeating the Russians in World War I. But when Germany lost the war he blamed the Jews, establishing a precedence that the Nazi used to try to exterminate them putting more than 6 million to death.

27. Widenor, *Henry Cabot Lodge,* p. 512.

28. Louis L. Snyder, *Hitler's Third Reich: A Documentary History* (Chicago: Nelson-Hall, 1981), p. 212. On June 26, 1999, the *Arizona Republic* reported that original copies of the Nuremberg Laws were kept in the Huntington Library vault in California.

29. Ibid., p. 211

30. It is interesting to note that this clause was similar to the grandfather clause that was used in the southern United States during the struggle for civil rights beginning in 1957 to deny African Americans the right to register as voters.

31. Synder, *Hitler's Third Reich,* p. 213.

32. World Almanac, *World Almanac and Book of Facts* (New York: Funk and Wagnalls, 1996), p. 785.

33. Hoopes and Brinkley, *FDR and the Creation of the UN,* p. 13.

34. Ibid.

35. Snyder, *Hitler's Third Reich,* p. 113.

36. Ibid., p. 84.

37. Ibid., p. 291.

38. Ibid., p. 293.

39. Ian Kershaw, *The Nazi Dictatorship: Problems and Perspectives of Interpretation* (London: Edward Arnold, 1985), p. 17.

40. Ibid., p. 19

41. Quoted in William van Til, *Education: A Beginning* (Boston: Houghton Mifflin Company, 1974), p. 46.

42. Ibid., p. 421.

43. This author has detailed the emergence of dictatorship in Africa at the end of the colonial period. See Mungazi, *The Mind of Black Africa.*

44. Widenor, *Henry Cabot Lodge,* p. 221.

45. Ibid., p. 223.

46. Ibid., p. 228.

47. Arthur Link, *Wilson: Campaign for Progressivism and Peace, 1916–1917* (Princeton, NJ: Princeton University Press, 1965), p. 35.

48. The History Channel, "Mysteries of History: Hitler's Secret Diaries," TV Broadcast, August 25, 1999.

# 3

# Conditions of Education After World War II

We wish to reaffirm our faith in fundamental human rights, in the dignity and worth of the human person, and in equal rights of men and women and of nations large and small.
                                            Preamble to the UN Charter, 1945

## DEVELOPMENTS FOLLOWING THE END OF THE WAR

The end of World War II in 1945 altered the way people all over the world thought about themselves, their nations, and the world itself. The use of the atomic bomb to end the war ushered in a new perspective from which people began to view themselves in relationship to the use of technology. While the bomb ended the war, it created an entirely new political environment in which human problems were seen in relationship to military power as the only viable solution to the problems of conflict and relationships among nations. The bitterness felt by both the victorious Allies and the vanquished Axis powers transformed man's mental and intellectual ability into a new and dangerous thinking that "might is right." For the first time in human history, people came face to face with a dilemma: Which is more important, the utilization of human reason to resolve problems among nations, or the utilization of military power to sustain the notion of peace through strength?[1]

Although the United States had tested the atomic bomb in New Mexico on July 16, 1945, American scientists grossly underestimated the extent of the damage that the two bombs dropped on Japan caused. When the first bomb was dropped on Hiroshima on August 6, 1945, it killed 70,000 people and injured many more. It also left a radioactive effect that lasted for years. Three days later, on August 9, the bomb that was dropped on Nagasaki killed 36,000 people. The total damage caused by the two bombs was of such huge proportion to any weapon that had been used in the past that it surprised even the best scientists. That the world had now entered the nuclear age also transformed people's perceptions of themselves, their society, and the world in ways that had not been done in the past. What was man and human life in this kind of environment? Where would this enormous power lead the world? Did the presence of such a weapon mean security of the world or its potential destruction? These are the questions that went through the minds of people as they reflected upon the destruction caused by the two atomic bombs.

One question is obvious and is pertinent to this study: What did the introduction of an atomic military arsenal mean to human relations and relationships among nations? Nations saw this enormous power as the only modus operandi. The implications of this new situation were incalculable for the world as a whole. It meant, among other things, that the more developed nations became militarily stronger the more they exerted greater influence on the nature of the relationships between them and other nations.[2] Now, did this mean that nations were prepared to go to any length to ensure their military power as the only form of their security? For the next twenty years many national programs, such as social services, were either neglected or relegated to the process of building military might. The formation of the Warsaw Pact in May 1955, in response to the formation of the North Atlantic Treaty Organization (NATO) in April 1949, created a new system of alliances in which the cold war acquired new powerful and dangerous dimensions.

The promotion of socialism by the Warsaw Pact members as a new political ideology and the determination of NATO members to foil it also created a new environment in which relationships among nations were seen in the context of the ideological conflict that was created between NATO and the Warsaw Pact nations. The reality that came out of this ideological conflict is that nations, even those that could not afford it, were forced to align themselves with either of these military organizations to insure their own security. The system of secret alliances that had been the major cause of conflict in Europe before the outbreak of the war was being played out once more. While this was happening, nations continued to neglect the real issues of national and world security, such as social services, education, political reform, economic development, and trade. This means that although the war had come to an end, the decision to introduce new ways of thinking about military power in the nuclear age posed problems for humanity that had not been faced before.

## PROBLEMS OF RELATIONSHIPS AMONG NATIONS IN THE NUCLEAR AGE

The notion of military power as the only way to ensure peace among nations was not only eroding the application of human reason to resolve problems, but was also slowly transforming the atomic age into the nuclear military technology age. The frightening reality of this situation is that instead of limiting membership in the nuclear club to Warsaw Pact and NATO countries, nuclear capability was steadily being acquired by nations from the Third World.[3] How realistic was it, therefore, to expect that nuclear power would insure the security of the world under these conditions? Since the end of the war in 1945, nations have been increasingly thinking in terms of resorting to human reasoning to find solutions to problems of relationships among nations.[4]

To make this approach to the problems of human existence viable, nations began to believe that the development of education, quite different from what it was prior to the outbreak of the war in 1939, must become a major commitment made by all nations. The purpose of this chapter, therefore, is to discuss some features of educational development that in 1945 nations believed should form part of the new thrust for the reconstruction of a new world order[5] based on the application of human reason, understanding, and cooperation. It examines how the major features of education influence the thrust for national development of new thinking enshrined in the UN principles.[6]

## THE INAUGURATION OF THE UNITED NATIONS AND HOPE FOR PEACE AMONG NATIONS

The outbreak of the war in September 1939 was an event that not only changed the nature of relationships among the people of the world but also demanded an appraisal of old values cast in a new environmental setting. What was at stake was not only that the Axis powers sought to rule the world, but also how human relationships of the future would be determined and how social institutions would be designed to function in response to human needs. The use of the atomic bomb to end the war created new problems in relationships among nations. The confusion and fear of destruction by atomic weapons, combined with the concern of the victorious Allies about atomic weapons, posed new questions about the extent to which nations were prepared to use this awesome and destructive power to protect national interests. The fact is that the existing world had been altered permanently by questionable perceptions about the future. Instead of insuring world peace and security, the use of the atomic bomb compounded old problems and created new ones.

The world of 1945 was no more secure than that of 1939. Into what directions was it moving?

The challenge before the world was to review the situation as it was at the end of the war and set a new agenda for action to insure world security. Before nations endeavored to reshape the fabric of a new order in the presence of this immensely destructive power, they decided to engage in a collective effort to examine the past in order to understand the present and plan the future. As the war came to an end, both the victorious nations and the vanquished Axis powers decided to form an organization known as the United Nations (UN). But this must be seen in the context of several events that began to unfold between 1941 and 1944. Among them are two that deserve mention and a brief discussion. The first event is the Atlantic Charter of August 14, 1941, in which President Franklin D. Roosevelt of the United States and Prime Minister Winston Churchill of Britain declared, "We respect the right of all peoples to choose the form of government under which they will live, and we wish to see sovereign rights and self-government restored to those who have been forcibly deprived of them." The second event is the Dumbarton Oaks Conference of October 1944.[7] This conference worked out details to establish the United Nations in a climate that was needed for equality among nations. Following discussions that had been started in August, representatives from the Soviet Union, Great Britain, China, and the United States agreed on conditions for the founding of the United Nations. Meeting at Yalta in February 1945, Churchill, Roosevelt, and Stalin went further to define the structure of the proposed UN. They agreed to convene a conference in San Francisco to begin on April 25, 1945, to prepare a charter for the UN, mindful of the enormous consequences of the demise of the League of Nations in 1920.

Exhausted by the war, and unsure of the future, these four nations agreed to invite forty-one other nations to the San Francisco conference. By the time the UN Charter came into being on June 26, 1945, delegates representing fifty nations had signed it. With its ratification in October, the UN Charter was poised to alter the character of the relationships among nations. In 1946, John D. Rockefeller, Jr., believing in the cause for world peace, gave $8.5 million to the United Nations to buy the site it was built on in New York City. Construction of the building began in 1949 and, when it was completed in 1952, cost $67 million. The cooperation, enthusiasm, and support that came from all over the world suggest that the world community was now ready to accept the challenge of constructing a new world order.

The preamble[8] to the UN Charter was meant to ensure that all members understood and accepted their responsibility in this collective endeavor, as its drafters were quite sensitive to its implications for world peace and security:

We the people of the United Nations, determined to save succeeding generations from the scourge of war, which twice in our life-time, has brought untold sorrow to mankind, and to reaffirm our faith in fundamental human rights, in the dignity and worth of the human person, in equal rights of men and women, and of nations, large and small, and to establish conditions under which justice and respect for the obligation arising from treaties and other sources of international law, and to promote social progress and better standards of life in larger freedom, wish to practice tolerance and live together in peace with one another as good neighbors.[9]

The euphoria and excitement that were part of the response of nations throughout the world can be understood in the context of the hope they expressed for a lasting world peace. For nations all over the world this was a new day of hope that their people would not be subjected to political domination that had been their lot in the past. Some national leaders felt that the possibility of insuring a future different from the past was within their grasp, and a new collective effort would yield the results that would translate into a new world order in which the role of individual nations would not be viewed in terms of military might, but in terms of mutual respect because that was the goal to which the UN was committing itself.

But nations, big and small, powerful and weak, were not aware that the task of bringing about this hope was not an easy one at all. There were still lingering doubts that embracing the principles that the United Nations was now asking all nations to accept would insure their security. There were still nagging questions that this collective endeavor had not fully resolved. Would all nations rise to the occasion and identify themselves fully with the objectives and principles that the United Nations had enunciated? Would the victorious Allies give up their military dominance to embrace the concept of sovereignty of nations as an operative principle of equality between them? Would weak nations struggling for self give up their quest for meaning and military power as a means of insuring their security in favor of the protection of the values and principles of the United Nations under its aegis of collective security?

## ASSESSMENT OF THE PAST: CAUSES OF THE WAR

The excitement with which nations supported the inauguration of the United Nations and the hope that characterized their activity to map out a better future were tempered by the equally nagging feeling that in spite of the claimed commitment by nations to embrace its principles, conflict in the world was likely to break out again in the future. For this reason, the delegates assembled in San Francisco decided that, before they asked nations to embark on the collective task of reshaping the future, they needed to take a journey into the past to examine developments that had brought the world to the brink of self-destruction twice in the century. The belief that one must study the past to understand the present and plan for the future was a central component of their strategy. Painful as this exercise was, they felt it had to be undertaken in order to take all relevant dimensions into account in planning that future.

Addressing the 282 delegates to the conference from forty-six nations President Harry S. Truman, who succeeded President Franklin D. Roosevelt who had died suddenly on April 12, 1945, observed:

You members of this conference are to be architects of a better world. In your hands rests our future. By your labors at this conference, we shall know if suffering humanity was to achieve a just and lasting peace. We who have lived through the torture and the tragedy of two world conflicts must realize the magnitude of the problem before us. We do not need far-sighted vision to understand the trend in recent history. Its significance is all too clear.[10]

Of course, Truman did not refer to his decision to use the atomic bomb to end the war. This was foremost in the minds of most delegates, and they wanted him to suggest how nations were going to prevent a holocaust that this latest military technology was sure to cause in the future, unless they knew exactly how to prevent it. That Truman did not address this critical issue later haunted nations as they tried to structure relations between them in the years following the end of the war.[11]

However, the first step toward this encounter with the past was to make an assessment of what had caused the war in 1939. The delegates to the San Francisco conference went much further than accepting the popular view that the war was caused by the reckless policies of the Axis powers. They examined a broader field from which to understand human behavior in order to deal with all relevant aspects of their efforts to plan for the future in a more realistic and comprehensive manner. To do this they reached four basic conclusions regarding conditions they identified that existed in all nations as contributing to causes of the war.

The first conclusion was that ignorance, poverty, and greed often caused conflict among people. These three pillars of the negative monument of human weakness had often combined to create a climate of conflict, both inter- and intranationally. Ignorance of the needs and feelings of other people, of what it takes to build a peaceful and happy society, and of the conditions that controlled people of other nations often become a prime factor in selfish behavior. Selfish behavior itself leads to greed. Once one has the power, one can use greed to exploit those who are in a vulnerable position in society. Exploitation then leads to poverty of those who are exploited. Exploitation breeds resentment, and resentment eventually leads to conflict. The recognition of these three factors as causes of conflict means that mankind must assume the responsibility of eliminating them in order to create a new climate of peace.

It is ironic that coming out of the Industrial Revolution of the nineteenth century, ignorance, poverty, and greed were the very negative features of society that technological advancement was expected to eliminate. On the contrary, they intensified in contemporary world settings. The recognition by the delegates to the San Francisco conference that these negative features of human existence had been a major cause of the war meant that a new effort had to be made to eliminate them if the future was to be different and more meaningful than the past. But they fully recognized that they needed to employ new strategies to achieve this objective.[12]

The second conclusion was that nations and their people prior to 1939 failed to understand each other because neither their leaders nor their citizens were educated sufficiently to understand human issues fully or the conditions that controlled relationships between them. Remembering that up to 1939 educational opportunity was the privilege of a few, the recognition of this reality led to the conclusion that if nations were to avoid conflict in the future, a new collective effort had to be made to educate people, both national leaders and citizens alike, to help them understand their respective responsibilities in developing democratic societies. This endeavor required rethinking the objectives and content of education itself. Educational practices of the past had to give way to educational programs based on new theoretical considerations.[13]

This self-appraisal led to the recognition that one basic objective of education in the postwar era was to produce more rational human beings whose thought processes and behavior patterns were influenced by reason and rationality, rather than by emotion. This line of thinking was influenced by the ideals arising from the Age of Reason or the Enlightenment, and was based on the belief that educated individuals could become controlled by a rational thought process and therefore would be less likely to do anything wrong because their sense of what is right or wrong was much sharper than those who were not as well-educated. Among the prominent spokesmen of the Enlightenment was Thomas Jefferson, president of the United States from 1801 to 1809. Himself a well-educated man, Jefferson saw human behavior as a product of education, and he argued that society had a duty to provide education to elevate people to a higher plane of reason and rationality and so reduce their tendency to make behavioral errors.

Indeed, Jefferson so believed in the value of education in promoting people's ability to exercise proper reason and rationality that he felt it would liberate everyone from the timeless oppression of irrationality. He thought that with education mankind was poised to scale down oppressive forces and rise up to envisage itself for the benefit of society. In a letter dated April 24, 1816, addressed to Du Pont de Nemours, Jefferson left his mark on the importance of education when he argued the following: "Enlighten the people and the tyranny and oppression of both body and mind will vanish like evil spirits at the dawn of day."[14] This was, indeed, a testimony of a founding father of a nation struggling for self and a man and leader whose own experience had shown him that without proper education man and his society were always victims of oppression and tyranny, and that to educate people is to liberate them from the scourge that undermined their potential for greatness. Having experienced the devastation of the war, it is not surprising that the delegates to the San Francisco conference embraced this line of thinking in their efforts to ensure future world peace and security.

The third conclusion was that discrimination and prejudice based on race, gender, and religion had always been a scourge that marred relationships between nations and their people. While they recognized that Nazi efforts to exterminate the Jews was the ultimate manifestation of racial hatred and prejudice, this negative aspect of human behavior was found among all nations, although it was more pronounced in some than in others.

It was not until 1955, however, with the increasingly painful evidence of discrimination, that the international community concluded that society needed to make a new thrust to eliminate it. Nations such as Great Britain and the United States, which had often been considered the citadels of democracy and the beacons of freedom, suddenly found themselves at the center of controversy generated by the various forms of discrimination and prejudice. In 1944, Gunnar Myrdal, the Swedish sociologist and researcher, appropriately called the situation in the United States an American dilemma.[15]

The fourth conclusion was that governments prior to the outbreak of the war were run by exclusive elite groups that cared little about the conditions of their people. In the same way, the opportunity for economic development was an exclusive right of a few people. As the Industrial Revolution progressed into the twentieth century, the rich were getting richer and the poor were getting poorer. This reality still exists to this day. In 1967 the Otto Kerner Commission, appointed by President Lyndon Johnson to investigate why African Americans were in a state of rebellion, raised an alarm when it submitted its report saying that the United States was moving in two opposing directions, one white and rich and the other black and poor, and that if this trend continued the country faced a grim future.[16]

The delegates to the San Francisco conference took these realities into consideration in concluding that discrimination of some people, whether it was racial, religious, gender, or economic, was repugnant to the principles of national development and that it had to be eliminated by making efforts to provide equality of educational opportunity. Such programs as affirmative action and positive discrimination have been demonstrated efforts to eliminate this scourge in human experience. But the fact that discrimination has continued to exist in all nations underscores the importance of finding solutions to it, so that nations can put it behind them as they endeavor to chart a new course in their search for a *safari* to a destination of human fulfillment. This is the only viable means to national development and international peace and security. The recognition that discrimination and prejudice were the prime cause of inequality in society led to the conclusion that they were the basic cause of conflict both among people of the same country and among nations.

Indeed, in this collective self-examination, delegates to the San Francisco conference also recognized that there are other adverse effects of discrimination and prejudice which they identified as contributing causes of conflict in the world. They concluded that the practice that nations had been pursuing in regarding some people and their nations as less important than others implied that equality as a basic operative principle of social justice was reserved for a special class of people, and that those who were excluded from it were less than human. Those who practiced discrimination and prejudice neglected one important consideration—that is, discrimination and prejudice combined to form cancer cells that often destroyed the vital tissue of national life and depleted the most important resources that any nation needs to ensure its own development. Indeed, discrimination and prejudice have always been a manifestation of a sick and degenerate society. It is not surprising that delegates to the San Francisco conference concluded that extending equal educational opportunity in all nations was essential for global peace and security.

While the delegates to the San Francisco conference readily recognized that discrimination and prejudice have always been two features of human existence that have persistently retarded efforts toward national development and often cause untold misery, they did not have a formula to eliminate them. The horrors caused by the Nazi perpetration of discrimination and prejudice are only a small part of the evidence showing that a society based on these two adverse conditions, created by man himself, robs itself of the opportunity to build a progressive social system that enables its people to recognize the vitality and dignity of every person in it. Idealistic as they were in engaging in this painful rendezvous with the past in order to plan the future, the delegates were not aware that problems of discrimination and prejudice would continue to ravage the beauty and glory of the human person far into the future.

One graphic description showed the cruelty of discrimination and prejudice toward a young couple belonging to the untouchables in India at the hands of the upper class as late as 1990. After suffering from brutality and humiliation because of her social class, Kuchchi told her husband Dhanraj that she was no longer willing to endure the indignities and cruelties that members of her social class had suffered for many years. Arjun Singh, a member of the upper class, and also a local political lord, ordered the elimination of Dhanraj because he protested the humiliating treatment that his wife had received.[17]

The fact that this tragedy occurred in Uttar Pradesh, the constituency of the prime minister of India, V. P. Singh, underscored the grim reality that discrimination and prejudice are well and alive forty-five years after the decision of the San Francisco conference that they must be eliminated. That Dhanraj's tragic death did not invoke public outrage suggests the extent to which the people accepted discrimination and prejudice as a way of life. This undercut the hope of a new start in collective efforts to build a new world order along the lines that the San Francisco conference had defined. It is equally disturbing that the United Nations itself failed to take these tragedies to reaffirm the principles that it so eloquently defined in 1945. However, the reason for taking this high road to identify inadequacies in national programs as collective causes of the war was to prepare delegates to accept collective action to solve problems of the postwar era.[18]

The vote this world body took in November 1990 to sanction the use of force to compel Iraq to withdraw from Kuwait is in itself a tragic action and a violation of one of its sacred principles—never to resort to force to resolve conflict. Does this suggest that the United Nations is now reversing itself in suggesting that these principles were good only during the years following the conclusion of World War II? Must nations assume that they are at liberty to resort to military force to resolve international problems? Perhaps the United Nations needs to reevaluate itself and its goals. Perhaps it has outlived its usefulness. Perhaps it needs to redraw its charter to remove the overwhelming power that permanent nations in the Security Council have in exercising vetoes. What that veto power clearly shows is that some nations are more important than others. Nothing is more dangerous to relationships between nations than the belief in this notion.

Further, there are two frightening realities that one must understand about discrimination and prejudice. The first is that they can deliver a deadly blow against those they select for victimization. The second is that India is not the only country in the late twentieth century to endure this scourge. The resurgence of Ku Klux Klan (KKK) activity in the United States, beginning in 1978; ethnic violence in the Baltic states of the former Yugoslavia; the continuing tragedy of apartheid in South Africa until 1994; and the surge of racial violence in France and Great Britain in 1992 are all examples of the pervasiveness of discrimination and prejudice in the world today. Indeed, conflicts among ethnic groups in Africa and between whites and Africans in South Africa are a direct result of the application of the policy of apartheid.[19]

Elsewhere in Africa the situation is no better, as corruption by government officials, nepotism, and other irregularities have become the order of things. In a letter dated March 14, 1991, addressed to this author, a bright, hardworking, and ambitious student in Sierra Leone expressed the problems that he and other students in similar positions are facing:

You see, sir, in Sierra Leone education has become a matter of privilege, not of right for the citizens. Scholarships are only awarded to the children and relatives of top government officials or civil servants. A system of nepotism and corruption has taken over the operations of the government. Because I do not have a relative working for the government I have no means of continuing my education beyond what I have done. God only knows if I will ever have the opportunity I desperately need. The government has abandoned its responsibility to its own people, and we are paying the price. Sir, I need your help![20]

In a similar manner the conclusion of the San Francisco conference that discrimination and prejudice were a major cause of social conflict is evinced by the effects of apartheid on the inability of whites to see the need to end it and to recognize that while they might derive short-term political benefits from it, they were placing their own long-term interests and those of the country in jeopardy. The effect of apartheid on the people of South Africa is quite consistent with the conclusion of the San Francisco conference that discrimination and prejudice in any nation pose a threat to international peace and security. Since its official introduction in 1948, the policy of apartheid has victimized both its perpetrators and its subjects. The tragedy of this infamous racial policy is that those who designed it were unable to see the devastating consequences that it posed, not only for South Africa but also for the world as a whole. Where does this lead the world?

## PLANNING THE FUTURE: DEFINING NEW OBJECTIVES

The conclusion of the San Francisco conference that the development of education throughout the world was the only viable means to end national inequality and, thus, international conflict led to the hope that a thrust for educational development would help eliminate the problems that society faced: poverty and ignorance, prejudice and discrimination, and political oppression. For the first time in human history, universally human beings began to place hope in the realization that ending inequality of educational opportunity was within their grasp and that the future carried prospects for self-fulfillment. This hope also meant that

origin of birth, social class, and other considerations that had perpetu-
ated inequality in society would no longer be used to determine who
received an opportunity for educational development. The belief that a
little black girl of humble origin in a remote rural area of Africa and a
little white boy in an exclusive suburban neighborhood in a Western
society stood on the same and equal plane to launch their educational
*safari* represented the dawn of a new era that led to new endeavors to
realize new national goals.[21]

To make this hope a reality, nations began to make plans, especially
in three essential areas. The first was that because existing systems and
programs were insufficient to meet the projected needs of a changing
society, educational expansion must become a national commitment and
a high priority; the reason for this strategy was that educational development is essential to all other forms of national development. The second was that economic development was needed during the critical stage
of the new thrust for educational development to invest in it, but that at
some point in the future, economic development and educational development would have a symbiotic relationship. The third was that educational opportunity was essential to seeking an improvement in the
quality of life of all the people, and that it would enable them to play a
dynamic and constructive role in the political process.[22]

The thinking that popular participation in the political process was
essential to political stability as a condition of social development led to
the conclusion that this participation was not possible without adequate
education. Without political stability, a climate of national development
would not be created. This was how educational development made the
practice of democracy possible. The idea of political elite groups who
had controlled and exploited the dispossessed and oppressed masses had
to give way to a new thinking that political stability was possible only
within a national environment of popular participation under the principle of freedom of expression. This made educational expansion an imperative of the hope for the future.

The delegates in San Francisco conference also concluded that this rendezvous with the past, as an expression of hope for the future, would
have little meaning unless all nations took specific action in setting goals
and making concerted efforts to fulfill them. Among these goals we must
cite and briefly discuss six. The first goal was that nations must invest
in educational development with specific reference to seeking an improvement in the curriculum and making it comprehensive enough to
allow students to learn about other people in the world. It was believed
that knowledge of other people was essential to global peace and security.[23]

The second goal was for all nations to set 1960 as a target date for
achieving 100 percent literacy. The reason for this objective was that basic

literacy was the only viable basis of the development of the individual as an essential component of national development. The development of the individual manifested itself in a variety of ways that would constitute elements of national development. They include economic well-being, freedom of political expression, and participation in national affairs so that no group of individuals would have a monopoly on political power at the expense of other groups.

Indeed, nations of the postwar period began to realize the grim reality that the oppression that illiteracy imposed on the individual would soon translate into an oppression of the nation itself. Simply stated, this means that no nation can ensure its own development if its people are still in the grip of illiteracy. The generation of new ideas, the creative activity of the human mind, the ability to see oneself as an essential and viable element of society—all these emanate from an ability to envisage oneself. Literacy has been recognized as the touchstone of self-actualization. Without literacy any activity, mental or physical, would have little meaning to the development of the people and their nation. This was the reason for setting 1960 as the year of eliminating discrimination in all its forms, especially race, gender, and religion, throughout the world.

The third goal was to develop adequate educational facilities, such as classrooms, improved teacher training programs, and the supply of adequate educational equipment. Prior to the outbreak of the war in 1939, these facilities were totally inadequate or altogether wanting. The training of teachers was considered especially essential to providing adequate educational facilities. Moreover, teachers understood the purpose of education better than perhaps any other group, and they inspired their students with confidence for the future. They understood the problems of human understanding in general and the nature of relationships that were intended to improve the human condition. They sharpened their students' perceptions of both themselves and their world. Teachers in the postwar era were therefore expected to demonstrate unquestionable competency in discharging their responsibility to their students and to show a clear understanding of the importance of the dynamics of human relationships beyond the local level.

In order to fulfill their duties well, teachers need tools that enable them to function effectively, not only within the limits of an educational environment, but also with the expectations of society itself. As of 1945 teachers were expected to see the value of education beyond the classroom and to impart this—to their students and to the members of a larger community—in a way that it was understood to benefit to society. It was quite clear to the members of the international community that the tools that the teachers needed to enable them to do a good job were in the form of facilities. The responsibility for providing these facilities was not that of teachers, but of nations. This means that all nations were called on to do nothing less than their best in providing these facilities so that teachers could discharge their responsibilities fully.

The fourth goal was to extend educational opportunities to both men and women, boys and girls, on the basis of equality. The reality that, due to cultural traditions, some nations had a bias for educational opportunity in favor of men and boys had to be discouraged because, as the argument went, a nation with only educated men was like a cake baked on one side. The thinking that society needed both men and women to make progress suggested the need to end all forms of bias against the educational advancement of women. It also suggested that bias had to be eliminated in both education and society itself.

The fundamental consideration relative to the need to end all forms of bias against the educational development of women was that, as long as this bias continued, educational opportunity offered on the basis of gender would inhibit the ability of schools to discharge their proper responsibilities to their students. Besides, it would inhibit the ability of women to do their best and would psychologically condition them to believe less in themselves and their potential. Society has always paid a price for this negative traditional approach to the question of education. Now, the conditions of the postwar era demanded efforts to eliminate this bias.

The fifth goal was to encourage families to do their best to enable their children to go to school. In many countries of the world, it had been the practice before the outbreak of the war for parents to depend on their children to make a contribution to the family's economic well-being. It was stressed that parents must adopt the attitude that encouraging children to go to school was the best way of preparing for the future. This, combined with the commitment of national leaders to stress education, made it possible to plan for a future quite different from the past. Parents who had missed an opportunity for education now began to see its value for the future of their children in an entirely different way.

This dramatic change of attitude toward the importance of education was the ultimate manifestation of the critical assessment or appraisal of the meaning of the past to the present in order to plan the future. In Africa, this change of attitude toward education was fully recognized by the colonial governments. In colonial Zimbabwe, for example, a high-ranking colonial official acknowledged in 1961: "The rather apathetic prewar outlook of the African masses towards education was rapidly being transformed into a general and urgent realization that education was the essential tool for gaining a foothold in a competitive civilized world."[24]

For Africans, tragic as it was, the war had transformed their thinking from accepting the colonial condition as inevitable into questioning its assumed values. They now began to see colonial systems not as something that they had to accept in order to ensure their survival, but as institutions that entailed negative features designed to engulf their existence and which they felt had to be eliminated in order to plan the future. This realization created a new environment in which they saw themselves, not as mere caricatures of human beings that the colonial condition had made them believe to be, but as a group of people with a potential and resources that had not been tapped for the good of all. This new level of awakening was the beginning of the rise of African nationalism. Indeed, the world of 1945 was poised for an unprecedented quest for new meaning through educational endeavors.

The sixth goal was that all nations must initiate carefully planned campaigns to provide adult literacy programs. The conclusion that adult education was important was a result of the view that those who had missed the opportunity for education earlier in their lives must make a contribution to national development without waiting to complete their education in the way regular students were expected to do. The approach to the question of adult literacy was also an outcome of the belief that those who had missed an opportunity for education earlier must not endure the perpetual life sentence of illiteracy, because every adult person has a critical contribution to make to the development of society.

The idea that adult education was an integral component of the thrust for national development had a special appeal to the participants of the San Francisco conference in their efforts to pass a set of resolutions that would guide nations as they engaged in this collective task of planning the future. While the enthusiasm for this endeavor was embraced by individual nations, especially those struggling for development, its success lay in a collective effort to identify problem areas and to make plans to resolve them. The reality was that no single nation had sufficient national resources to successfully launch the campaign alone.

## RESPONDING TO NEW HOPE

To suggest that nations of the world recognized the importance of a new thrust for educational development is to conclude that they went beyond the level of raising hope for its role in shaping the future. They envisaged a world system of social justice based on the belief that equality of educational opportunity was the touchstone of a peaceful and secure world. But a number of things happened as a result of considering education as a panacea for all social evils. The very fact that nations placed their total confidence in education as the chief instrument of resolving all human problems posed risks that they did not foresee.

If education succeeded in this endeavor, then it would indeed become a panacea of all other ills in all of human experience and existence. But if it failed, it would dash the aspirations and hopes that they were trying to promote as the ultimate solution to all problems. In planning this undertaking, nations were not willing to consider the real possibility that they would encounter problems they did not anticipate. But for the moment, considering these problems was not something that they had to take into account, because the excitement of a new era was too much to offset the enthusiasm that was at the base of their thinking and action.

Among these outcomes was that parents began to encourage their children to go to school in the hope that education would offer them opportunities in a way that was not done in the past. By 1960, the year nations collectively set as a target date for achieving 100 percent literacy, enrollment, especially in the urban areas, had doubled. But still there were as many children who were denied admission because there was not enough room and facilities. It is ironic that the first sign of a new crisis in education in the world came as a result of the action of the nations themselves in raising a new hope for a changed world. Along with the dramatic increase in enrollment came a dramatic increase in population itself. This put severe limitations on financial resources needed to support the development of education. The following figures show literacy in relationship to total population as of 1990[25]:

| Country | Population | Literacy |
|---|---|---|
| Africa | 470,600,000 | 41% |
| Japan | 123,230,000 | 99% |
| U.S. | 247,498,000 | 95% |
| Soviet Union | 287,015,000 | 98% |

One major problem that nations encountered is that, in spite of the efforts they made to eliminate illiteracy, this scourge continued to handicap national development, which they had planned as the only viable means to a world of peace and security. That no country has succeeded in eliminating illiteracy helps explain how difficult the problem really was, and still is. In 1990 there was serious concern that illiteracy throughout the world was steadily increasing, including Western nations,[26] for a number of reasons, such as rising population, declining economies, inflation, instability in global trade, political strife and a lack of adequate strategies to eliminate it, and continuing conflict in national priorities.

There was yet another consequence of this hope for the future through education. Inequality, that dark spot on the trail of human endeavor, had persisted in various forms. In Western countries inequality based on race and gender showed no signs of abating. The efforts of the U.S. Supreme Court to end this form of inequality came first in the postwar period in 1954 in the famous *Brown* decision.[27] That racial inequality has persisted in the United States, a nation that espouses the philosophy of equal opportunity for all people as a central tenet of its social system, suggests the critical nature of this problem. That in recent years problems of racial inequality have resurfaced in Europe, especially in Britain and France, explains the inability of nations to resolve one of the fundamental issues delegates in San Francisco identified as essential to national efforts to map out a strategy of dealing with inequality in the world.

Indeed, one of the most notorious examples of racial inequality is the system of apartheid in South Africa. Since its introduction unofficially in 1652[28] and officially in 1948, the policy of apartheid has caused a level and extent of bitterness rarely known in the history of mankind. The enactment of the Bantu Education Act in 1953 caused so much pain among the Africans that their education lost the meaning for which it was created. On this dimension of apartheid, Leo Marquard of South Africa wrote:

Such acts of parliament as the Group Areas Act, the Population Registration Act, the Immigration Act, the Mixed Marriages Act, the Extension of University Education Act, and the Industrial Conciliation Act, all discriminate between different racial groups in South Africa. While some provisions of these acts entail serious economic hardships, their main purpose is to achieve as much social and racial separation as possible.[29]

The South African parliament at Cape Town represented one of the most vile institutions known to mankind designed to ensure perpetual oppression of Africans. In 1953, Hendrik Verwoerd, prime minister of South Africa from 1958 until his tragic death in 1966, argued as the minister of Bantu affairs, which had responsibility for education of the Africans:

Native education should be controlled in such a way that it should be in accord with the policy of the state. If the Natives are being taught to expect that they will live their adult life under a policy of equal rights with whites, they are making a big mistake. The Natives who attend school must know that they will be the laborers in the country.[30]

By the time of the Soweto uprising in June 1976, apartheid had become a religion that was to guide the Afrikaners and the government of South Africa into a total and absolute belief in their assumed superiority and the inferiority of Africans.

Indeed, apartheid reduced black South Africans to the level of bare existence, presumed incapable of showing any positive attributes of being human. Until its end in April 1994, in spite of the stated intention of the San Francisco conference to end all forms of racial inequality in society, including education, apartheid continued to cast a long shadow in the endeavors of the world community to plan the future in a way that is different from the past. It is not surprising that South Africa has been paying the price of underdevelopment in more painful ways than other nations. Until 1994 when the government of South Africa[31] finally succeeded in removing this national scourge, South Africa continued to slide on the perilous road of uncertainty and conflict, denying itself an opportunity to tap the priceless human resources it needed in order to make national progress possible.

Inequality in educational opportunity based on gender was as pervasive as that based on race. Differences in ways societies have treated men and women have been the practice for thousands of years. From biblical societies and Greek and Roman cultures, through the Thirteen Colonies of North America, to modern societies, men and women have often been treated differently both in education and society simply because they are different.[32] At all levels of education women have not been afforded equal opportunity. The following figures show that women have received less educational opportunity than men[33]:

**Percentage of Women in Total Enrollment, 1965–1980**

| Region | Primary | | Secondary | | Higher | |
|---|---|---|---|---|---|---|
| | 1965 | 1980 | 1965 | 1980 | 1965 | 1980 |
| Developed | 49 | 49 | 50 | 51 | 38 | 47 |
| Developing | 41 | 43 | 32 | 39 | 27 | 34 |

The reasons given for inequality in education due to gender vary. Among them are that women are weaker physically than men, that they are less intelligent and less creative than men, that their real place is in the kitchen. It is true to say that educational inequality based on gender is more acute in developing countries than in developed nations.

However, the problems of overall inequality are as acute in developed nations as they are in developing nations. For example, the United States has had to resort to such controversial programs as affirmative action to end that inequality. By 1990, women in the United States, on the average, earned 65 percent of what men earned; this shows that, indeed, the United States still has a long way to go to eliminate this negative feature of its society. The existence of inequality based on gender in the United States also shows that this is still a serious problem for the world.

If there is an area of life in which all nations need to cooperate in order to find lasting solutions, it is in making a collective effort to end inequality based on gender. In many Third World nations, such as those in Latin America, Africa, and the Islamic nations, differences in the treatment of men and women in dividing educational opportunity are part of cultural traditions and are so hard to eliminate. The presence of allied troops in Saudi Arabia in 1990 made it possible to observe the extent of inequality that exists between men and women there. They learned, for example, that women are not allowed to drive cars and to have bank accounts in their own names without permission of their husbands.

That, in their enthusiasm to plan the future, the delegates to the San Francisco conference attempted to develop strategies of dealing with inequality shows how idealistic they were in seeking ways of eliminating a climate of conflict between nations caused by inequality. It was obvious by 1965 that disappointment was the consequence of a new hope. While the delegates to the San Francisco conference recognized the pervasive nature of inequality in both society and education, their inability to find a workable formula for its solution reduced the confidence of both the delegates and the nations they represented in a collective strategy in dealing with one of the most serious problems in human existence. However, failure to find a solution to this problem did not mean they would stop trying; it simply meant that efforts to find an answer be continued. The reality of the problems that all nations faced is that these problems were rooted in the cultural traditions that they felt could not be altered without threatening the fundamental basis of society itself. This is why many of the problems that nations identified in San Francisco have still not been solved.

## THE WILLIAMSBURG CONFERENCE: REVIEWING PROGRESS OF THE PAST

In 1967 nations felt that no sufficient progress had been made in solving the problems that the delegates to the San Francisco conference had identified and the objectives that they had set. They therefore decided to convene another conference to review the situation and to establish new goals and strategies for their implementation. Unlike the San Francisco conference, which included mainly government officials, the Williamsburg conference included politicians, civic leaders, educators, economists, parents, and interested individuals. All assembled in Williamsburg, Virginia, in October 1967 to assess the condition of education throughout the world and to decide what new actions must be taken to solve the many problems all nations faced. They did not think they should begin where the San Francisco conference left off.[34]

The Williamsburg conference was also different from the San Francisco and other preceding conferences in one important respect: it was not run on issues raised by conflicting positions of various papers, but on a single working document that had been sent to participants before they arrived in Williamsburg. The document centered on two basic issues: how to eliminate illiteracy and how to end inequality in both education and society. The conference approached both issues from a practical standpoint. With respect to the first issue, participants concluded that illiteracy had not been eliminated because nations failed to convince their people of the practical value of equality in both education and society. The feeling was that granting equality in these two critical aspects of national life would erode a system of social values and cultural practices that had been in place for so long.

The participants in the Williamsburg conference also recognized that nations had not made a concerted effort to solve the problems they were facing. This is why they recommended that nations intensify their efforts to demonstrate that extending equality and eliminating illiteracy were both essential to national progress. One method of seeking to accomplish this fundamental objective was to turn over the responsibility of education to local communities, where everyone was encouraged to contribute ideas for improvement. The logistical matters of running programs were also believed to be best handled at the local level.

But in this seemingly innovative approach to these issues of national development, the participants to the Williamsburg conference appear to have neglected a critical factor of their success—financial outlay—and that local communities were not in a financial position to discharge this responsibility. However, these local communities would be asked to keep records of all activities. As local businessmen and farmers, for example, would need to know how to keep records, they would demonstrate the practical value of literacy and so help combat illiteracy.

The Williamsburg conference also recognized that the change in demography and social structures—the migration of people from rural settings to urban areas in search of employment opportunity—made it necessary to acquire basic literacy in order to function in a new socioeconomic environment. This meant an initiative must be made to provide facilities so that local communities can pool their resources to combat illiteracy. The participants to the Williamsburg conference concluded that nations must increase their budgets for education in general and literacy in particular because it was essential to other forms of national development. In addition to placing emphasis on formal education, nations were encouraged to initiate new adult literacy programs to insure that no segment of the community was neglected. To make this investment would require a commitment to the thrust for a new start. Nations were therefore urged to make their economies stronger than they had been in the past.

The Williamsburg conference also concluded that educators alone must not be expected to assume the responsibility of seeking improvements in education, but that all segments of all nations should share the responsibility for providing adequate facilities so that education could serve the purpose for which it was intended. Industry, religious organizations, financial institutions, and private organizations must all cooperate in a national effort to fight illiteracy and inequality. Indeed, the conference also recognized the need to resolve a growing serious problem—that is, the inability of nations to adapt national programs to new conditions. Changes in technology, political thought processes, institutional structures, and industrial development all demanded fundamental changes in the way nations structure their educational systems.

To seek solutions to an increasing number of problems, the Williamsburg conference made other suggestions. The following are among them: Nations must cooperate more closely in the future than they had done in the past. Developed nations must offer their assistance to developing nations because it is in their own interests to do so. Nations must place education higher on the national agenda and allocate more finances than they had done in the past. Nations must recognize the importance of initiating innovation in their educational system because, "if it clings to conventional practices merely because there are traditions that cannot be changed, that system is a satire of education itself. From the standpoint of society, the resources invested in perpetuating such a system are misused resources because a higher proportion of students will emerge ill-fitted to serve well either themselves or their society."[35]

Indeed, the Williamsburg conference warned developing nations not to import educational systems from developed countries without making necessary adjustments to suit local conditions. Its members must have recognized that in their enthusiasm to initiate national developmental programs, developing nations erroneously equated the educational systems in developed countries with development itself. They neglected the reality that due to many years of effort nations had taken into account other important considerations, such as establishing informal education and eliminating rural-urban conflict, a major cause of underdevelopment in many developing nations. In realizing that the thrust for educational development must not be removed from the thrust for economic development, the Williamsburg conference fully acknowledged that manpower development was a critical component of this strategy.[36]

The importance of the Williamsburg conference is not in its accomplishment but in its representative character and its ability to articulate elements of a new start in the endless quest for new educational meaning. Its participants did not try to discredit the efforts of the San Francisco conference to come to grips with a very serious situation that the entire world faced. But, while it recognized the critical nature of this situation, the Williamsburg conference also failed to produce a magic formula to solve the problems that were being compounded by a combination of forces that the San Francisco conference did not envisage. But one must not conclude that the Williamsburg conference was a failure, because it was not. To attract people from all walks of life, to pinpoint the nature of the problem, to lay out the prerequisites of finding solutions—all these combined to enable the conference to make an indelible imprint on the crisis that mankind was facing in the struggle for self.

Indeed, the Williamsburg conference represents a fresh start in the human drama of survival.[37]

## SUMMARY AND CONCLUSION

In spite of the enthusiasm that characterized the approach of nations to education following the end of the war in 1945, there were a number of problems that had to be resolved in order to encourage national development as a prerequisite to world peace and security. The conclusion that the delegates to the San Francisco conference reached—that world security and peace were possible only if nations endeavored to give their people a viable education—signified the beginning of a new strategy to seek solutions to age-old problems of human conflict. While this strategy had a real potential, the inability of nations to make education what it should be translated into an inability to find solutions to problems of human conflict.

The exercise in self-appraisal that nations engaged in at San Francisco, painful as it was, was a gallant effort to put that thrust into proper perspective in order to ensure a future better than the past. Tragic as it was, the war itself was an eye-opener to the grim reality and reminder that nations faced a greater danger of conflict in the future than they had experienced in the past, unless they utilized education to seek a better understanding of each other in order to avoid conflict. The outbreak of hostilities in the Persian Gulf in January 1991 was a grim reminder of this reality. But, in order to make it possible for nations to understand each other, they have to make sure that they design educational programs that bring it about. Without resolving the problems that this chapter has discussed, it is not quite possible to eliminate the possibility of that conflict.

The crisis in education after the war in 1945 suggests that, in spite of the efforts that nations have made to solve them, problems of national development and international relationships have continued to intensify. By the time of the crisis caused by Iraq's invasion of Kuwait in August 1990, there was nothing to suggest that nations had learned the lessons of war. That many people in the Arab world accused Kuwait of amassing a fortune for the exclusive use by a few sheiks suggests the need to reevaluate the ideas the San Francisco and Williamsburg conferences put forward for discussing the thrust for education can be made anew to sustain both international and national principles that are essential to human development and peace.

## NOTES

1. Donald K. Grayson, "Human Life vs. Science," in Thomas Weaver (ed.), *To See Ourselves: Anthropology and Modern Social Issues* (Glenview, IL.: Scott, Foresman, 1973), p. 32.

2. The UN Charter provided for an extraordinary power known as the veto to five major nations to stop any resolution in the Security Council. These nations are Britain, France, United States, Soviet Union, and China. In this manner the five major nations have exercised great influence in the conduct of relations among nations.

3. In 1999 it was reported that India and Pakistan were poised for a confrontation over a border dispute that has been cause of conflict between them for many years and that each nation had nuclear weapons in its arsenal.

4. Grayson, "Human Life vs. Science," p. 33.

5. Indeed, on January 16, 1991, during an address to the nation, President George Bush argued that the reason the United States had launched an attack on Iraq for invading Kuwait on August 2, 1990, was to create a new world order.

6. This study avoids the use of terms like "international education" because there are variations in the educational process that do not define education in the same way either in its meaning or its intent and practice. What is important is for nations to design education to enable students to learn about people in other lands.

7. Both the Atlantic Charter and the Dumbarton Oaks Conference are discussed in considerable detail in Chapter 6 of this book.

8. Ironically, Jan Christiaan Smuts, the prime minister of South Africa, a country that would soon become notorious for its racial policy of apartheid, is credited with drafting the preamble.

9. Preamble to the UN Charter, June 26, 1945.

10. Townsend Hoopes and Douglas Brinkley, *FDR and the Creation of the UN* (New Haven, CT: Yale University Press, 1997), p. 184.

11. In 1999 U.S. President Bill Clinton was urging the Republican-controlled Senate to ratify the nuclear test ban treaty that nations had agreed upon in light of rising tension between Pakistan and India, both of which were reported to have developed nuclear capability that would threaten the security of the world. But for political reasons the Senate voted on October 14 to reject the treaty, raising serious doubts among nations about the U.S. commitment to peace and security of the world.

12. Philip Coombs, *World Crisis in Education: The View From the Eighties* (New York: Oxford University Press, 1985), p. 31.

13. Ibid., p. 33.

14. Quoted in William van Til, *Education: A Beginning*. Boston: Houghton Mifflin Company, 1974, p. 141.

15. Gunnar Myrdal, *An American Dilemma: The Negro Problem and Modern Democracy* (London: Harper and Brothers, 1944), p. 15.

16. Dickson A. Mungazi, *The Evolution of Educational Theory in the United States* (Westport, CT: Praeger Publishers, 1999), p. 174.

17. *Time*, May 28, 1990, p. 37.

18. Ibid., p. 38.

19. Dickson A. Mungazi, *The Last Defenders of the Laager: Ian D. Smith and F. W. de Klerk* (Westport, CT: Praeger Publishers, 1998), p. 148.

20. Letter to the author from a student in Sierra Leone, March 14, 1991. For a detailed discussion of problems caused in Africa by corruption, see, for example, Dickson A. Mungazi, *The Mind of Black Africa* (Westport, CT: Praeger Publishers, 1996), p. 169.

21. Dickson A. Mungazi, *Educational Policy and National Character: Africa, Japan, the United States, and the Soviet Union* (Westport, CT: Praeger Publishers, 1993), p. 14.

22. Coombs, *World Crisis in Education*, p. 31.

23. Ibid., p. 32.

24. Southern Rhodesia, *The Report of the Commission of Inquiry into Discontent in the Mangwende Reserve* (James Brown, Chairman) (Salisbury: Government Printers, 1961), p. 77.

25. World Almanac, *World Almanac and Book of Facts* (New York: Funk and Wagnalls, 1991).

26. PBS, *A Chance To Learn*, documentary film presentation, 1989.

27. U.S. Supreme Court, *Brown vs. Board of Education of Topeka*, 347 US 483, 1954. The *Brown* decision was a landmark ruling, stating that separate educational facilities for different races were inherently unequal.

28. For evidence to support this conclusion, see Dickson A. Mungazi, *The Struggle for Social Change in Southern Africa: Visions of Liberty* (New York: Taylor and Francis, 1989), p. 74.

29. Leo Marquard, *The Peoples and Policies of South Africa* (London: Oxford University Press, 1969), p. 129.

30. Alex La Guma (ed.), *Apartheid: A Collection of Writings of South Africa by South Africans* (New York: International Publishers, 1971), p. 46.

31. At the time, the government of South Africa was led by F. W. de Klerk who had succeeded Pieter W. Botha as president in 1989. Under extreme pressure from the international community and the Africans themselves, de Klerk began to negotiate with the African National Congress for the ending of apartheid. For details see Mungazi, *The Last Defenders of the Laager*.

32. Coombs, *World Crisis in Education*, p. 224.

33. Unesco, *Statistical Yearbook*, 1982 cited in Philip Coombs, *World Crisis in Education*, p. 225.

34. Ibid.

35. Ibid., p. 6.

36. Mungazi, *Educational Policy and National Character*, p. 18.

37. Ibid., p. 19.

# 4

# *Fundamentals of Education to Ensure Understanding Among Nations*

Proper education for whites will benefit Negroes as much as proper education for Negroes will benefit whites. . . . Henceforth there must be one school house for both former slave master and former slave.
Booker T. Washngton, 1884

## EDUCATION AND HUMAN UNDERSTANDING

For many years the expression "international education" has been employed to relate to a variety of cultural and educational activities intended to improve understanding and cooperation among nations so as to eliminate or reduce the prospects of conflict.[1] Originally applied to formal education beginning at the conclusion of World War I, the definition of international education now includes activities initiated by both government and nongovernment organizations in order to facilitate to the maximum level of cross-cultural understanding and assistance any form of educational development. This is considered compatible with the ideals of human understanding and cooperation. The development of related aspects, such as an effective means of communication and the advancement of technology and science, is intended to serve human needs.

While the introduction of the concept of international education to university settings as a discipline is a relatively new phenomenon, its magnitude cannot be minimized, especially during the age of nuclear technology. Informed people all over the world now understand that the survival of the human race hangs perilously on the cliff of self-destruction unless nations themselves learn to live in peace and in mutual trust of each other.[2] This is where international education plays a crucial role. But in order to accomplish this objective, all nations must understand that international education must be structured in such a way that it has broader implications beyond itself.

The purpose of this book is to show that international education plays an important role in bringing people of the world together in mutual trust and cooperation in order to avoid conflict and to improve chances for world peace. But that is not the extent of the value of international education; it also serves other important purposes and functions, such as creating bridges to human endeavors and individual aspirations in the context of a global environment that recognizes people as integral components of the universal human family. This study also examines the various factors that come into play in an effort to bring this about. The critical nature of international education that one needs to understand is that it makes all human beings aware of themselves and the values of being members of a dynamic global society. Without an essence that makes it possible to perceive human issues from this perspective, our sense of both ourselves and the world is blinded.

It is true to say that while conflict has been part of human experience, the search for solutions to it also has been its parallel development. As one examines some major events in human history, one sees the evidence to support this conclusion. As early as 510 B.C., Buddha taught his followers the importance of exercising sensitivity in structuring relationships with other people. About that same time the Chinese philosopher Confucius stated the elements of his philosophy of human relations that have become known as the *Golden Rule*: "What you do not want done to you, do not do to others." It is for this reason that Confucius went on to argue that because human relationships are far more important than any other aspect, man must endeavor to reach complete understanding of others. To accomplish this objective, man must assume the responsibility of designing an education that would enable him to attain it.[3]

Confucius also believed that in using the concept of human understanding as a basis of educational development, humanity was quite capable of discovering the inner source and meaning of world unity. As Confucius saw it, world unity was evident in humankind's quest for a new spirituality, the very essence of what it meant to be human. As modern humanity understands it, the concept of human spirituality also means that unless one learns to live in harmony with the universe, one is unlikely to live in harmony with oneself. Therefore, Buddha and Confucius concluded that education was the main channel through which humanity relates to man as an outcome of the harmony that must exist between oneself and the universe.

It is from this perspective that modern humanity recognizes the imperative of creating harmony with ourselves; the universe cannot be removed from our environment. Once this kind of environment has been created, the ambivalence that manifests itself in human behavior is substituted for by an intellect that replaces the thinking that one human fears another human because one does not know humanity. The notion that "might is right" as a modus operandi in global relationships gives way to the need to end provincialism and nationalistic patriotism based on irrational chauvinism.

The thinking that one major objective of education must be to understand the universal human seems to have acquired a new meaning as early as the Middle Ages. At that time the Christian church added a new dimension of viewing the importance of education, not only to enhance religious values as a basis of meaningful life, but also as a means by which man sought to understand other people. This is why Bishop John Amos Comenius ordered that church leaders make a new effort to embrace the concept of humanity through educational endeavors.

In 1658 Comenius wrote *The Visible World* in which he stressed two essential components of human life as a focus of education. The first component was his belief that man was not free until all men were free, and that to ensure this freedom, education was crucial. The second component was that since human life was made more meaningful by the application of logic and reason under the influence of religious values, it was in man's best interest to study the essential nature of human views of himself in order to understand his own mind.[4] Therefore, argued Comenius, ability to understand other people enables one to seek cooperation in various forms of human endeavor.

Although, during the height of the Roman Empire, especially in the time of Nero (A.D. 37–68), Christians were persecuted for promoting religious values that would have been essential in efforts to create better understanding of humans, the ambivalence of religion that had Moslems fight Christians made it possible for the universal man to see the senselessness of the confrontation. When Comenius suggested that a college be started to study issues of relations among nations and dedicated to human advancement based on mutual respect, the concept of educational understanding acquired new and powerfully persuasive dimensions.[5]

Within a few years of this development, informal exchange of both knowledge of the universal human being and learners and teachers began to take place in various centers that were being established in Europe and Africa.[6] By this time the concept of the universal human being had become the object of thinking in terms of designing an education that would make it an operative principle in human relationships. Students and teachers alike were slowly but steadily becoming aware of the value of understanding and cooperation across national boundaries as an outcome of the educational process. It is therefore not surprising that the Renaissance gave birth to the Age of Reason, during which people began to see themselves as being capable of creating an ideal society based upon the values of its institutions. These values could be developed only if people understood the common bonds that brought them closer to the concept of the universal human being. In this kind of setting, the universal human being of the Age of Reason came to believe that because it was possible to create an ideal society, social evils and conflict so characteristic of earlier times would be eliminated.

Throughout this period, people placed considerable faith in education as a panacea of all human problems. In the United States the chief spokesman of the Age of Reason was Thomas Jefferson, the third president of the United States, who served from 1801 to 1809. Jefferson championed the cause of education in order to ensure world security and peace. Although he was an uncompromising patriot, Jefferson saw the United States in the context of its role in seeking a lasting world peace for the benefit of all humankind. His call for an education to "enlighten the people and the tyranny of the oppression of both mind and body will vanish like evil spirits at the dawn of day"[7] became the cornerstone of his belief in the ability of humanity to eliminate negative features of human existence. It also became the basis of his argument in favor of establishing the University of Virginia, which became a reality in 1819.

The political turmoil that began in Europe in 1832 eventually led to the Franco-Prussian war of 1870, paving way for the powerful Otto von Bismarck to assume power in Germany. By the time that World War I broke out in 1914, relations among nations were based on secret treaties and alliances. The concept of human understanding through education had given way to the concept of military power. Leaders of European nations were now motivated by the consideration of national interests, rather than by global interests; by the need to exert power and influence, rather than by principles of mutual respect; by greed, rather than by sharing resources. During the age of the Great Industrial Revolution, nations in a state of underdevelopment were subjected to colonial governance with severe consequences for all.

The violence and brutality with which European nations subjected the people of Africa to colonial domination, in order to obtain raw materials for example, raised new and serious doubts about the role of education in promoting human understanding. From their inception, the colonial governments were motivated by the objective of promoting their own political and socioeconomic interests at the expense of those of the Africans. By their very nature, the colonial systems rendered the concept of human understanding through education meaningless as the Africans were trained to function only as laborers.

Therefore, the denial of meaningful educational opportunity became the green pastures in which the milk cows of colonial systems grazed. Albert Schweitzer, the famous German missionary to nineteenth-century Africa, described the extent of the suffering that the Africans endured at the hands of their European colonial conquerors, saying, "Who can describe the misery, the injustice and cruelties that the Africans have suffered at the hands of Europeans? If a record could be compiled, it would make a book containing pages which the reader would have to turn over unread because their contents would be too horrible."[8]

If there was any aspect of the colonial period that exemplified this suffering more than any other, it is the fact that the concept of human understanding had no application to colonial conditions. This is why colonialism anywhere is condemned more for its negative features than for any claim of its positive attributes. It is not surprising, therefore, that bitterness remained the only form of relationship between the Africans and the colonial governments.

Indeed, the outbreak of World War I in 1914 suggested to people in less developed areas the conclusion that the claim that Western civilization was superior to any other civilization was not substantiated by actual facts. The destruction of both human life and property left injured human feelings that could not be healed. The deliberations at Versailles following the end of the war were marked by conflicting positions taken by the victorious Allies on the question of what to do with territories of the vanquished. Some argued that they should be divided among them under the notion of "to the victor belong the spoils." This suggests the incompatibility of their views and thinking.

When President Woodrow Wilson succeeded in convincing the Allies to consider the interests of the people in these territories, because it was in their own best interests to do so, a new level of thinking emerged which enabled the participants to see human events from the point of view of their importance to global interests. When the League of Nations was finally formed in 1920, Article 22 specified, "For those colonies which are still inhabited by people not yet able to stand by themselves under the strenuous conditions of the modern world, there should be applied the principle that the well-being and development of such people form a sacred trust of civilization."[9]

While this line of thinking was appropriately directed toward better human understanding, it lacked a broader perspective from which to embrace the concept of the improvement of man as an outcome of education because the objectives of education were not clearly defined. This is one major reason why the League of Nations did not survive beyond 1935, setting the stage for the outbreak of World War II in 1939.

## THE IDEAS OF RABINDRANATH TAGORE IN PERSPECTIVE

It sounds strange that in modern times the search for education to realize the importance of human understanding came, not from the members of the Western civilization, but from those of less developed nations. It is for this reason that Rabindranath Tagore, a leading philosopher in India and the 1913 recipient of the Nobel prize for literature, expressed some ideas that were relevant to the search for education to realize the critical nature of human understanding. We must briefly discuss the implications of Tagore's ideas related to the role of education in promoting human understanding.

Writing *The Unity of Education* in 1921, only one year after the founding of the League of Nations, Tagore concluded that because Western nations utilized education to engage in empirical thought process, rather than in magic, they could conquer the world militarily.[10] But Tagore went on to argue that the inherent weakness of the Western perception of human relationships was an inability to recognize the importance of the existence of other cultures and their potential to contribute to the common good of humanity, as well as the form of education they used to achieve a balanced socioeconomic order.

This inability, concluded Tagore, to see the viability of both other cultures and the systems of education in them threatened the fundamental concept of man as the final act of creation with value that transcends national boundaries.[11] The tendency among Western nations to create horizontal relationships between Western nations and non-Western nations leads them to the conclusion that other societies and cultures are inferior. An aggressive behavior comes out of this attitude, that in turn makes it unlikely that contributions made of people of these cultures will be appreciated.

Tagore argues that the demise of the League of Nations must be seen in the context of what he calls the cultural arrogance of some Western nations who are under the assumption that they are superior to Third World Nations. Out of this form of arrogance human irrationality emerged to create new psychological problems that placed serious limitations on human intellect itself.[12] Therefore, the problems of global peace and understanding have constantly been imperiled more by the erratic behavior of some Western nations than by anything else. Indeed, a close study of Adolf Hitler's behavior would substantiate Tagore's conclusion.

The net result of this pattern of behavior is that it creates conditions in which people fear themselves because they do not seem to understand the principles which must govern their lives. When provincial patriotism, such as the United States experienced during the McCarthy era in the

1950s, becomes our modus operandi, we substitute rationality with increasing chauvinism that tends to embrace blindly a new level of irrationality. This situation generates an environment in which human conflict becomes inevitable. This is why neither Neville Chamberlain nor Adolf Hitler could formulate policies with the implications they would have in larger areas of human relationships.

One can see that this is the kind of situation that created conditions for both World War I and World War II which left behind them a trail of bitterness that would not be resolved. The action of the warring parties to substitute education for military technology has, in recent times, translated into the acquisition of military power and its use to resolve human problems. But the truth of the matter is that resorting to military means to solve human problems has never been a viable method of finding solutions.

Tagore concludes that Western nations need a new form of education more than any other people, and offers some suggestions about the content of that education. Among other things, he suggests that Western nations must embrace the kind of education that prepares students for world citizenship. It must prepare and enable students to participate in events designed to improve their understanding of the universal human being. It must arouse human compassion in all youth so that they learn from examples that reach into the heart of all people. And it must have them rise above the peripherals of human thought process to grasp the lofty ideals that make the human being the supreme act of creation.

Once education makes this possible, a student learns the importance of interdependence of all people regardless of their origin or culture. This helps the student to appreciate and accept people of other cultures as equals because they belong to the same human family. The emergence of this new attitude facilitates the creation of better systems of communication, trade, and cultural exchange programs (to name only a few examples) that are essential to human understanding on a global level. This is how an environment of human understanding is created. This is how solutions to the problems of human conflict can be found. Tagore decries the practice by some Western nations that "education has been used mainly by the mighty to increase their power and by the modern states to fan the fire of nationalism."[13] Tagore is also actually advising Western nations to rethink their value systems to embrace the kind of education that he is suggesting in order to end the perilous road to human conflict.

In discussing Tagore's ideas of education to realize the importance of the universal human, one must ask the question: What are the possible results of accepting the suggestions that he is making? One is immediately led to the conclusion that if a genuine effort were made to accept and implement these suggestions, some important results would accrue to the universal human being in general and to Western nations themselves in particular because they have more to gain. It would mean, among other things, an educational system that would help all people recognize their common interests and destinies as a result of understanding each other.

This effort was directed at increasing the awareness of nations and their people about the importance of accepting diverse national and cultural groups as a national enrichment, and at eliminating the intolerance that has marred human and national relations. It was also intended to produce a new universal human being who would yearn for a universal meaning beyond the mere acquisition of technological power and knowledge as the person endeavors to substitute provincial nationalism with international perceptions of human existence.

This approach to education would enable the new universal human being to make an effort to set all men free from want, from fear of political domination, of economic exploitation, of military threat as a form of political domination as individuals aspire to raise human intellect above the level of the ordinary to embrace something far more sublime within the setting of the spirit of human enterprise. It would make it possible for the universal human being to seek a stronger union with the universe in which human spirituality surges to new heights of human efforts to place the world on a lasting foundation of human understanding and security.

The reality of this endeavor would compel human beings to seek a new form of fellowship both with themselves and their universe as the ultimate player in an emerging world order with unity of all people as its focus and in an association that extends far beyond the petty political alliances that have contributed to the adverse conditions that have led to human conflict. In this kind of human setting the Golden Rule and its application would become a new universal religion that the universal human being finds comfortable in embracing as a new modus vivendi. If this happened, then the human ethical consciousness would rise to envisage all people as having a positive role to play in shaping the character of the new social order. This is why Confucius says this enables all men and women to become brothers and sisters. The ambivalence that tears people apart would be virtually eliminated.

In a letter dated September 16, 1934, addressed to Professor Albert Murray of Britain, Tagore expressed deep concern over man's inability, through indiscretion, to see the peril in which he was placing the world by his irrational behavior that he equated with provincial nationalism as a substitute for education.

I find much that is deeply distressing in modern conditions. I am more conscious of the inevitable and inescapable moral links which hold together the fabric of human civilization. I cannot afford to lose my faith in the inner spirit of man, nor in the sureness of human progress. Man, in his essential nature, is spiritual and not entirely materialistic. We have seen Europe spread slavery over the face of the earth. Exploitation becomes easier if we can succeed in denying educational creativity and generate a callous attitude toward those who are its victim.[14]

The central point of Tagore's argument is that while the attitudes of Western nations toward other societies have had a negative effect on human relationships, it is basically the inability or the unwillingness of all people to place human values on an environmental plain that reduces the prospects of conflict. That is why he went on to argue:

Western humanity, when not affected by its unnatural relationship with the East, preserves a singular strength of moral conduct in the domain of its social life, which has great inspiration for us all. In human greed for political power we are apt to ascribe the fact that human tendency towards separateness to accidental circumstances in the creation of new relationships between all people.[15]

This is the situation that demanded a new approach to education. The emergence of tyrannical governments, the denial of civil liberties to certain classes of people, the violence and the decadence which pervade society "combine to betray the consciousness in the mind of man of the inescapable collective responsibility"[16] to rethink the structure and the content of a new educational system to reflect the demands of the universal human being.

## THE STUDY OF CULTURE TO IMPROVE HUMAN UNDERSTANDING

Because the world consists of different people belonging to different cultures, peace and security of the world can be ensured only by accepting the concept of cultural diversity as a demonstration of human understanding. Writing in 1990 on the importance of the role of education in seeking to strengthen cultural diversity as a thrust for national development and enrichment, Young Pai of the University of Missouri observed: "Educators generally agree that education takes place in a specific socioeconomic context. But we are not always clear and precise about the myriad of ways in which cultural factors influence the process of schooling and learning."[17] What Pai is suggesting is that culture furnishes the best environment in which education must be cast, both a student's own culture and other cultures he should study.

This is the line of thinking that Gennadi Yagodin, a Russian thinker of Mikhail Gorbachev's time, took into account in expressing the value of culture as a prerequisite of the fundamentals of education, saying, "To develop education in isolation from national culture means to regard students as people without kith and kin."[18] Yagodin goes on to suggest that when students receive an education that is based on their own culture, they are likely to pursue it to understanding other people and their culture. Out of this approach comes an understanding of people in general. Yagodin argues that this understanding cannot be attained for its own sake, it serves a very important function in bringing people of the world to share common values that eliminate conflict.

Yagodin also argues that understanding is important in helping people to cooperate in seeking solutions to complex problems of contemporary world.[19] These problems are many and include, to name just a few, economic development, population explosion, terrorism, trade, monetary systems, travel, and world hunger and food production. Nations need to cooperate in finding solutions to these problems, because no nation can go it alone. Understanding culture also makes it possible to understand a people and its other national institutions, such as system of government, mode of production, family systems, geography and history, and materials it uses as a means of trade with other nations.

One must therefore conclude that because education cannot be removed from the culture of students, culture itself has a profound influence on students as they seek to understand other people. This is what Bertrand Russell, a British philosopher, had in mind when he argued toward the end of his life that schools have a responsibility to teach students to understand people who are different from themselves and their culture.[20] This approach to education requires acceptance of what has become known as multicultural education.

Human relations in the contemporary world have become so complex that nations are constantly afraid that any slight misunderstanding would trigger a major conflict. While the end of the cold war has somewhat eased that prospect, the possibility still exists of an outbreak of conflict because there are now new issues that can cause it, such as competition for depleting resources. Since the end of World War II in 1945, nations, under the guidance of the United States and Unesco have endeavored to create a climate that enhances understanding among them and so avoid the possibility of conflict. This level of understanding is evident in efforts to understand not only nations, but also individuals within them. Because nations consist of people, to understand them is to understand the people who are part of nations. To understand people is to understand their culture. Young Pai suggests that it has been universally recognized that a people with strong cultural foundations has nothing else on which to build a dynamic and vibrant society.[21]

Bertrand Russell adds to this line of thinking:

The sentiments of an adult are compounded of a kernel instinct surrounded by a vast husk of education. Throughout education, from the first day to the last, there should be a sense of intellectual stimulation based on cultural imperatives. The thing above all, if democracy is to survive, is that the teacher should endeavor to produce in his students a level of understanding and the kind of tolerance they need to accept those who are different from themselves.[22]

Margaret Mead, the American anthropologist, concluded in 1932, after extensively studying the culture of the people of Samoa, that while cultures are different, they are equal and that any difference must not imply that one culture is superior to another.[23]

This author has observed that some school districts in the United States argue that they do not need multicultural educational programs because they do not have students from ethnic minority groups. Such school districts fail to recognize that multicultural education is highly desirable in all schools, big or small, whether or not they have minority students. In a statement adopted on March 11, 1980, the Nebraska Department of Education stated: "Developing the curriculum which promotes a realistic view of minority people is a task that involves all school systems, not merely that with minority students."[24]

Those schools which have made an effort to implement an effective multicultural educational program beyond the limit of social studies have actually provided an enjoyable and meaningful educational experience that yields tangible results in many respects. To have an effective multicultural educational program, a school must make adequate curriculum provisions at all levels and in all areas of study. This enables students to gain a thorough and complete knowledge of history and the contributions of racial or ethnic groups to the development of their country. When such knowledge becomes an operational base of studying other societies and their culture, it enriches the educational experience of students as they begin to see how societies are more similar than different.

If a school wishes to introduce the study of African Americans as an example of studying culture and its values, what would it consider an appropriate place to begin? It may wish to study the history of African Americans who have made a considerable contribution to the development of the United States. The following may serve as good examples: Crispus Attucks was the first to die in the Boston Massacre. Daniel Hale Williams was the first physician to perform open heart surgery. Charles Drew was the physician who first discovered blood plasma. Matthew Benson traveled with Commander Perry to discover the North Pole. George Washington Carver discovered hundreds of products from peanuts. In recent years Robert Weaver and Patricia Harris served as secretary of urban affairs in the federal government, and Thurgood Marshall was appointed as a member of the U.S. Supreme Court.

These examples are not intended to suggest that only famous African Americans should serve as examples of individuals who could form the basis of a new approach to the curriculum, but as examples of individuals from diverse backgrounds who have made contributions to the development of the United States. What is important in the inclusion of these examples is that their inclusion would give African American students a sense of belonging, and nonminority students a new understanding of the inclusive nature of the curriculum as representing the importance of the diversity of the nation. It would help to erase the conventional prejudice that is often the basis of discrimination in society.

This approach also illustrates another very important point: multicultural education does indeed enhance the educational experiences of all students. Parents, school officials, and members of the community must insure that all students make their educational endeavors from the perspective of appreciating cultural diversity as a positive attribute of their society, both historical and contemporary. They should be taught to view the achievements of various people in society as an inspiration in their own efforts. This is why in 1899 John Dewey suggested, "What the wisest parent wants for his own children is what the community wants for all its children. Any other idea for the schools is narrow, and, if acted upon, destroys our democracy."[25]

Until the middle of the twentieth century, the theory of the "melting pot" had a considerable influence on educational thought and programs in the United States. Immigrants were expected to discard their cultural heritage in favor of adopting what was considered conventional American culture and values, whatever they were. But it became apparent that what was considered "the American culture" was, in fact, a mixture of cultures because there is no single culture other than language. Today thinkers dispute the theory of a melting pot. During the height of the civil rights movement beginning in 1957,[26] the notion of the melting pot as a social theory was rejected in favor of a more viable theory of cultural pluralism. Today the theory of the melting pot has little relevance to the educational process.

It will be seen that the thrust for multicultural education, if properly approached, enables students to gain a deeper understanding and appreciation of the value of their heritage as a basis of understanding other cultures. This perspective becomes a strong base on which to build a solid foundation of education and society for the future, enshrined in the concept of cultural diversity as a thrust for national enrichment. Officials of some school districts argue that a separate unit of only a few class sessions on minority cultural studies in the social studies curriculum is enough to reflect the concept of multicultural education. This is not how multicultural education should be viewed. This is why the Nebraska Department of Education took pains to explain the proper approach: "Multicultural educational programs must permeate all areas of study provided for the student."[27]

This line of thinking about education to ensure understanding suggests that schools must operate under the principle that teaching about the achievements of some individuals of different ethnic groups would demonstrate the importance of embracing multicultural education. In teaching about this achievement, schools must make sure that students get a broad overview of the conditions, social environment, history, and hopes of people of all ethnic groups. The students' own aspirations, goals, and objectives must not be overshadowed by an attempt to teach about the achievements of Booker T. Washington or Caesar Chavez, for example.

Young Pai suggests that this approach would indicate that multicultural education enables students to become aware of the fact that "the proponents of the counterculture movement in the mid 1970s argued that though the United States achieved an unprecedented economic affluence through the achievement of ethnic groups, the country continued to emphasize economic success and production as a result of the dominant racial group."[28]

## SETTING EDUCATIONAL OBJECTIVES

A discussion of education designed to promote human understanding must, of necessity, involve a corresponding discussion of some strategies to implement it. One way of designing the kinds of strategies that would yield an anticipated outcome in this education is by considering the curricular structure from preschool to college. The basic assumption underlying this line of thinking and approach is that it enables students at all levels to realize that the educational process entails far more than the need to explore the concept of education to ensure human understanding. Barbara Biber has outlined basic goals of the preschool directed toward understanding the universal human being.

One goal is to establish both short-term and long-term objectives of education. The short-term goals should include three that seem to stand taller than others. The first is to help children map out their immediate space so that they gain an understanding of the importance of beginning to orient themselves toward their spatial universe and to acquire a subsequent working knowledge of the world.

The second short-term goal is to assist children in understanding the importance of the various roles that people play in sustaining the integrity of their society, such as the letter carrier, the nurse, the grocer, the doctor, the truck driver. Early in their educational process children should be taught to appreciate that the different roles that people play sustain the structure of society itself. Once they understand this basic truth, children can gradually translate that understanding to embrace the roles that people play to produce the resources the people of the world need to lead a happy and prosperous life. Oil from the Middle East, minerals from South Africa, grain from the United States and Canada— all contribute to an understanding of the importance of the role of various people of the world to create a balanced world order of trade.

The third short-term objective is to help children understand that just as their local community is made up of various people, the world community is made up of people with different lifestyles, cultural values, ethnic backgrounds, and racial origins.[29] Biber suggests that when properly handled, children can demonstrate clear understanding of these basic concepts. Once they embrace them as part of their educational development, they are likely to have them form part of their attitudes and perception of the world. This is how this strategy can yield some tangible results.

The objectives of the primary school become a little more advanced because they should include an appreciation of some of humans' greatest achievements in science, such as aviation and medicine, communication, technology, and travel. Once students demonstrate an appreciation of these achievements, they will have an appreciation of man himself and of the fact that no race has a monopoly of human talent because success and failure are known to all people.[30] Failure to recognize the contribution of other ethnic groups in areas of national endeavor, including economic development, undermines the national morale that is required to place the country on a strong foundation of development. To ignore national factors that impede the ability of all ethnic groups to contribute to all areas of national development, such as racial discrimination, is to ignore the very important factor of efforts directed at national development itself.

This reality suggests two conclusions. The first is that there are social and economic consequences of continuing the perception of society that is exclusively structured on the basis of stressing only the contributions of majority ethnic groups in the area of national endeavor. The second conclusion is that while there are some common disabilities suffered by members of minority ethnic groups, multicultural education must relate to important contributions that all ethnic groups have made to national development. Failure to recognize this contribution would derail national programs as minority groups feel their contribution is not appreciated. National conflict usually arises out of this social environment.

The awareness of this reality would make it possible for students to recognize early in life and education that they live in a country and world inhabited by other ethnic groups, and that their contributions to national endeavor are as important as those of any other group. The acquisition of this understanding becomes an important factor that helps students to recognize their common heritage, which they feel obligated to sustain, preserve, and pass on to the next generation. Above all else, students introduced to this kind of educational environment are more likely to eliminate the racial prejudice of earlier generations in their personal relations with people of other ethnic groups. They also come to realize that those who are influenced by race appear to lack confidence in themselves.

## COOPERATION BETWEEN THE SCHOOL AND THE COMMUNITY

The concept of "multigroups" in multicultural education demands total commitment by both the school and the community. Each community has an obligation to support its schools in efforts to provide students an effective education, knowing that students who come out of these schools will exercise responsibility not only for that community, but also for the world. If German students had been introduced to this kind of educational environment, they would have had an opportunity to know a different set of values which they would have utilized to see Jews in a positive light and would have been able to recognize their potential in the development of Germany. They would have transformed hatred into understanding.

Instead of seeking conquest of the world, Nazi party members would have accepted cultural diversity as an enrichment of human society. Instead of regarding themselves as an Aryan race, they would have accepted other racial and ethnic groups as viable in building relationships that were based on cooperation in an effort to solve problems that were affecting all nations, such as the Depression, the practice of secret alliances that became the main cause of World War II, and the lack of trust among nations because of the desire for power. In the end it was the German people themselves who paid the ultimate price. Just as there was a collective responsibility among Germans for the behavior of the Nazi party, there is a collective responsibility for the community to make education a success. The question is whether national leaders in Germany today have learned from the tragedy of the past.

Cooperation between the school and the community in making education the best it can be takes the kind of cooperation to bring about what Barbara Jordan calls "common good for the community."[31] Common good enshrines the concept of mutual respect of cultural differences as a whole and as a fabric from which a community can be knitted into a garment of unified cohesion and purpose. For this to happen, total equality in the treatment of members of society is critical. Such an approach enables teachers and members of the community to cooperate in helping students to objectively examine various problems that exist in their community as a preparation for seeking solutions that the world faces.

Unless members of a community give mutual respect to each other, their problems will always appear greater than they really are. The greatness of any society comes from the recognition of diversity of cultural backgrounds of its people. The community that recognizes the vitality of cultural diversity finds it easier to cooperate on what needs to be done to give students an effective education that prepares them well to play their roles in the larger context than their community. The community therefore plays a critical role in developing cultural diversity as a platform on which to base effective educational programs.

It can be argued that much of ethnic cultural expression and manifestation that relate to experiences of the ghetto, poverty, and discrimination are characteristics of the nature of existence of deprived people who have lost their sense of cultural values because they have been denied an opportunity to interact with people of other ethnic groups. For them life has lost its meaning and all they see is crime and degeneration, which leave them in the shadows of an exclusive society. In years before the end of apartheid in South Africa in 1994, the Africans had lost all sense of what it meant to be human. For many, crime or resorting to the culture of violence had become a way of life. That was all they knew. It is still going to take quite some doing to bring this tragedy to an end.

The result of denying development to any one ethnic group is that members of all ethnic groups are denied an opportunity to know each other as human beings with a potential to make society great. An effective multicultural education would seek to eliminate this situation and restore the sense of purpose that generates a new level of both individual and collective identity so essential to the building of a national character. Without a national character, no ethnic group can hope to place itself on a solid foundation on which to build a future.

Minority groups express experiences through various forms of media. By utilizing appropriate music lessons of a particular ethnic group, for example, the school creates a meaningful channel through which students and members of the community come to understand and appreciate ethnic cultural music and the emotions it expresses and the message it carries. Mildred Dickerman explains why this is important: "Until this experience enters the school as a significant record, students will continue to lack the means of relating themselves and their background to the goals of formal education."[32] The school cannot achieve this success by itself; it will need the support and cooperation of the community.

In seeking to make a positive contribution to conditions of peace through understanding in the world, students should endeavor to become models of their own code of ethics and behavior based upon what they learn in both the school and the community. If the community does not support the school, students may lose proper perspective of their role in society. This creates an environment of conflict from which no one benefits. This is why, in 1990, the government of South Africa recognized this fact and decided to change the course of national development. The community has a responsibility of supporting the school in designing a curriculum around clearly defined goals and objectives that would promote these codes of ethics. Such goals and objectives must seek to promote a sense of belonging based on the concept of individuality and shared community values. With students' objectives fulfilled there comes a sense of pride, achievement, and purpose in living.

## CREATING THE ENVIRONMENT FOR INTELLECTUAL DEVELOPMENT

We must now turn our attention to another important aspect relative to the effect of traditional stereotypes regarding the intellectual potential of minority groups as a result of environmental factors. For many years cultural attributes and different characteristics of minority students were regarded as deficiencies in intellectual and academic potential. Some educational thinkers speculated that minority groups were inherently academically inferior. Today educational thinkers, such as Young Pai, argue that environmental factors play a leading role in developing or retarding intellectual development of all people.[33]

Controversial as the role of environment is to intellectual development and educational success, the educational system should not take chances with potential achievement of students. However, to expect the student from the ghetto to perform at the same level as a student from the upper middle class is to expect the impossible and would place him under severe strain. It cannot be done. This is not to suggest that students from lower socioeconomic levels must not be expected to perform at a higher level, but to caution that when the environment is neglected, one cannot expect performance at a high level. The fact that members of minority groups were denied an opportunity for cultural enrichment through creative activity suggests the need to improve the environment as an important factor in nurturing intellectual development of students.

Through economic and intellectual deprivation, the vast majority of members of minority groups have had limited access to the stimuli that generate human spirit to search for knowledge. Philip A. Cusick suggests that some educational theorists, such as R. N. Nelson, place great emphasis on values, culture, and social background of students as important stimuli to intellectual development.[34] Therefore, to assume that a student from the ghetto has less intellectual capability than a student from the middle class on the basis of his achievement on any given test is to be blind to the important role that environmental factors play on intellectual development and academic achievement. Environmental factors, including associations students have with each other, determine whether students fail or succeed. One of the major functions of the school and the community is to create an environment in such a way that students have a greater opportunity for success than the potential for failure.

This fact was recognized by the U.S. Supreme Court in 1954 when it stated, "To separate Negro children from others of similar age and qualifications solely because of their race generates a feeling of inferiority as to their status in the community that affect their hearts and minds in a way unlikely ever to be undone."[35] Since the *Brown* decision researchers have argued that when kept away from the prejudicial influence of adults, children can recognize no factors that impede their ability to have meaning and mutually beneficial relations with children of any race or ethnic background. This is a critical environmental factor that makes a difference between success and failure in education and, as adults, success or failure in relations with people of other countries.

In the post-Revolution era in the United States, for example, as members of minority groups were denied equal opportunity for advancement through education, the dominant ethnic group claimed to have intellectual superiority over them. In 1845 Frederick Douglass observed the effect of racism when he said that what white America did not realize was that the destiny of black America was the destiny of the country itself.[36] Things did not start to change until the beginning of the civil rights movement in 1957. Members of minority groups felt rejected and alienated. Their sense of purpose and motivation was dulled or lost entirely in the mire of racism. During that period racism became detrimental, not only to achievement of deprived members of minority groups, but also of the dominant group itself as well.

Americans sadly found that if racism was a major factor of achievement in the nineteenth century it was even more so in the twentieth century. In 1964 Martin Luther King, Jr. described what racism did to black America as a reflection of what it was doing to the nation itself. Taking Birmingham, Alabama, of Bull Connor's time as an example, King observed:

If your power of imagination were great enough to enable you to place yourself in the position of the Negro baby born and brought up to physical maturity in Birmingham, you would have pictured your life in the following manner: You would be born in a Jim-Crow hospital to parents who lived in the ghetto. You would attend a Jim-Crow school. It is not really true that the city fathers had never heard of the Supreme Court's school desegregation order.[37]

What Douglass and King said suggests the conclusion that intellectual development and academic achievement must be regarded in terms of environmental factors that are conducive to their development. Black

Americans did not seek integration of schools just to be with whites; they knew that as long as schools remained segregated they would never have equal opportunity for development. That is a critical environmental factor that they had to take into consideration in launching the civil rights movement. Therefore failure or success must not be seen from an ethnic perspective, but must be viewed from factors that constitute a set of conditions that create an environment from which students are expected to function in school. During the period of the civil rights movement, increasing demands were made on educational institutions to recognize differences in cultural backgrounds of students as a national positive attribute and an enhancement of the cognitive process of all students. Judgment and evaluation of their academic performance had to be based on environmental and cultural factors, not on any assumptions of hereditary deficiency or traits.

To help in assessing student potential, schools needed to involve parents and members of the community for the good of all students. In 1970 Lee Montgomery described the need for this involvement:

Parents want to be partners with teachers in the development of all levels of education for their children. There are two major factors for this desire. The first is the desire to have cultural differences recognized and appreciated. The second is that they wish to impress upon teachers that they must appreciate the style of speech, the mode of dress, the Afro, the habits, the beads or the medallions which are popular and or indigenous to some Americans.[38]

For this positive approach to occur, the community must take a positive attitude toward cultural pluralism. Racism or cultural prejudice of any kind must be eliminated from the minds of the people in order to afford every child an equal educational opportunity. The Kerner Commission clearly saw the need for this when it stated in 1968, "What white America has never fully understood, but what the Negro can never forget, is that white society is deeply implicated in the ghetto. White institutions maintain it, and white society condones it. Racial prejudice has shaped our history decisively, and it now threatens our future."[39]

This is a serious indictment of a nation that prides itself on its efforts to promote human rights across the world. For many years racism was a characteristic feature of American life. In 1978, for example, *Time* reported the following facts: National unemployment reached 5.8 percent of the labor force. Yet among Mexican Americans the rate of unemployment reached 8.9 percent, and nearly 40 percent among black Americans. At the same time the school dropout rate among Mexican Americans was reported to be as high as 85 percent. Their average income was $7,000 per year.[40] Some people have made the argument that national governments must assume a major responsibility for creating a national environment that makes it possible for all people to achieve at their highest level. This is substantiated by the conclusion that Lord Acton, a British statesman, reached in 1862: "A state which is incompetent to satisfy different races condemns itself. A state which labors to neutralize, to absorb, or to expel them destroys its own vitality. A state which does not include them is destitute of the chief function of government."[41]

## THE TEACHER'S ROLE IN PROMOTING UNDERSTANDING

The message that these developments have for the classroom teacher is quite clear. While the schools are charged with the responsibility of eliminating all forms of prejudice in their functions and in the nature of education they provide, it is the classroom teacher who exemplifies by his or her conduct and attitude the nature of relationship students have with people of other cultures. This will be a prerequisite of developing good relationships with people of other countries as adults. If it is true that charity begins at home, the thrust for understanding among nations must originate in a local school district. The classroom teacher can play a decisive role in that thrust.

The classroom teacher can better achieve educational objectives by promoting the spirit of understanding needed to develop mutual respect among students and in society. This understanding is essential to cooperation needed to achieve defined goals and objectives. In a teacher's efforts to promote understanding and cooperation in the classroom, the teacher must constantly be aware that those individuals who exhibit prejudice based on race, particularly in terms of superior-inferior attitude, cause a systemic destruction of essential elements of good human relationships.

In engaging in this kind of activity, individuals who are insensitive to prejudice force a loss of an opportunity for building a community influenced by reason and understanding. These are the elements that are needed to ensure understanding of people in other countries. Cooperation comes from this understanding. Classroom teachers should also be aware that in their interactions with students no reference must be made, either deliberate or implied, to the notion of one ethnic group being superior to another. Classroom teachers must also realize that students need to be made aware of their responsibility to maintain the cultural heritage of all students and to promote related values so that they retain their ethnic and cultural identity.

In 1978, writing an introduction to an annotated bibliography on multicultural literature in Nebraska, this author observed:

The teacher must become a channel of ethnic and cultural values among her students. In the context of educational activity she must remain totally alert to attitudes that may detract her responsibility so she can be quick to detect some negative racial elements that often become a barrier to efforts to define and implement elements of cultural and ethnic understanding leading to cooperation.[42]

Charles Payne, professor of multicultural education at Ball State University, added, "For all teachers to adequately demonstrate understanding of the importance of all cultures requires that more students from different cultures be included in the process of education. If education is viewed only as fragmented units study it will quickly lose its purpose, and therefore, meaningless."[43] James Boyer, nationally recognized authority on multicultural education in the United States, listed five important components of a successful multicultural education as (1) incorporating content data about minority groups, (2) including an understanding of the Third World thought process, (3) recognizing content of both European and other nationalities, (4) emphasizing relationships between people of different cultural backgrounds, and (5) recognizing varied sources of content materials in reviewing current curriculum materials for their ethnic and diversity objectives.[44]

Although the concept of multicultural education was unknown during his time, Booker T. Washington articulated his philosophy of something close to it when he spoke in 1884 before the National Education Association conference held in Madison, Wisconsin:

Proper education for whites will benefit Negroes as much as proper education for Negroes will benefit whites. Let there be a Negro with the virtue of his superior knowledge and the white man will come to him to learn. In the process former slave holders will conquer two hundred years of prejudice against the Negro. Henceforth there must be one school house for both former slave master and former slave.[45]

Eleven years later, in 1895, Washington echoed that philosophy in Atlanta. Speaking at the Cotton and International Exposition he said,

As we have proved our loyalty to you in the past, we shall stand by you with devotion, ready to lay down our live[s] on defense of yours in a way that will make the interests of both races one. In all things purely social we can be as separate as the five fingers and yet one in as the hand in all things essential to mutual progress.[46]

Indeed, Washington was advocating a form of education that he believed would generate mutual respect among different races in the United States. To conclude that Washington was ahead of his time in this regard is to suggest that he projected a vision of the country rare among African Americans of this time. Today, in order to provide an education that is different from Washington's time, we design goals and objectives that address the process by which students seek to understand humanity by understanding their fellow students. To understand humanity is, in essence, to appreciate the socioeconomic and moral values that set human beings apart from other living species. In this regard, social studies can play a major role in developing understanding among people of the world. In the same way, the study of literature from other lands can help expand students' horizons and their perceptions of the world.

The need for studying other cultures appears to have been recognized at most college campuses across the world. But the objectives that must influence its structure have yet to be fully defined. At the college level, the main objective is to enable students to understand the dynamics and mutuality of human relationships. Studying cultural variation as well as political and socioeconomic systems enhances the prospects not only of understanding various cultures and peoples of the world, but also the importance of cooperation beyond national boundaries. The important thing to remember here is that once objectives have been fully defined, an appropriate curricular content can be designed to fulfill them. Endeavors to develop an educational system to realize the importance of human understanding is in effect too important to relegate it to a lower level of the educational process. It must take the center stage of the educational process itself.

## SUMMARY AND CONCLUSION

What has been discussed in this chapter leads to the conclusion that the world of today has a potential for both greatness through education and destruction through ignorance and conflict. The advent of nuclear technology leaves no doubt that if conflict breaks out, the human race faces a real possibility of annihilation. It is therefore within the power of humanity itself to stop this from happening. From the discussion in this chapter, one is led to the conclusion that the best way of doing so is by seeking to understand the universal human being. This is the line of thinking that the British poet, John Donne, took into account when he wrote, "No man is an island. . . . Every man is a piece of the continent. . . . Any man's death diminishes me because I am involved in mankind."[47]

One can see that Donne believed that no human being can exist without relationships with other people. He felt that each human being is part and parcel of the global family, and that any conflict within an individual society is likely to translate into conflict between nations. Therefore, people of the world not only depend upon each other for survival, but also need to strive toward maintaining a balance between ideals of the individual nations and those of a world community.

What has been discussed in this chapter also leads to the conclusion that since our task as human beings is to live together on this planet on the basis of peace and cooperation, schools must be given the responsibility to teach students ways and means of working together to solve the problems of human existence, first in their community, and then in the world. Without education to acquire understanding of the importance of human interaction, emotion and irrationality can displace the critical elements of reason. No one can pretend that problems of the world can be solved in an environment of this kind. World peace and human cooperation must constitute a fundamental objective of education.

The reality of contemporary human existence demands that education become a component of the search for solutions to human problems. An essential component of the curriculum to realize human understanding is its efforts to give both a sense of unity and a perspective in which the individual person sees himself in relation to the universal human being. This is why the United Nations created Unesco in 1946 to promote education so as to facilitate the search for understanding among people of the world. Because Unesco has played a major role in this undertaking, we need to discuss its structure to appreciate how it operates and to understand its efforts to initiate change in that structure in order to improve its effectiveness.

## NOTES

1. David Scanlon, *International Education: A Documentary History* (New York: Teachers College Press, 1960), p. 1.

2. Ibid., p. 3.

3. Robert Ulich (ed.), *Education and the Idea of Mankind* (Chicago: University of Chicago Press, 1964), p. 3.

4. Ibid., p. 8.

5. John W. Waldon, *The Universities of Ancient Greece* (New York: Charles Scribner's Sons, 1910), p. 17.

6. Ibid., p. 8.

7. William van Til, *Education: A Beginning* (Boston: Houghton Mifflin Company, 1974), p. 12.

8. *The Christian Century*, October 8, 1975.

9. Article 22 of the League of Nations, January 20, 1920.

10. Rabindranath Tagore, "The Unity of Education," in Ulich, *Education and the Idea of Mankind*, p. 2.

11. Ibid., p. 13.

12. Ibid., p. 15.

13. Ibid., p. 13.

14. Rabindranath Tagore, letter dated September 16, 1934, addressed to Professor Albert Murray of Britain.

15. Ibid.

16. Ibid.

17. Young Pai, *Cultural Foundations of Education* (Columbus: Merrill Publishing Company, 1990), p. v.

18. Gennadi Yagodin, *Towards Higher Standards in Education Through Its Humanization and Democratization* (Moscow: Novosti Press, 1989), p. 17.

19. Ibid., p. 19.

20. Van Til, *Education: A Beginning*, p. 13.

21. Pai, *Cultural Foundations of Education*, p. 16.

22. Van Til, *Education: A Beginning*, p. 419.

23. P. A. Cusick, *The Egalitarian Ideal and the American High School: Studies of Three Schools* (White Plains, NY: Longmans, 1983), p. 18.

24. Nebraska Department of Education, "Position Statement on Multicultural Education" (Lincoln: Department of Education, 1980), p. 3.

25. T. Wilson, *Towards Equitable Education: A Handbook for Multicultural Consciousness for Early Childhood* (Palo Alto, CA: Ujama Developmental Education Publications, 1976).

26. This date is often considered the beginning of the civil rights movement in the United States because Martin Luther King, Jr. and Rosa Parks initiated the bus boycott in Montgomery, Alabama, to protest racial discrimination.

27. Nebraska Department of Education, "Position Statement on Education," p. 13.

28. Pai, *Cultural Foundations of Education*, p. 28.

29. Barbara Biber, "Understanding Mankind Through Preschool," in Ulich, *Education and the Idea of Mankind*, p. 71.

30. Ibid., p. 72.

31. Wilson, *Towards Equitable Education*, p. 96.

32. Mildred Dickerman, "Teaching Cultural Pluralism," in J. Banks (ed.), *What Educators are Saying* (Washington, DC: National Council for Social Studies, 1973) p. 20.

33. Pai, *Cultural Foundations of Education*, p. 30.

34. Cusick, *The Egalitarian Ideal and the American High School*, p. 30.

35. U.S. Supreme Court, *Brown v. Board of Education of Topeka*, 347 US 483, Washington, DC, 1954.

36. Frederick Douglass, *Narrative of the Life of Frederick Douglass* (New York: New American Library, 1845), p. 75.

37. Martin Luther King, Jr., *Why We Can't Wait* (New York: New American Library, 1964) p. 47.

38. Lee Montgomery, "The Education of Black Children" in N. Wright (ed.), *What Educators Are Saying* (New York: Hawthorne Books, 1970), p. 25.

39. Quoted in R. Daniels and H. Kitano, *American Racism: Exploration of the Nature of Prejudice* (Englewood, NJ.: Prentice-Hall, 1970), p. 1.

40. *Time*, December 16, 1979, p. 15.

41. Quoted in Daniels and Kitano, *American Racism: Exploration of the Nature of Prejudice*, p. 3.

42. Dickson A. Mungazi, *Annotated Bibliography of Multiethnic Conceptual Literature* (Lincoln: Nebraska Department of Education, 1978), p. 1.

43. Charles Payne, "Preparation of Multicultural Teacher," paper presented at a conference on multicultural education, Lincoln, Nebraska, June 12, 1978.

44. James Boyer, *Administration's Checklist for Ethnic and Multicultural Curriculum* (Manhattan: Kansas State University, 1978), p. 4.

45. E. T. Thornbrough, *Booker T. Washington* (Englewood Cliffs, NJ: Prentice-Hall, 1989), p. 59.

46. Booker T. Washington, *Up From Slavery* (New York: Doubleday, 1916), p. 218.

47. Charles M. Coffin (ed.), *The Complete Poetry and Selected Prose of John Donne* (New York: Modern Library, 1952), p. 441.

Photo 1. Woodrow Wilson, President of the United States from 1913 to 1924. "We are not put into this world to sit still. We are put into it to act in a new age to lead the world to its salvation." Photo: National Archives No. 36, 1999.

Photo 2. Henry Cabot Lodge and Theodore Roosevelt, partners in opposing Woodrow Wilson. "Lodge and Roosevelt intensely disliked Woodrow Wilson's entire program and believed that their opposition to his role in the formation of the League of Nations was in the best interests of the United States." Photo: National Archives No. 165-WW-441F/29, 1999.

Photo 3. Council of Four of the Versailles Peace Conference, May 27, 1919. From left to right: Vittorio Orlando (Italy), David Lloyd George (Britain), Georges Clemenceau (France), and Woodrow Wilson (United States). "An association of nations must be formed for the purpose of affording mutual guarantees of political independence and territorial integrity to great and small states alike." Photo: National Archives No. 722, 1999.

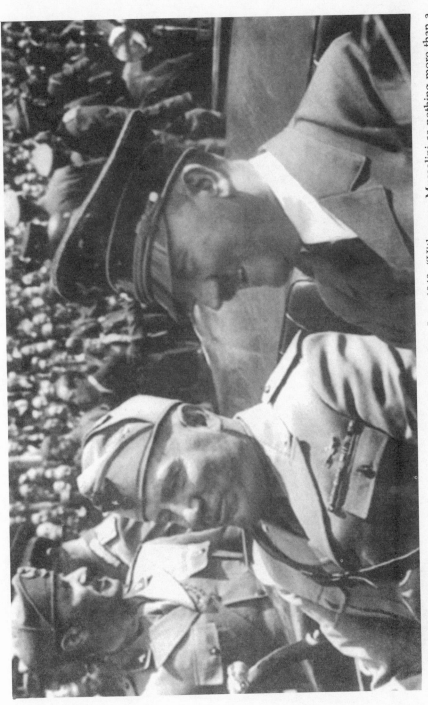

Photo 4. Benito Mussolini and Adolf Hitler in Munich, Germany, June 1940. "Hitler saw Mussolini as nothing more than a surrogate or subordinate who was paving the way for his grand entry into the arena of new geopolitics in which he would rule supreme. For Hitler the world was what it was by the act of his will." Photo: National Archives No. 746, 1999.

Photo 5. Paul Joseph Goebbels, Nazi Minister of Propaganda, and Heinrich Himmler, Nazi Head of Police and Gestapo, June 1935. "Members of the Nazi Party shared a belief in the supremacy of the German people as an Aryan race. Under this belief they committed atrocities against Jews, sending 6 million to their deaths." Photo: National Archives No. 131-12-2/242-HBA-651, 1999.

Photo 6. Emperor Hirohito and Admiral Isoroku Yamamoto, architect of attack on Pearl Harbor, December 1941. "When Japan launched a surprise attack on Pearl Harbor, the United States had no choice but to enter the war." Photo: National Archives No. 208-N-43408/80-JO-79462, 1999.

Photo 7. Big Three at Yalta Conference, February 1945. From left to right: Winston Churchill (Britain), Franklin Roosevelt (United States), Joseph Stalin (Soviet Union). "While World War II brought the Soviet Union and Western nations together in the pursuit of a common objective to defeat the Axis powers, rivalry among them later ensued during the era of the cold war." Photo: National Archives No. 750, 1999.

Photo 8. General Douglas MacArthur, Supreme Allied Commander, signing formal Japanese surrender on the *USS Missouri* in Tokyo Bay, September 2, 1945, and Field Marshall Wilhelm Keitol of Germany signing German surrender at Russian Headquarters in Berlin, May 7, 1945. "The defeat of the Axis powers made it possible to establish peace which would afford all people an opportunity to live out their lives in freedom from fear and want." Photo: National Archives No. 1363/1353, 1999.

Photo 9. Trygve Lie of Norway, Secretary-General of the United Nations from 1946 to 1952, welcoming Dag Hammarskjold of Sweden, Secretary-General of the United Nations from 1952 to 1961, at New York Airport in 1952. "The secretary-general is the chief executive officer of the United Nations." Photo: National Archives No. Q59-G-155, 1999.

Photo 10.  The United Nations headquarters in New York ("The creation of the UN made it possible for the world to achieve a lasting peace."); U.S. space capsule, Friendship 7 ("The U.S. space program was designed to ensure that exploration of space was intended to foster understanding among nations."); South African Parliament in Cape Town with the famous Table Mountain in the background ("The international community took exception to the fact that the South African Parliament passed some of the most oppressive laws known to man under apartheid."); and a billboard warning against AIDS in Zambia ("Problems of the world have become so complex that no nation can solve them alone.") Photos by the Author, 1995.

Photo 11. White House conference room, where decisions affecting the world are made, and Parliament of Kenya, in Nairobi, where the struggle for democracy continues. "The practice of democracy is universal, it is not an exclusive possession of any one country." Photos by the Author, 1976, 1995.

Photo 12. Three girls are happy to begin high school at Hartzell Secondary School, Mutare, Zimbabwe. "For a little black girl in a remote part of Africa and a little white boy in the suburbs of New York to recognize that they stood on the same plane of equal opportunity for education represented the dawn of a new era." Photo by the Author, 1972.

# 5

# Education for Understanding Among Nations: Focus, Problems, and Solutions

Any definition of national development must not be imposed on any ground, but must be open to collective input to have real meaning and benefit to the nation because it benefits the individual as a condition of initiating understanding among nations

Ralph E. Dodge, 1963

## THE INDIVIDUAL AS THE MAJOR FOCUS OF EDUCATION

History shows that there are three recipients of a good education: the individual, society, and the world community in that order. This chapter discusses this sequence of the function of education as it is designed to serve the needs of the individual, society, and the world community. Asked during an interview with the author in July 1983 to define the purpose of education, the late Rev. Ndabaningi Sithole, veteran political leader in Zimbabwe, responded,

Education provides the individual who has certain ideas and feelings a means of articulating self-expression. Self-expression is an indispensable condition of being fully human. Before one acquires education it is impossible for one to exercise that self-expression sufficiently and in a logical manner. Education gives the individual a wide scope and a depth to one's thinking. It is an instrument of self-fulfillment. It converts a person into a human being with solid qualifications to pursue the goals that one defines.[1]

One can reach the conclusion that the primary purpose of education is to prepare the individual to meet his own needs. Among these needs is to exercise self-expression, which comes in various forms that include an ability to be independent in sustaining conditions of living. Self-expression distinguishes the human being from other living species because the human being is not a silent creature.

Some thinkers have expressed ideas that relate to the function of education as it is intended to benefit the individual as its primary recipient. Paulo Freire, the famous writer from Brazil, takes this line of thinking in presenting his view of what education must be designed to do. He suggests that self-expression itself invokes in the individual an ability to exercise critical thinking to acquire skills in communicating ideas consistent with the essence of being fully human.[2] Like other thinkers, Freire is among those who argue that the individual is the primary recipient of education so that he is able to sharpen his skills to meet his needs. He also argues that the individual who is able to fulfill his needs becomes an asset to society.

In 1845 Frederick Douglass, the great African American civil rights leader, recognized the purpose of education for himself as an individual. He described his efforts to ensure it:

I lived in Master Hugh's family about seven years. During this time I succeeded in learning to read and to write. In accomplishing this I was compelled to resort to various strategies. I had no regular teacher. My mistress, who had kindly commenced to instruct me, had, in compliance with the advice and direction of her husband, to not only cease to instruct me, but had also set her face against my being instructed by any one else.[3]

Douglass went on to discuss the decision made by his master's wife to stop teaching him literacy, saying that he was thrown into the cave of mental darkness and that was why he was determined not to let that happen because, he said, the light of life was a beacon that summoned his willpower to overcome adversity. He concluded that success of the individual in any area of human endeavor lay in his effort to see purpose in his own life.[4]

The effort that Douglass made to secure education leads to the conclusion that since it is the individual who decides how best to prepare himself for the future, factors that influence his efforts must be related to the purpose that only he must define in pursuing it. In 1972 Samora Machel, president of Mozambique from 1975 to 1986, expressed his philosophy of education in a way that addressed its purpose in a universal sense relative to its importance to the individual:

We must never think of man as a form of automation who must receive and carry out orders irrespective of whether he understands them or has assimilated them, but as a viable individual who has defined purpose in his life to do what he must do to meet his own needs. In securing the quality of education that enables him to meet his own needs the individual meets those of society.[5]

Machel went on to add that when the individual is unable to exercise freedom of choice of what to study, he loses the focus of his education. As a result the education he receives is irrelevant to his meeting his needs and therefore irrelevant to meeting the needs of society.[6]

John Dewey's philosophy of progressive education, which had attracted the attention of leading thinkers and educators worldwide, is based on some fundamental principles about the student as an individual learner. He readily recognized that students vary greatly in regard to their rate of learning, their interest in what they study, and the strategies they utilize to learn concepts. Dewey argued that those responsible for education must take these variations into account in providing facilities for students to pursue their education on the basis of individuality. Under his philosophy of progressive education, Dewey considered a good teacher as the one who recognizes these principles so that students are not pressured to learn at the same rate and the same subjects. Dewey concluded that applying principles of progressive education ensures success of education far more than traditional education,[7] which is too rigid to provide flexibility that enables students to be individual learners.

Individuality—that operational principle of educational success that must be designed to seek the promotion and development of the individual as its primary focus—must be provided for in the educational process because its acquisition is critical to creativity. If education is not approached from this perspective, it loses its value for both the individual and society. If education, like salt, loses its flavor by losing its values to the individual, how can it be used to benefit society? Nations have increasingly come to understand that as the individual benefits from education because it is approached on individual basis, society becomes its ultimate beneficiary.

## EDUCATION AND SOCIETY

When Mikhail Gorbachev became president of the Soviet Union in 1984 he introduced two new terms of reference in discussing national programs he was initiating: *glasnost* (openness) and *perestroika* (reform). In doing so Gorbachev was reversing the policy that had been in part of the Soviet Union for seven decades since the Bolshevik Revolution of 1917. Gorbachev had recognized the error of policy since that time. He also recognized that in their enthusiasm to introduce radical change, the Bolsheviks introduced a policy that placed the needs of the state ahead of those of the people. In the seven decades between the revolution and

Gorbachev, the Soviet Union regarded education of the individual as a means of ensuring the security of the state before it ensured that of the individual.

The Bolsheviks expected the individual to subordinate himself to the needs of the state. When the state was secure, the Bolsheviks concluded, then it would ensure the security of the individual. Gorbachev was the first national leader in the Soviet Union to recognize that for education to serve the needs of society it must serve those of the individual first.[8] He also understood that education must be reformed so that it becomes relevant to the needs of the individual in order that it becomes relevant to society.[9] *Glasnost* and *perestroika* were introduced in an effort correct that imbalance.

Gorbachev was quite clear in his perception of the importance of education for the individual and society. He was not abandoning socialism at all, but was trying to improve its effectiveness by initiating what he considered to be an innovative program. He understood that in attempting this experiment, he was taking a big risk. But he felt that it was better to take risks than to continue leading a nation that was trying to implement a policy that was not relevant to conditions of the time. He remembered that in 1928 Joseph Stalin forced people into communes in which they were expected to utilize education to produce more for the benefit of the state.

Although the literacy rate in the Soviet Union increased from 8 percent in 1928 to 40 percent by the time of his death in March 1953, Stalin had to enslave his people to carry out his policy.[10] Gorbachev concluded that this was not national development. In his thinking that education must benefit the individual as a condition of benefiting society, Gorbachev was coming into line with the universal thinking and practice.

In recent years a number of thinkers, organizations, and government agents across the world have expressed ideas stressing the belief that only education that benefits the individual benefits society. Let us take a few examples to illustrate the accuracy of this conclusion. In 1977 the National Commission on Education in Botswana observed, "Education is at the center of national life of any society because it is intimately involved with its culture and values, its political system and economic development."[11] The Commission goes on to conclude that the primary purpose of education is to ensure that the individual is properly educated in order to serve his own needs as a condition of serving those of society, and that the individual cannot serve the needs of society unless he serves his own needs first.[12]

The question that one must ask is: How does education serve the needs of society as an outcome of serving the needs of the individual? The answer is very clear. By earning a decent income to enable the individual to be self-sufficient, he contributes to the national economy. By participating in the political process, such as the simple act of casting a ballot in elections, he helps to strengthen the democratic process. By participating in the affairs of his community he helps to give his society a national character.

In 1963 United Methodist Bishop Ralph E. Dodge, who served in Zimbabwe from 1956 to 1964, saw national development in terms of the role of education as it gives the individual freedom to participate in various aspects of his society to create a stable political system that affords equal opportunity to all. Dodge concluded

Citizens of every country should have access to all the essential information regarding the policy of their government so that they play a constructive role in seeking its improvement. Any definition of national development must not be imposed on any ground, but must be open to collective input to have real meaning and benefit to the nation because it benefits the individual as a condition of initiating understanding among nations.[13]

Dodge was arguing that only when education is designed to serve the needs of the individual can it serve the needs of society.

Countries all over the world, including those whose leaders do not observe democratic principles, have come to recognize that governments stand to benefit more than anyone else from their educated citizens. Governments therefore have a major interest in educating their people as individuals. The more the people are educated the more they help create a happy society. Progressive governments now realize that by providing facilities and resources for people to secure education, they are actually creating conditions of national development. National development cannot occur with exclusion of the individual. Among other things, the ultimate outcome of national development underscores the structure of relationships between the people and their government in forming a partnership for progress. The thinking that education gives value and worth to society only because it gives value and worth to the individual is a fundamental tenet of the philosophy of the relationship that must exist between the two.[14]

At the beginning of his administration in 1901, Theodore Roosevelt addressed the importance of education for the individual as a condition of serving the needs of society: "Education must light the path of social change. Social and economic problems confronting us are growing in complexity. The more complex and difficult those problems become the more important it is to provide a broad and complete education to all students."[15] It is quite clear that Roosevelt was recognizing the value of education to society because he recognized its value to the individual. Over the years in the United States, education was based on this fundamental principle because since the days of the reform movements of

Horace Mann and Henry Barnard, succeeding generations of Americans have seen its utilitarian value to the individual.

The famous Swiss educator and psychologist Jean Piaget discussed the importance of education to society because, he concluded, it was important to the individual: "The principal goal of education is to create men and women who are capable of doing new things, not merely repeating what other generations have done, men and women who are creative, inventive, and who are discoverers."[16] One can see that Piaget is stressing his view of the function of education that in order to serve the needs of society it must serve those of the individual first. In this context he is also arguing that society has a responsibility of constructing the environment that permits students to be discoverers in various areas of human endeavor to serve the needs of society. Like other thinkers Piaget is also suggesting that only when education serves the needs of the individual does it serve those of society.

## EDUCATION AND UNDERSTANDING AMONG NATIONS

There is a third function that education must serve in order to complete that sequence, and that is to ensure understanding among nations. Immanuel Kant took this perspective when he argued in 1781, "The purpose of education is to train children, not only with reference to their success in the present state of society, but also to a better possible state in accordance with ideal conception of humanity."[17] There is no doubt that Kant was arguing for designing an education that, in serving the needs of the individual and his society, would also serve the needs of world community. To Kant's line of thinking Joan Fagerburg, director of the Office of Students from Other Countries at Northern Arizona University, adds a critical dimension:

The Office of Students from Other Countries at Northern Arizona University is dedicated to an education designed as a necessary preparation for today's life-long experience in a culturally diverse world with its clear message for understanding among nations. For this reason it is the mission of both this office and university to serve and assist students from sixty-three different countries to serve the needs of a world that has become what has appropriately been known in recent years as a global village.[18]

In the modern world the thinking that education must address problems of relationships among nations has emerged as an important consideration because national leaders have increasingly become aware that their nations need other nations to develop. This reality demands a demonstration of understanding in order to cooperate in seeking solutions to problems of development. Soon after Zimbabwe gained independence in 1980, Dzingai Mutumbuka, the minister of education and culture in the new government that Robert G. Mugabe led, articulated a theory of education that was intended to address the need to demonstrate understanding of people of other nations: "We are developing a new alternative system of education along a new perception that it must produce a new man richer in consciousness of humanity. This is the only way a new nation makes life better and more meaningful for the world."[19]

As the presidential elections of 1928 got under way in the United States, many Americans believed that Herbert Hoover, the Republican candidate, did not seem to understand conditions that existed in the country and the world. Among those who held this view was educator John Dewey. As voters were about to go to the polls, Dewey, then sixty-nine years old, not only supported the candidacy of Alfred E. Smith, Hoover's Democratic opponent, but he also criticized Hoover for failing to demonstrate clear understanding of the issues of the sagging economy and relationships between the United States and other nations. Dewey also accused Hoover of not being able to present an effective policy to address problems affecting domestic and world relationships whose application would ensure the development of the country and the security of the world. Dewey went on to add to his criticism of Hoover: "If he has any human insight, dedicated by consciousness of social and world needs, into the policies called for by the day-to-day life of his fellow human beings, either in domestic or international affairs, I have never seen the signs of it."[20] Dewey particularly criticized Hoover for failing to articulate an educational policy that, when implemented, would address critical issues both at home and abroad. The decline in morale and the threat of Communism were problems Dewey believed would be addressed by designing and implementing an effective national educational policy and he concluded that Hoover had none.

Dewey's concern was based on his argument that "lying just below the optimism, apparent prosperity in a binding image of the roaring twenties, there seems to be an influence of a strong undercurrent of dissatisfaction ready to surface as the whole creed of complacence is the greatest force that exists at present in maintaining unrealities of the social tone."[21] Dewey then predicted that Hoover's economic policies would lead, not to two chickens in the pot and a car in every garage of every American family, but to an unprecedented economic disaster. However, the Republicans believed that Hoover had what it took to lead the country into the era of great economic prosperity, and so refused to consider the ominous signs of impending doom. Dewey's understanding of critical issues facing the United States and the world was rare.

## PROBLEMS OF RELATIONSHIPS AMONG NATIONS

During the period of rapidly rising tensions among nations beginning in 1931, compounded by a declining economy, especially the position of teachers, many locals of two national organizations, the American Federation of Teachers (AFT) and the National Education Association (NEA), united in order to do something to resolve problems of relationships among nations. In August 1935 the Baltimore Teachers Union passed a resolution stating:

Whereas the danger of an impending war threatens more and more ominously aggravated by a suicidal race in preparing arms and other war materials, and whereas such organizations as the ROTC, CMTC, CCC, etc., are indoctrinating our youth in the military and nationalist spirit, therefore be it resolved that teachers counteract such preparation by the doctrine of peace and internationalism for the settlement of national disputes and international conflict. Be it further resolved that armament expenditures be diverted to educational channels for the benefit of children and under-educated adults. Be it further resolved that this convention urge the AFT to reorganize a nation-wide opposition to imperialist war bringing together all organizations opposed to war.[22]

It is not surprising that those who saw the peril of Nazi and Fascist imperialism regarded the resolution as supporting Hitler and Mussolini. However, the failure of the Munich conference between Hitler and Neville Chamberlain on September 20, 1938, cannot be attributed to the beliefs of this kind, but to Chamberlain's appeasement of Hitler.[23]

To make sure that the Baltimore Teachers Union was not misunderstood, it passed another resolution the same day:

Whereas fascism is a reactionary force in society interested in the destruction of all liberal and progressive thinking about trade unions, fraternal organizations, and political parties, and whereas fascism incites the population against minority races and groups, and whereas fascism is spreading an international network of reaction and race hatred awakening in this country, be it resolved therefore that this convention reiterate its unalterable opposition to fascism. Be it further resolved that the teachers, as directors of the union, use their influence in combating fascist thought and activity. Be it further resolved that the extension of credits or loans to the Nazi government by the United States be condemned and that the AFT request the U.S. government to prevent such credits or loans.[24]

It is clear that the Baltimore Teachers Union saw events in Europe as constituting a serious threat to peace in the world and wanted to do something to stop it before war engulfed the world. The outbreak of the war on September 1, 1939, transformed the way people thought about themselves and their world.

The Japanese sudden and surprise attack on Pearl Harbor on December 7, 1941, a day that President Franklin D. Roosevelt said would live in infamy, forced the United States to end its neutrality. In January the president underscored the importance of four freedoms he believed must be preserved for all people: "In the future day, which we seek to make secure, we look forward to a world founded upon four essential human freedoms. The first is freedom of speech and expression everywhere in the world. The second is freedom of every person to worship God in his own way. The third is freedom from want. The fourth is freedom from fear."[25] It is clear that even when his nation had been attacked, President Roosevelt demonstrated understanding the need to preserve human dignity in all its aspects.

In 1944, while the war was raging, the United States was placed under a world spotlight which demanded understanding of itself if it hoped to show understanding of the world. The publication in that year of Gunnar Myrdal's *An American Dilemma: The Negro Problem and Modern Democracy* invoked a sense of urgency to do something to confront the problem of racism in all its dimensions. In his well-documented study Myrdal predicted that unless racial discrimination soon ended, the United States was likely to encounter serious racial and social problems in the not-so-distant future. Mrydal suggested the causes of this social conflict:

The crowdedness in the Negro ghettos, the poverty and the economic insecurity, the lack of wholesome recreation and education are factors which all work in the direction of fostering anti-social tendencies leading to conflict. Racial discrimination in opportunity for school facilities is as spectacular as it is well known. The current expenditure per pupil in daily attendance per year in elementary and secondary schools in ten southern states in 1935 and 1936 was $17.04 for Negroes and $49.50 for white children.[26]

This difference meant that African Americans were receiving less educational opportunity than white Americans, a fact that contributed to both the *Brown* decision in 1954 and the beginning of the civil rights struggle in 1955. The United States had become of age. Now, the country could begin to address problems of its relationships with other nations.

## ESSENTIALS OF THE CURRICULUM

An essential consideration of education designed to ensure the concept of human understanding and cooperation is that the curriculum should give both a sense of unity and a perspective in which the individual student sees himself in a positive light in relation to his concept of the universal man. In this kind of setting the student also sees the world as the only viable basis of a meaningful educational experience. But to see himself in a positive light demands that the curriculum acquires a fundamentally positive image of both the student as an indispensable component of the global society and the value of the concept of the universal man.

These realities combine to create an environment in which the student perceives what is happening in the world as a definite outcome of human thought process. This suggests another critical essential element of the curriculum: it must enable the student to envisage a changed world in which he plays a major role. A changed world, in the context of his perception of it, must involve a set of activities which are designed to promote the concept of human cooperation beyond national boundaries. This means that from its inception, the educational process must provide the student a high level of confidence in both himself and the future.

The widespread lack of confidence in themselves in the late 1970s came about as a result of the students' belief that the existence of nuclear weapons offered no future. That this reality was so damaging to students' educational effort and motivation is evinced by the steady decline in SAT scores and other measures. Therefore, the curriculum to ensure human understanding cannot simply happen, it has to be so carefully structured that it inspires the students with confidence for the future as a result of collective effort. It must also be designed to fulfill some fundamental objectives consistent with a positive image of both oneself and the universal man. These essential elements of the curriculum require a full cooperation among all levels of the school administrative structure to ensure that nothing is left to chance.

## CURRICULUM CONSIDERATIONS

The question that one must consider is: What considerations must those responsible for the educational process take into account to realize the essentials of human understanding and cooperation? The answer demands a discussion of ideals necessary to find solutions to the problems of human relations. Robert Mueller puts the answer in the perspective of the reality of human existence when he writes, "To bind the human family together, to foster its further ascent, to prevent it from losing ground and falling into the abyss of despair, we must have a constant vision, a dream for the human family, the universal man. We will swim forever in the present sea of complexities unless we are shown the shore."[27]

What Mueller seems to suggest is that the educational process serves no purpose if students do not learn about human conditions in various parts of the world or about any culture in an artificial sense of their meaning without getting directly involved in events that affect people all over the world. This suggests that the curriculum must be structured in such a way that students learn from it the critical components of what it takes be fully human and to understand conditions that govern human life on a global scale. This is one way in which they become active participants in shaping the course of world events. The involvement may take different forms, such as demonstrating peacefully at the South African Embassy against apartheid. This enables the students to know and understand more, not only about apartheid itself, but also about themselves as major players in the drama of human relationships.

It is a known fact that students all over the world are adversely affected by a limited educational experience within their own system. The responsibility that schools have in designing educational programs must be understood in the context of the educational objectives themselves and the strategies needed to fulfill them. In undertaking this task schools must ask themselves two basic questions: First, when it comes to seeking a knowledge of people in distant lands, what must students study? Second, how must teachers teach in order to enable their students to become part of the world in which they live? The answer to the first question involves the nature of that curricular content, and the answer to the second question involves teaching strategies. The reality that comes out of this endeavor is that the education the students receive is designed to prepare them for the role only they can play in seeking an improvement in human understanding.[28] This is so important and vital to both the educational process and the students that it must never be taken for granted.

One can see that by its very nature, the curriculum must include essential elements of human existence in the world, such as patterns of population increase, life expectancy, literacy, per capita income, or gross national product as indicators of the universal conditions that intimately affect the universal man. These are also important indicators of the direction that nations are taking in an endeavor toward national development. They also indicate the extent to which nations are able to offer services to their people, such as health, communication, education, and an improved standard of living. Therefore, the educational process that comes out of these curricular considerations enables students to understand how geographical as well as cultural and socioeconomic factors influence the political, economic, and social shaping of national systems. These in turn influence the behavior of nations and attitudes toward each other. They also influence the patterns of relationships between nations and people as individuals.

These curricular considerations also enable the school to become aware of the need to educate students to acquire basic skills to enhance a fundamental human principle of fair play as a binding thread to a genuine article of faith in human interaction. This is what Martin Luther King, Jr. had in mind when he argued in 1965: "We have inherited a large house, a great world house in which we have to live together in peace, black and white, Eastern and Western, gentile and Jew, Catholic and Protestant, Moslem and Hindu. It is a family duly brought together by ideals, cultural diversity, mutual interest because we can never again live apart."[29]

Indeed, the problems of the world have become more complex, especially in the nuclear age, than any time in human history. The crises of rising population, massive starvation, pollution of the environment, depletion of resources, the increasing number of the homeless and the poor, the surge of illegal drugs, and a new wave of racism, to name only a few, neither acknowledge national boundaries nor respect any human institutions. The task of education is to equip students with basic tools needed to confront them all, or human life as we have known it steadily will be placed in a perilous situation.

What this suggests is that in designing a curriculum for the global age we can no longer afford to think and behave in terms of mere isolated provincial or national interests, but in terms of the needs of the world community. The survival of the human race now hangs perilously on the cliff of enormous global problems that we all face. A collective action entailing consideration of human cooperation and understanding seems to be the only viable means to save the world from possible catastrophe. An important reality that the curriculum must take into account is the view that political and socioeconomic systems used throughout the world, though seemingly different, actually depend on each other. Therefore, schools, through the application of universal concepts of understanding the universal man, must endeavor to impart to all students an understanding of the critical bonds that exist between various peoples of the world to make them conscious of the need for cooperation, not in terms of political ideology, but in terms of perceiving issues that affect human existence.

Indeed, no one must try to believe that embracing the concept of the universal man brings the Communist ideology and Western ideology into the same line of thinking and behaving. Rather, it would enable both to recognize the mutuality of their interest in seeking an improvement in the conditions that affect human life everywhere. Gorbachev seemed to understand the importance of this line of thinking as he endeavored to initiate fundamental socioeconomic and political reforms in the Soviet Union. The Western democracies must actively assist all such crucial events to insure world peace and security.

In considering the curricular structure for education to insure understanding of the universal being, it is important to keep in mind the essential nature of the value of enabling students to appreciate the fact that man must live in harmony with himself to ensure harmony with the universe. Therefore, any efforts to conquer some aspects of nature, such as limiting the effects of tornadoes or continuing research on cancer or birth defects, are futile unless one first endeavors to understand the conditions that control one's self in relation to the universe. One's acceptance of nature enables one to live in harmony with it. This is how human society can develop a socioeconomic potential without hurting the delicate environmental balance needed to sustain life.

This approach helps students understand that the destruction of the rain forest hurts not only the people who live in it, but all people throughout the world. Therefore, the curriculum must make it possible for students to appreciate the fact that to endeavor to understand the universal man is, indeed, to make efforts to learn how to protect the environment in which they live. This demands a demonstration of an ability to accept responsibility for careful utilization of the world's resources as an integral part of it.

Gerald Weinstein and Mario Fantini seem to take this line of thinking toward the curriculum for the global age when they argue, "The pervasive emphasis on cognitive power and its separation from the real effect poses a threat to our society in that educational institutions may produce cold, detached individuals uncommitted to humanitarian goals and so are unable to think in terms of large human condition."[30]

In applying this thinking to the process of constructing a curriculum aimed at understanding the universal being, one sees a critical component of the educational process itself, and that is, it carries implications that suggest that the schools must not treat concepts of the curriculum as just a body of knowledge to be acquired for its own sake, but as important tools that must be utilized to promote the cause of human cooperation as the only viable means of sustaining the interests of the universal being. In this manner, choices of what is learned become important strategies needed to accomplish objectives and working toward outcomes which are compatible with the essence of human fulfillment.[31]

David Hicks and Charles Tawnley emphasize this point of view regarding the curriculum and go on to argue that human relationships can have meaning only if they are intended to ensure mutual understanding, respect, and acceptance. Hicks and Tawnley add:

Whatever view of knowledge we focus on, it is clear that human relationships must offer something more than mere facts. Knowledge should enable students to extend their activity beyond acquiring it. It should equip them with skills needed to accept those who are different as a viable world modus operandi. Knowledge must offer something more than a peripheral view of both man and the world itself. It must offer understanding, respect, and acceptance of the universal human being.[32]

This perspective suggests a critical dimension of the curriculum beyond itself. It means that students are placed in an environment which demands tolerance, cooperation, acceptance of diversity, and the formation of positive attitudes toward societies other than their own. This means that all school authorities must also understand another important dimension of their responsibility, and that is to teach students to appreciate the fact that the concept of the universal man implies an ability and a willingness to see issues of human existence beyond the local level. They should teach students to appreciate the fact that all people, as members of the human family, must share the joy and the responsibility of freedom based on shared human and social values. Discussing the importance of ending racism in the United States as a condition of establishing an environment of understanding among nations, the Bahai Assembly stated in 1991,

Racism is the most challenging issue confronting America. A nation whose ancestry includes every people on earth, whose motto is *E pluribus unum* (from many to one), whose ideals of freedom under law have inspired millions throughout the world, cannot continue to harbor prejudice against any racial or ethnic group without betraying itself. Racism is an affront to human dignity, a cause of hatred and division, a disease that devastates society.[33]

It is quite possible that the students who come out of this educational environment and system are more likely to appreciate the importance of human understanding and cooperation along the lines this book suggests, because the curricular content includes components that make it possible to see things from this point of view. If all students are exposed to these curricular components, they are in a better position than previous generations of students to embrace the view that all people are equal and that while competition should remain an essential element of human development, it is cooperation in some important areas of human endeavor that is likely to yield better and lasting results for the benefit of all. This is the kind of outcome that international education would offer to all people.

## PROBLEMS OF UNDERSTANDING CULTURAL AND SOCIOECONOMIC DEVELOPMENT

There is no doubt that informed people of the world, whom the educational process must endeavor to include, now realistically understand and appreciate the fact that the world itself is invariably enriched by the diversity of its cultures. Unfortunately the vast majority of the people of the world do not see this cultural diversity from this perspective. That is why there has been serious conflict between the Afrikaners and the Africans in South Africa, between the Hindus and the Moslems in India, and, more recently, between Armenians and Azerbaijanis in the Soviet Union.

The extent of this conflict and the harmful effects it has caused wherever it has existed is the reality that the new president of South Africa, F. W. de Klerk, seemed to take into consideration in 1988 as he and his government took a hard look at a time when the policy of apartheid was leading the country to a major national disaster. The knowledge that apartheid had created a scourge of bitterness among the people of South Africa led de Klerk to reevaluate it in the context of the world condemnation of it. Nowhere in South Africa was the effect of apartheid more profoundly felt than in education.

The creation of the Bantu Education Act in 1953 placed South Africa on the high road to an incredible national conflict. Over the years the agony of racial bitterness reached a level that had to be resolved in order to reestablish mutual trust among the people as the first essential step toward making efforts to find solutions to the problems of human relationships. This is the extent of the crisis that compelled Nelson Mandela to remark, as soon as he was released from prison on March 2, 1990, after serving a prison term of twenty-seven years, that apartheid had to go because it was a crime against humanity.[34] In 1989, the South African government spent $50.00 per black student compared to $1,000.00 per white student, combined with strict racial segregation to alienate the whites from the blacks and make them complete strangers to each other.

When, on February 2, 1990, de Klerk announced the unbanning of the African National Congress (ANC) and other political parties and the decision of his government to release Mandela, there was a new hope that South Africa, in making efforts to end apartheid, would return to national behavior acceptable to the community of nations. Since 1960, South Africa, under the leadership of Hendrik Verwoerd, had been considered an outcast due to the application of the policy of apartheid. Now, in this hour of hope, South Africa had to realize that education is the key to finding solutions to its problems, and that the first step toward that end would be to dismantle apartheid immediately in order to restore the confidence of all the people in the richness of their cultural heritage.

But because of the bitterness created by many years of the application of apartheid, South Africa needed to move aggressively to put in place elements needed to find solutions. Nations of the world with goodwill toward the people of South Africa came to its assistance so that the transition from an Afrikaner political domination to an African majority government could be made with as little disruption as possible. This is how education can play a crucial role. Unesco stood ready and willing to render its assistance in the critical developments that would undoubtedly take place in this troubled country. De Klerk's hope that "the period of seasonal violence is over, the time for reconstruction has arrived,"[35] could only be realized within the framework of efforts to redesign the educational process so that its people were trained to play the role they must in order to create a new society. If apartheid was not dismantled, both in education and in society, education in South Africa could not be allowed to prepare the people of South Africa to play their appropriate role in the transformation of their country. In this context the racial bitterness and cultural conflict that had been the South African way since 1948 would find new ways of expressing themselves in all aspects of national life to the extent that South Africa would enter a new phase of trouble and conflict. When apartheid finally came to an end in April 1994, the dawn of a new day heralded the beginning of a new era of human understanding and cooperation.

In 1994, in order to find a common ground so that the people of South Africa could solve problems of national and human development, South Africa, like other nations, understood the imperative of endeavoring to educate all its people to understand and accept the importance of promoting the development of the individual based upon his cultural identity and a national collective system of values. Now, the challenge before all its people is to accept an opportunity to learn that ignorance of socioeconomic and cultural realities in the postapartheid era are detrimental to national efforts. Indeed, the introduction of its own form of multicultural education can become a panacea of the social evils that the application of apartheid created over many years and can heal the painful wounds of racial conflict that South Africa endured for so long.

Experience in other countries, such as the United States, seems to suggest that multicultural education can help eliminate ignorance and, at the same time, help in focusing on some important aspects of national life that cannot be addressed through political action alone. It creates an environment of mutual trust between people of different racial backgrounds. It builds bridges to effective human communications. It generates in the people a new level of confidence in their ability to plan the future. It offers a new perspective from which to seek common approaches to national problems. These are among the realities that South Africa must now accept as it makes new efforts to create a nonracial society. This is an endeavor which the international community has argued South Africa must make to be reaccepted as a member.

To demonstrate the tangible benefits of this approach, South Africa, as well as other nations that are struggling for development, must place emphasis on instructional materials that are free from any bias and stereotypes that have been used to perpetuate negative attitudes toward the Africans.[36] This approach must permeate the entire curricular structure from preschool to college and in all areas of study. This will make it possible for students to generate a new meaning of self in the context of global perceptions of their role in a community of nations. Clyde Marten takes this line of thinking when he argues, "Multicultural education helps students gain some ideas of the way people of other countries feel about themselves and about their problems. It helps eliminate stereotypes and enhances socioeconomic perceptions based on the cultural diversity of its people as a national enrichment."[37]

There is no question that any education intended to help in resolving problems of socioeconomic, political, and cultural conflict between people goes a long way in helping create new bonds of human understanding and cooperation. Indeed, these are the considerations that South Africa and members of the international community must take into account in making new efforts to redefine new elements of their efforts to understand the universal being.

## EDUCATION OF WOMEN AND THE WORLD COMMUNITY

A discussion of international education cannot be complete without addressing the educational opportunity for women all over the world. When, a few years ago, the United Nations declared an international year of women, the world organization knew that throughout human history, the position of women in the global society had often been less than that of men. Today women still hold positions inferior to those of men and the argument advanced for this is that women are not as educated as men. Modern society seems to ignore in this argument that being mothers, women are often the first teachers of their children, and that to educate them properly means, in essence, to educate the future generation of young people. The values they impart to their children will become essential as they play their role in society and, thus, their role in the world.

Because so many personality traits are implanted in children by the time they are five years old, they will need mothers to teach them to deal with their rapidly changing global environment. Throughout the world women have many household responsibilities to carry out in addition to working outside the home. In these positions, women are paid far less than men. The fact of the matter is that it is quite difficult to expect women to become involved more in society unless the curriculum is structured to meet their specific needs.

In many respects women are as much victims of tradition and culture as they are a product of the action of society itself. There is no doubt that the role that women should play in society today is determined by the level of their educational attainment. But custom and tradition tend to favor men more than women. "To promote men and their status and demote women, to build men as masters of the home, village, nation and the world and to relegate women to lower status because tradition and culture demand it is to ignore the importance of change in society."[38] The Margaret Thatchers of the world are very few and their role is one of trying to make men appear more successful at their own expense. Conditions of the times combine with other considerations to demand a change in this traditional attitude in order to realize the essence of the universal being.

Perhaps this is why in 1981, Sarudzai Churucheminzwa, a young Zimbabwean woman, took this into consideration in expressing her feelings when she recalled:

As I grew up I strongly resented the attitude of my society, which deliberately underestimated women's capabilities to mold a universal society. Such an attitude deprived many women of an opportunity to give assistance where they could and all incentives to cultivate their talents as human beings. My brothers gained a lot of experience, physically and intellectually. Because of this they began to challenge me. I was even embarrassed, when at school, we had heated arguments about why women were regarded as biologically less intellectual than men. To deny women an opportunity for educational development is to deny the world community an opportunity for its own advancement.[39]

It is not surprising that the entire school process itself has been one of disappointment as it has considerably lowered the self-esteem of young women. In this situation many young women with ambition have become frustrated by the attitudes of their society, and the sacrifices that they make to ensure a meaningful education often lead them to dead-end situations. What is needed therefore is a fundamental change of attitude toward the education of women in order to realize the importance of educating them properly. This task can best be accomplished by initiating a global strategy.

## POPULATION INCREASE, HUNGER, AND EDUCATION

Among the major problems that the world is facing is the threat of world hunger and uncontrollable population increase. Indeed, hunger and famine have become world problems for a long time. Frances Moore Lappe takes this line of thinking when she writes: "Hunger is a screaming siren telling us that something is terribly amiss in the global social order created by population explosion."[40] The world has seen horrifying pictures of starving masses in Ethiopia, the Sudan, and Mozambique, but with the technology at its disposal the world community is still unable to resolve the problems created by this scourge.

Throughout the world conditions of living have reduced children to a position in which malnutrition has permanently damaged their physical and mental capacity to grow and develop. In both developing and developed countries the effect of hunger and malnutrition are felt first by children because their bodies need a balanced diet in order to grow and develop. Compounding this problem is population explosion which forces a destruction of the environment.[41]

Hunger and the population explosion both seem to suggest two critical approaches to find possible solutions. The first is that all nations must recognize that they do not have sufficient resources by themselves needed to solve their problems. Therefore, international cooperation would enable nations to set a common agenda for action so that they can pool their resources and direct them toward areas of greatest need. The second is an educational system that places emphasis on common features of national development, which in turn ensures global development. Periodic conferences on education, the structure it should take, recognition of the major global world, and methods of improving agricultural production could help find answers to problems of global peace. The twin problems of hunger and population increase are far too serious to be left to chance. The global community has an obligation to redesign an educational system that adequately responds to both.

## SUMMARY AND CONCLUSION

What has been discussed in this chapter suggests two basic conclusions. The first is that the world must move closer to understanding and accepting the importance of cooperation or face the real prospect of a devastating human conflict. The essential element of ending human conflict is a demonstration of the understanding of the universal man. The world must see the change that is taking place in Eastern Europe and the prospects of peaceful change in South Africa as constituting a set of human events that must be accepted from a positive point of view as a manifestation of the understanding by its members of the concept of the universal being.

This is not to suggest a mere theoretical perspective from which to seek an understanding of humanity, but to make a clear call to broaden the human base to ensure cooperation based on an endeavor to sustain mutual human and global interests. This is how global peace can be maintained. It is in the interest of the global community to help those nations that are struggling for meaningful change that a harmonious global common direction can be structured. The international community must become actively involved in this kind of endeavor, rather than stand on the sidelines and watch a perilous course take its direction to the detriment of all humanity.

The second conclusion is that any change in human condition and interaction has much more meaningful implications for global security when education becomes a central component of its structure and operation. International education, as it has been defined in this study, becomes a major instrument with which nations, as members of the global community, can accomplish the objectives that are critical to international peace and security. Our task, as members of the human family, is to endeavor to make it a reality by having it address the needs of the human being. Once this reality becomes accepted by all, the universal being can then direct its efforts toward other equally challenging endeavors to place one on the higher plain of life that one deserves. This is a challenge we must accept and a call we must answer.

These conclusions suggest that international education reduces the likelihood of a global conflict. The universal being gets to understand one's self better through education than by any other means. Therefore, any change in human conditions and relationships poses much more meaningful implications for global security when education becomes a central consideration in an endeavor to accept the concept of the universal being. It is in the best interest of the international community itself to promote the educational development of all people. It must not seek military might. Instead it must seek to promote human understanding.

## NOTES

1. Ndabaningi Sithole, interview with the author (Harare, Zimbabwe, July 22, 1983).

2. Paulo Freire, *Pedagogy of the Oppressed*, trans. Myra Bergman Ramos (New York: Continuum, 1983), p. 62.

3. Frederick Douglass, *Narrative of the Life of Frederick Douglass an American Slave by Himself* (New York: New American Library, 1845), p. 52.

4. Ibid., p. 45.

5. Samora Machel, "Leadership Is Collective Responsibility, Responsibility Is Collective," speech given at the Joint Meeting of Frelimo in Maputo, Mozambique, February 2, 1972 (Mozambique Ministry of Information).

6. Ibid.

7. John Dewey, *Experience and Education* (New York: Collier, 1938), p. 17.

8. A. Putintsev, *U.S.S.R.: Perestroika* (Moscow: Novosti Press, 1990), p. 12.

9. Ibid., p. 14.

10. Dickson A. Mungazi, *Educational Policy and National Character: Africa, Japan, the United States and the Soviet Union* (Westport, CT: Praeger Publishers, 1993), p. 38.

11. Botswana, National Commission on Education (Gaborone: Government Printer, 1977), p. 17.

12. Ibid., p. 18.

13. Dickson A. Mungazi, *The Honored Crusade: Ralph Dodge's Theology of Liberation and Initiative for Social Change in Zimbabwe* (Gweru: Mambo Press, 1992), p. 57.

14. Dickson A. Mungazi and L. Kay Walker, *Educational Reform and the Transformation of Southern Africa* (Westport, CT: Praeger Publishers, 1998), p. 154.

15. William van Til, *Education: A Beginning* (Boston: Houghton Mifflin Company, 1974), p. 419.

16. Ibid., p. 417.

17. Van Til, *Education: A Beginning*, p. 418.

18. Joan Fagerburg, Director of the Office of Students from Other Countries at Northern Arizona University, statement of mission (Flagstaff, October 27, 1999).

19. Dzingai Mutumbuka, "Zimbabwe's Educational Challenge," paper presented at the World Universities Services Conference, London, December 1979 (Zimbabwe Ministry of Information).

20. Herbert Kliebard, *The Struggle for the American Curriculum, 1893–1958* (New York: Routledge and Kegan Paul, 1987), p. 180.

21. Ibid., p. 181.

22. The Baltimore Teachers Union, Resolution on the Danger of War, August 10, 1935 (The AFT Files, Walter Reuther Archives of Labor, Wayne State University, Detroit).

23. Louis L. Snyder, *Hitler's Third Reich: A Documentary History* (Chicago: Nelson-Hall, 1981), p. 291.

24. The Baltimore Teachers Union, Resolution on the Danger of War.

25. Franklin D. Roosevelt, The State of the Union Message, January 6, 1941.

26. Gunar Myrdal, *An American Dilemma: The Negro Problem and Modern Democracy* (London: Harper and Brothers Publishers, 1944), p. 332.

27. Robert Mueller, *New Genesis* (New York: Doubleday, 1982), p. 19.

28. Ibid., p. 20.

29. James Washington (ed.), *Testament of Hope* (New York: Harper and Row, 1986), p. 67.

30. Gerald Weinstein and M. Mario Fantini, *Toward a Humanistic Education: A Curriculum of Affect* (New York: Praeger Publishers, 1970), p. 27.

31. Ibid., p. 29.

32. David Hicks and Charles Tawnley (eds.), *Teaching World Studies* (New York: Longman, 1982), p. 174.

33. Bahai Assembly, *The Vision of Race Unity: America's Most Challenging Issue* (Wilmette, IL: Bahai Publishing Trust, 1991), p. 1.

34. Nelson Mandela, a statement to the press on March 2, 1990, SABC-TV.

35. F. W. de Klerk, speech to the South African Parliament in Cape Town, February 2, 1990, SABC-TV.

36. A specific case in point is the documentary film "The Search for Sandra Lainge: Education in South Africa," SABC-TV, 1981. This shows a strict application of apartheid.

37. Clyde Marten, *A Venture in International Understanding* (Austin: The University of Texas Press, 1985), p. 132.

38. Zimbabwe, *First Women's Seminar* (Harare: ZANU Information Office, 1981).

39. Ibid.

40. Frances Moore Lappe, "Democracy and Dogma in the Fight Against Hunger," *The Christian Century*, December 10, 1986, p. 15.

41. "Why Africans Go Hungry," *Scholastic Update*, January 27, 1989.

# 6

# Unesco, Education, and Understanding Among Nations

Since wars begin in the minds of men, it is in the minds of men that the defense of peace must be constructed.

Unesco Charter, 1946

## THE DUMBARTON OAKS CONFERENCE AND THE FOUNDING OF THE UNITED NATIONS

This chapter discusses the efforts that United Nations Educational Scientific and Cultural Organization (Unesco) has been making since its founding in 1946 to exert a positive effect on conditions of the development of education and understanding as prerequisite of peace among nations. In doing so it first discusses the founding and functions of the United Nations itself. At first nations anticipated that the war would come to an end between 1942 and 1944. In 1944 Britain, the United States, and the Soviet Union convened a conference to be held at Dumbarton Oaks in Washington, D.C. to begin on August 21 to prepare for the founding of an organization among nations to be known as the United Nations.[1]

The U.S. delegation was led by Secretary of State, Cordell Hull, the Soviet Union delegation was led by Ambassador to the United States, Andrei Gromyko, and the British delegation was led by Foreign Secretary Sir Alexander Cadogan. Recognizing that the action taken by the U.S. Senate in rejecting U.S. involvement in the formation and operation of the League of Nations following the end of World War I was a mistake, the U.S. delegation at the Dumbarton Conference was quite enthusiastic in being part of laying ground for the creation of an organization intended to keep peace among nations following the end of World War II.[2] The Dumbarton Oaks Conference worked out details of how the United Nations was to be structured and how it would function.

As the conference began the task of putting together the structure and functions of the proposed organization among nations, President Franklin D. Roosevelt instructed his delegation to adopt a hard-line position on Germany to impress upon its people that they carried a collective guilt in their failure to restrain their leaders from waging a "barbaric assault on civilization."[3] But his advisers cautioned him to remember that any punitive measures taken against the German people would invoke a negative response among members of the international community, because many people were talking about the need to exercise moderation in order to succeed in creating an organization that would keep peace in the world.

With a delegation of eighteen people, including six from the army and navy, the United States dominated the Dumbarton Conference. But operating within the spirit of moderation that was part of the deliberations about the future, the U.S. delegation toned down its tendency toward adapting a hard-line position. This would prove to be beneficial at the San Francisco conference that convened to reconstruct the world after the war in 1945. Delegates to the Dumbarton Oaks Conference did not want to consider how the war was going in order not to lose sight of that future. There was difference of opinion as to whether deliberations should reflect progress of the war toward a conclusion. Cadogan and Gromyko argued that the conference must not ignore the conduct of the war because its end would help determine how the United Nations would function. Hull argued that whatever the outcome of the war was, it should not influence the structure and functions of the organization because it should be influenced by how the war was going. Hull was highly sensitive to the fact that when President Woodrow Wilson presented his plan for the future of the world, World War I was still going on. This put the U.S delegation in an uncomfortable position. In the end the U.S. delegation succeeded in persuading the other delegations to see things from its perspective, and the deliberations continued to a successful conclusion after solving some problems.

It was a miracle that the Dumbarton Conference succeeded in its task. It was nearly ruined by the action the Soviet Union took against Poland in August 1944. With its army on the edge of Warsaw to stop German forces from making another attempt to move toward Soviet territory, Radio Moscow urged a rebellion to speed up the liberation process from control by forces opposed to Moscow. Britain and the United States asked Stalin to intervene to stop the conflict. But Stalin declined, arguing that the rebellion was against Soviet interests in that part of Europe.[4] When the British and U.S. governments decided to airlift essential supplies from their bases in Italy to the insurgents in Poland, much of the supplies and materials were captured by German forces, threatening the Dumbarton Conference itself. Of course, Germany had indicated that it was not interested in any dialogue except on its own terms. It was interested only in conquering and ruling the world.

German forces intercepted most of the materials airlifted to insurgents in Poland loyal to Britain and the United States, while the Soviet Union and Germany killed millions of Poles from opposing sides.[5] This unfortunate incident reinforced the belief of the delegates to the Dumbarton Conference that they must continue their efforts to lay the foundation of the founding of the United Nations to make the world safe for democracy and peace as President Woodrow Wilson had stated toward the end of World War I. That Stalin declined to intervene in the carnage in Poland invoked a bitter exchange between him and Roosevelt. Right in the middle of deliberations, delegates to the Dumbarton Oaks Conference decided that the new crisis in Poland was serious and that they could not continue under the possibility of its escalation. Each delegation needed time to assess the situation and review its position.[6]

However, on September 7, 1944, Roosevelt had a direct discussion with Gromyko to see if differences between the delegations could be resolved to enable the deliberations to continue. In responding, Gromyko showed flexibility and understanding of the concerns of the U.S. delegation that it would not be beneficial to any side to continue discussion under the influence of new conflict when all sides were thinking that the war was coming to an end. Gromyko also persuaded Stalin to exercise understanding of the situation to enable him to support the continuation of the Dumbarton Conference in the belief that the creation of the United Nations would be in the best interests of all nations, including the Soviet Union.[7]

In the midst of a renewed hope for continuing the deliberations at Dumbarton Oaks there was a new problem. Gromyko suddenly demanded that the delegation from the Soviet Union in the UN General Assembly be increased to sixteen to offset the number of delegations from Britain and the United States. This is the position that Stalin himself had taken and Gromyko was merely expressing the position of his government on the issue. Both Stalin and Gromyko argued that the United Nations must have the number of civilian delegates more than the number of military delegates to eliminate the criticism that the proposed organization was another military alliance. Both Hull and Cadogan seemed to agree with that idea.[8] When the issue was resolved the Dumbarton Oaks Conference continued.

However, it soon became apparent that there were other differences of opinion about the structure of the proposed United Nations that seemed to present new problems. One issue was the question of the veto power that the five major nations[9] wanted to give themselves as permanent members to control the decisions of the Security Council. The Dumbarton Oaks Conference decided that in order to address all pertinent issues regarding the structure and functions of the United Nations, including the veto power of the five major nations, it was necessary to divide itself into three working committees.

The first committee was asked to work out the UN structure and functions. The second committee was asked to work out detailed procedures of resolving disputes among members by peaceful means. The third committee was asked to work out details of security procedures for the entire world.[10] Each committee took its assigned task seriously in order to minimize the possibility of the entire organization being rejected when nations assembled at San Francisco because parts of the proposed organization were inadequate.

When the Dumbarton Oaks Conference adjourned on October 3, 1944, delegates carefully considered detailed reports of the three committees and agreed on their recommendations, including the controversial issue of the veto power to be exercised by the five permanent nations. The conference agreed to recommend that an international organization known as the United Nations be inaugurated at the San Francisco conference. In reaching this decision the Dumbarton Oaks Conference singled out four issues it felt must be addressed in its recommendations.

The first issue was that membership of the General Assembly should be open to all independent nations. Colonies were excluded because they did not carry the responsibility of making decisions that would affect their relationships with other nations. Delegates also agreed that the United Nations should have broad role to play in search for solutions to problems of relationships among nations. Gromyko stressed this point to emphasize the need for collective action on issues affecting peace in the world.[11]

The second issue was the need to draft the charter to cover specific provisions and conditions of the structure and functions of the proposed organization. These conditions would include a clause prohibiting nations from resorting to military action to seek solutions to conflict among them.[12] They were expected to refer all disputes to a branch of the organization known as the Security Council for resolution. The Security Council, headed by the secretary-general as the chief officer of the United Nations itself, would act as the UN executive. The Dumbarton Oaks Conference also recommended that a court be established to resolve legal questions of ethnic conflict or strained relations among nations. Today the International Court at The Hague plays that role well.

The third issue was the voting procedure in the Security Council.

While voting in the General Assembly constituted recommendations, voting in the Security Council constituted decisions that had to be implemented. There, any issue was subject to veto power by any of the five permanent members. This means that no issue can be decided without unanimous support of the five major nations. The veto power was not subject to discussion or overrule. Aware that the veto power could be abused, the Dumbarton Oaks Conference accepted a resolution from the U.S. delegation for inclusion into its recommendations that "provision will need to be worked out with respect to the voting procedure in the event of a dispute in which one or more of the members having continuing tenure are directly involved."[13]

The fourth issue was the creation of an agent under the general supervision of the United Nations itself. This agent would be given the responsibility of promoting education, cultural understanding, and technological and scientific development in the world to make sure that nations had an opportunity to learn and understand each other to avoid conflict and to ensure cooperation in the maintenance of peace.[14] With these recommendations forming the thrust for its report the Dumbarton Oaks Conference felt that it had accomplished its assigned task and adjourned with high hopes that the war would soon be over and the world would soon look to the future of peace with great expectations.

## THE STRUCTURE AND FUNCTIONS OF THE UNITED NATIONS

On April 25, 1945, 283 delegates from forty-six nations began to arrive in San Francisco to attend a very important conference convened to undertake the task of reconstructing the world, anticipating that the war would end soon.[15] On June 26 delegates signed a document creating the United Nations out of the report and recommendations of the Dumbarton Oaks Conference. This section briefly discusses the structure and function of the United Nations to set the stage for a discussion of Unesco itself. The creation of the United Nations was the climax of developments that began to form with the Atlantic Charter, an eight-point document developed and signed by U.S. President Franklin D. Roosevelt and British Prime Minister Winston S. Churchill, on August 14, 1941. The form of the report of the Dumbarton Oaks Conference followed pretty much the elements of the Atlantic Charter.

Because the charter is relevant to the San Francisco conference, it is important to list here its provisions. The president of the United States and His Majesty's government in the United Kingdom deemed it right to make known certain common principles in the national policies of their respective countries.

1. Their countries seek no aggrandizement, territorial or otherwise.

2. They desire to see no territorial changes that do not accord with the freely expressed wishes of the people concerned.

3. They respect the right of all peoples to choose the form of government under which they will live, and they wish to see sovereign rights and self-government restored to those who have been forcibly deprived of them.

4. They will endeavor, with due respect for their existing obligation, to further the enjoyment by all states, great and small, victor or vanquished, of access, on equal terms, to trade and to raw materials of the world which are needed for their economic prosperity.

5. They desire to bring about the fullest collaboration between all nations in the economic field with the object of securing for all improved labor standards, economic advancement, and social security.

6. After final destruction of the Nazi tyranny, they hope see established peace which will afford to all nations the means of dwelling in safety within their own boundaries and which will afford assurance that all men in all lands may live out their lives in freedom from fear and want.

7. Such a peace should enable all men to traverse the high seas and oceans without hindrance.

8. They believe that all nations of the world, for realistic as well as for spiritual reasons, must come to the abandonment of the use of force. Since no future peace can be maintained if land, sea, or air armaments continue to be employed by nations which threaten, or may threaten aggression outside their own frontiers, they believe, pending the establishment of a wider and permanent system of general security, that the disarmament of such nations is essential. They will like-wise aid and encourage all other practicable measures which will lighten for peace-loving peoples the crushing burden of armaments.[16]

With these words the two leaders made Africans believe that they were, in effect, warning against continuing colonial conditions to the detriment of the development of the people they ruled. The charter and the Africans' interpretation of it would create serious conflict following the end of the war. However, the founding of the United Nations was based essentially on the report and recommendations of the Dumbarton Oaks Conference. The preamble to the UN Charter states: "Our representative Governments, through representatives assembled in the city of San Francisco, who have exhibited their full powers found to be in good and due form, have agreed to the present charter of the United Nations and do hereby establish an international organization known as the United Nations."[17] The purpose of the United Nations was stated

To maintain international peace and security, and to that end: to take effective collective measures for the prevention and removal of threats to peace, and for the suppression of acts of aggression or other breaches of the peace, and to bring about by peaceful means, and in conformity with the principles of justice and international law, adjustment or settlement of international disputes or institutions which might lead to a breach of peace.[18]

In addition to this broad objective, the United Nations also reflected contemporary thinking that the new organization should achieve goals that would sustain ideals and conditions of relationships among nations in the atomic age. Many people felt that it was designed to ensure the acquisition of knowledge and understanding so that it would become the center of harmonizing action among nations in attaining common purposes through dialogic interaction and the observance of principles of equality, tolerance, and sovereignty of all nations. They also believed that acceptance of cultural diversity was a critical function of the United Nations. This means that they expected the United Nations to be more inclusive than any other organization in the world. It was not too much to expect nations to observe a few simple operational principles, especially respecting territorial integrity of all nations and respect of the UN charter, particularly refraining from resorting to military force to resolve conflict. Nations were expected to give the United Nations their unconditional support, knowing that it was there to ensure peace among nations by expecting certain behavior from each nation. In turn the United Nations was expected to behave in certain ways, such as refraining from interfering in the internal matters of nations unless there was good reason to do so, such as gross violation of human rights and genocide.[19]

Chapter 2, Article 3 of the UN Charter addresses membership of the organization, stating that original members would be those nations which had participated in the conference at San Francisco or those that had previously signed the declaration of the organization's intent on January 19, 1942, or those who decided to sign the Charter at the San Francisco conference.[20] This means that membership in the United Nations was open to all peace-loving nations provided they agreed to observe the principles that it outlined, accepted its obligations contained in the Charter, and, in the judgment of the organization, were willing and able to carry out these obligations by observing conditions of its operational principles.

Chapter 3, Article 7 of the Charter also specified that the United Nations would have agencies and divisions to maximize the effectiveness of its organization and functions. Major UN divisions included the General Assembly, Security Council, Economic and Social Council, Trusteeship Council, International Court of Justice, Children's Fund, and Educational, Scientific and Cultural Organization. These were recommended by the Dumbarton Oaks Conference, knowing how critical they were to meeting the needs of the people in all nations. The composition of these divisions was also specified. The General Assembly would consist of all UN members. Each delegation would have no more than five members. The secretary-general[21] is the chief executive officer of the United Nations itself.

The current secretary-general, Kofi Annan of Ghana, is a man of considerable accomplishments. Born in Kumasi province, on April 8, 1938, Annan studied at the University of Science and Technology in Kumasi and completed his undergraduate work in economics at Macalester College in St. Paul, Minnesota, in 1961. From 1961 to 1962, he undertook graduate studies in economics at the Institut Universitaire des Hautes Etudes Internationales in Geneva. As a 1971–1972 Sloan Fellow at the Massachusetts Institute of Technology, Annan received a Master of Science degree in management.[22]

Annan joined the UN in 1962 as an administrative and budget officer with the World Health Organization in Geneva. Since then he has served with the UN Economic Commission for Africa in Addis Ababa, the UN Emergency Force in Ismalia, the Office of the UN High Commissioner for Refugees in Geneva, and at the UN headquarters in New York (as assistant secretary-general for Human Resources Management and security coordinator for the UN System from 1987 to 1990 and assistant secretary-general for Program Planning, Budget and Finance, and controller). In 1990, following the invasion of Kuwait by Iraq, Annan was asked by the secretary-general to assume a special assignment to facilitate the repatriation of more than 900 international staff and the release of Western hostages in Iraq. He subsequently led the first UN team to negotiate with Iraq on the sale of oil to fund purchases of humanitarian aid. It was a fitting recognition that on January 1, 1997, the General Assembly elected Annan as the seventh secretary-general of the United Nations.[23]

Chapter 15, Article 97 of the Charter states that the secretary-general is the chief executive officer and is elected by the General Assembly upon recommendation of the Security Council, and that he would be assisted by a secretariat also elected by the General Assembly.[24] The Security Council consists of the five permanent members, each with a veto power, and ten members elected by the General Assembly to serve a two-year term. A retiring nonpermanent member nation would not be eligible for reelection.[25] This section of the study discusses four divisions or agencies of the United Nations as examples of how it was organized to improve its effectiveness.

The Economic and Social Council had three major responsibilities to fulfill. It was intended to improve the standard of living in the world in an effort to eliminate poverty, which was identified at the end of the war as one of the major causes of war. It was also expected to ensure that all people had an equal opportunity for economic security so that they were free from want and deprivation. This division was also expected to facilitate the search for solutions to economic and social problems arising from trade relationships among nations. This division was also expected to influence nations to provide equal opportunity for economic and social development without any regard to race, religion, and gender,[26] other factors that were recognized as a cause of World War II.

The Trusteeship Council consisted of fifteen nations elected by the General Assembly for a term of three years. The council had the responsibility to make sure that nations appointed to administer these trust territories did so according to the requirements laid out by the United Nations. Trust territories were not colonies. The idea came out of the end of World War I, when Woodrow Wilson proposed the principle that "their well-being form a sacred trust of civilization,"[27] in order to prepare them for eventual independence. The administering nation was expected to submit annual reports regarding the progress being made toward independence. In 1945 many countries were under colonial rule and the United Nations asked the Trusteeship Council to make sure that those nations administering them made a sincere effort to prepare them for independence and to make sure that progress was being made toward that objective.[28]

The International Court of Justice was, and is, considered the principal legal division of the United Nations. The court consists of fifteen judges elected by the General Assembly, most of them from developing countries. Each member of the court serves a term of nine years with reelection to another term of nine years. No two judges can be elected from the same country. The main function of the court is to settle disputes among nations. The court meets at The Hague. It elects the president and vice president. Individuals cannot bring cases before the court unless they are sponsored or supported by their government.

The decision of the court is final and there is no appeal after it. Just as the president of the United States has responsibility to implement the decision of the U.S. Supreme Court, the Security Council has responsibility to implement the decision of the International Court of Justice. The court can also examine treaties reached between nations and make sure that they are legally binding and see if they are properly drawn. Chapter 14, Article 94 of the UN Charter requires that "members of the United Nations comply with the decisions of the Court. If any party to a case fails to perform its obligations incumbent upon it under a judgment rendered by the Court, the other party may decide upon measures to be taken to give effect to the judgment."[29]

There were other agencies that the United Nations established to improve its effectiveness in responding to human needs all over the world as a condition of ensuring understanding and peace. Among these are the Food and Agricultural Organization, which helps developing nations in seeking improvement in the methods of producing food. International Civil Aviation helps facilitate travel in the world to reduce problems of conflict over the question of air space. The International Labour Organization mediates in disputes between management and workers. The International Monetary Fund works closely with the World Bank to facilitate financial arrangements, such as loans given to developing countries to invest in their development. The Relief and Rehabilitation Council helps nations that have been hit by natural disasters such as earthquakes, typhoons, or hurricanes assess the extent of damage they have suffered and their need for relief and rehabilitation. The UN Children's Fund (Unicef) offers assistance to children made destitute by circumstances they cannot control.

The United Nations is particularly sensitive to the need to protect children for a very good reason. Any society that does not make sure that its children are protected and properly raised is doomed. This is why in June 1997 Kofi Annan stated his ideas of how to ensure the future of children in one critical dimension of their lives, saying from a broad perspective, "The world is beginning to recognize that conflict has many roots, that peace rests on economic and social stability. Creating such stability is not merely a matter of projects and statistics. It is above all, a matter of people, real people with basic needs: food, clothing, shelter, medical care and water."[30]

Before we discuss the work of Unesco we must draw some conclusions about the United Nations itself. From its creation in 1945 as a result of the report submitted by the Dumbarton Oaks Conference, through the turbulent period of the cold war, to the present, the United Nations has been subjected to severe pressure to act according to the interests of individual nations that have had agendas of their own. But the United Nations has remained faithful to its charter. Some nations have given it their total support, others have been less than loyal in giving that support. But all in all the United Nations has tried under very difficult circumstances to do its work in serving the needs of the world.

In drawing their study, *FDR and the Creation of the UN*, to a conclusion, Townsend Hoopes and Douglas Brinkley summarize the role that the United States must play in strengthening the United Nations:

The challenge to the American political system is to recognize both the fundamental importance of the United Nations Organization and its inherent limitations. The corollary is to acknowledge the enduring necessity for the dominant world power to play a steady balancing role both inside and outside the UN. The United States should take a leading role in an effort to strengthen and sustain the UN peace-keeping system that is deliberately designed to reduce the need for U.S-led military efforts.[31]

Now we must turn our attention to the discussion of the role that Unesco has played in advancing the quest for knowledge to ensure peace and understanding among nations. When Unesco was founded to begin its operation in December 1946, it became a lightpost of hope among nations that a new opportunity was about to make it possible for all people to learn what they believed they needed to make peace a reality of life in a rapidly changing world. All over the world people believed that the acquisition of knowledge would bring them to a new level of understanding of people in different parts of the world as a prerequisite of peace. Unesco was given the responsibility of promoting educational, cultural, and scientific development as a cornerstone of peace in the world by nations' conduct and behavior toward each other. The central tenet of Unesco has been to teach people in all nations that they must never assume that their own culture is superior to other cultures. Although Unesco did not say so directly, it was certainly aware that the assumption made by members of the Nazi party in Germany that Germans were an Aryan race led to the deterioration of relationships with people of other cultures.

## UNESCO IN PERSPECTIVE

This study has concluded that there exists a definite need to establish a means of improving the level and content of education throughout the world, and a way of breaking down the cultural and national barriers that prevent the world community from communicating and functioning as a more cohesive unit. The creation of Unesco represents the world's effort in forming an organization with a working knowledge of defining and fulfilling objectives relative to the quest for understanding of people of other cultures. Although Unesco has fallen short of its expectations, it has tried under very difficult circumstances to live up to expected criteria.

Indeed, Unesco has become a world organization that is characterized by political disharmony and divided by numerous conflicting nationalistic and provincial interests. However, it has endeavored to discharge its proper responsibility: the development and application of the concept of cooperation among nations in creating an environment conducive to the acquisition of knowledge or education so that the world community can live the reality of development and peace. The weaknesses that have led to Unesco's limited ability in the face of glaring inadequacies of its organizational structure explain the weaknesses of its parent organization, the United Nations itself. That Unesco's mission is entrenched in its operational charge—"Since wars begin in the minds of men, it is in the minds of men that the defense of peace must be constructed,"[32]— underscores the essence of its existence. Regardless of the problems that

Unesco has experienced recently, especially the withdrawal of the United States and Britain in 1985, Unesco cannot be regarded as a failure. The purpose of this chapter is to examine Unesco's operational principles, discuss some of the problems it has been experiencing, and offer possible solutions. This is done on the assumption that Unesco has an important role to play in making efforts to understand people in other societies.

## UNESCO'S OPERATIONAL PRINCIPLES

At the conclusion of the war in 1945, the necessary arrangements for establishing an organization based on cultural and educational cooperation were put in place. At that time the idea of forming such an organization was suggested by the Chinese.[33] It is ironic that until 1979, the People's Republic of China was not admitted into the UN because of political differences. The idea of forming a world organization with special focus on promoting knowledge through education to insure understanding was subsequently followed up with action by the Western nations, which had put forth a considerable amount of funds to enable Unesco to come into being.

That at its formation Unesco established a number of goals and objectives explains how seriously it regarded its task. Among these goals was to work hard to eliminate the ignorance its members knew existed about cultures other than one's own. In the process of eliminating such ignorance, Unesco tried to establish a more world peace-oriented cooperative based on understanding of the valued components of its institutions.[34] Unesco also was designed to serve as a centralized source for worldwide research in the areas of scientific and technological development and to assist in the development of educational systems throughout the world, especially in countries that needed the greatest amount of assistance, such as those of the Third World. The fact that Unesco put in place a machinery of fair determination through an assessment of needs, suggests its commitment to the cause it had accepted as its primary responsibility.

Another important principle that Unesco has utilized as a basis of its operation is that representation is based upon the action of the United Nations itself and that all member nations are represented in its decisions. Although Unesco's director-general assumes the responsibility of its operations and decisions, he does not make crucial decisions alone. This practice means that all members make an important contribution to the decision-making process in order to reflect its mission to the entire world. The process of determining needs is as complicated as it is fascinating. The general conditions of a country—its literacy rate, economic status, political systems, gross national product or per capita income, need for adult educational programs—are among some important considerations Unesco takes into account in deciding the kind of assistance a country should receive in its struggle for development.

In his assessment of the efforts and the effectiveness of Unesco in its endeavor to elevate the human being to a higher standard of living level, Marvin Stone presents an impressive argument:

One might think that the goals and ideals upon which Unesco was founded make it seem like a catch-all type of educational organization that would draw the countries of the world together. However, in reality, there has been much debate about the new problems Unesco has been trying to resolve and how it has inadvertently become a target of international conflict as opposed to a way of developing international understanding and cooperation. These problems, inherent in the U.N.'s structure, have become so great that they have caused serious conflict between nations. When the U.S. withdrew from Unesco in 1985, Unesco lost 25% of its operational budget, the amount that the U.S. had been contributing.[35]

## UNESCO'S PROBLEMS

There are a number of problems that Unesco has been facing, especially in recent years. These are the problems that forced the United States to withdraw from Unesco in 1985. Among the problems is the highly politicized nature of the organization of Unesco itself. From 1982 to 1984 the United States, Britain, Japan, the Netherlands, and West Germany became increasingly dissatisfied with the highly political atmosphere that Unesco was accused of cultivating.[36] These nations argued that in an atmosphere as politicized as they claimed Unesco had become, it was impossible to arrive at decisions that would benefit the entire world community. This argument had a powerful appeal to Western nations because many of Unesco's delegates had only their individual national interests in mind.

It is a sad truth that the general concern among these nations had moved away from seeking understanding and cooperation among nations toward nationalistic tendencies which the UN itself had identified in 1945 as one of the major causes of conflict in the world. Malcolm G. Scully concludes that these nations argued that a degree of politicizing Unesco had become so widespread in its operations that it had become singled out as "a prime example of the intrusion of politics into international assistance agencies."[37] While one can appreciate the fact that because Unesco stands on a high visible plain, it could not avoid the political implications of its operations. One must also recognize the perilous course that those who saw it from a political perspective were setting for it.

A specific example of exactly how politics can affect Unesco can be found in the controversy that surrounded the issue of Unesco's role in disarmament education. First, in 1953, Unesco felt that it could support the development of nuclear energy as a form of its commitment to educational research. But when, in 1955, it saw that some nations were developing nuclear capability to suit their military purposes, Unesco withdrew its support in protest. This created a situation in which some nations argued that the development of nuclear potential was a scientific matter that was well within its responsibility to assist.

The discussion on disarmament brought out a considerable degree of nationalistic sentiments that were contrary to Unesco's operational principles. On this particular issue, the United States and several other Western countries wished "to abandon the discussion on the controversial disarmament education, but the damage to the integrity of Unesco had been done."[38] The Soviet Union of the pre-Gorbachev era, on the other hand, supported the program because a large portion of it was "inspired by the Soviet Union and clearly designed to further its own national interests,"[39] and because its own technology of the postwar era was still relatively in a state of underdevelopment.

Being part of Unesco, which has attempted to operate under the assumption adopted by the United Nations that provincial nationalism has always been detrimental to understanding among nations, some nations, most of them Western, felt that they needed a strong military preparedness to defend themselves. They saw the provision of disarmament education as a threat to their security. But Third World countries, those nations that need Unesco's assistance the most, suffer the greatest from any political conflict that emerges from Unesco's operations because they inevitably lead to a detraction from its effectiveness.[40] The African saying, "When two elephants fight, it is the grass below that suffers most," is true in this case.

Other areas of concern for Unesco's effectiveness as a peace broker in the world have centered around specific actions and general trends within the organization that encounters one of its main purposes: the breaking down of barriers to understanding that have been erected by cultural ignorance, intolerance, and misunderstanding. One of these areas has been the debate regarding the degree to which the press should be allowed to function freely in the world in order to facilitate the free flow of information. George D. Stoddard suggests that one of the initial UN guidelines set up for Unesco was for it "to help people all over the world maintain free speech and free press,"[41] because these were considered essential to maintaining the freedom of the human being. This strategy was designed as a way of encouraging strong communication among nations by supporting the importance of the right of the individual to free expression.

In direct contradiction to this objective, Unesco decided to support a measure called the New World Information Order, which was designed to promote the freedom of the press as being synonymous with the freedom of the human being. The New World Information Order, more specifically, was designed to facilitate the amount and nature of the media coverage in and about the Third World. Marvin Stone concludes that the basis of this action was that "governments should license news reporters. If journals wrote anything the government did not know, they should not lose their license. What the government does not want known, as we have seen to our sorrow in several parts of the world, might be deprivation, starvation, mass arrests, torture and murder. These then can proceed without publicity or objection from anyone."[42]

Unesco's endorsement of the New World Information Order was quite clear evidence of its fundamental purpose as a facilitator of communication among nations. This is an excellent example of Unesco's commitment to its original charter. But this has remained a sore spot in relationships between it and the countries that do not respect democratic values. Indeed, the problems of human freedom are considered inherent in Unesco's organizational structure and in its discharging of its responsibilities.

This precarious situation has become one of Unesco's main problems and an area of controversy surrounding the director-general's position. In 1985 the director-general's methods of operation were seen as a major reason for the United States to pull out of Unesco. The United States, Britain, and other Western nations had actually accused Amadou Mahtar M'Bow, then director-general, of using his executive power to change the operational procedures of Unesco from one of equality among all member nations to one in which Third World nations exercised more power than Western nations. This unfortunate political perception of Unesco and M'Bow himself did not help in seeking solutions to the problems of understanding among nations.

Indeed, in 1985, M'Bow, from the Third World African nation of Senegal, was "the embodiment of the thinking that he manipulates so remarkably."[43] Jerome Dumoulin has concluded that "many important educational and administrative authorities have left Unesco because M'Bow's inability to accept criticism has created a climate of distrust, prejudice, intolerance, fear and servility."[44] These are the problems that the founding of Unesco was designed to resolve, and if M'Bow's official conduct carried a trail of these difficulties, how then could Unesco exercise much-needed leadership in promoting education, knowledge, and understanding during a critical period in human history?

The United States and Britain argued that since he took office in 1974, M'Bow's style of leadership manifested behavior patterns that were largely responsible for the controversy that was weakening Unesco's ability to discharge its duties fully, and that his resignation could bring those Western nations back into Unesco.[45] It is not difficult to see that Unesco was entering a period of major crisis that was handicapping its ability to function properly in accordance with its charter.

Some observers have argued that the problem that Britain, the United States, and other Western nations were having with M'Bow's leadership of Unesco was not that he was running the organization poorly or that he was using dictatorial methods to have his own way prevail at the expense of the principle of collective decision, but that he was from the Third World. It has been quite common for members of Western societies to perceive members from the Third World as representing an entirely new point of view that was diametrically opposed to that of their own. There was therefore a fundamental difference in perceiving priorities and problems that had to be resolved because there was a fundamental difference between Western societies and Third World societies in perceiving the world itself. The more serious difference lay in their respective perception of the direction that Unesco should take. Therefore, one must conclude that because M'Bow represented the acquisition of power that had always been the prerogative of Western nations, his official conduct posed a threat to the Western concept of exercising power on an international level. Therefore, M'Bow's style of leadership became a problem for Unesco and Western nations, not for M'Bow himself.

However, the divisiveness that M'Bow's style of leadership brought into Unesco's operations and functions had, by 1986, been compounded by the extremely controversial way in which it was managed. Charges of excessive spending, misappropriation of funds, and a general lack of accountability for Unesco's $370 billion annual budget combined with accusations that when M'Bow visited his homeland of Senegal, and wherever he went in Africa, he was received like he was a head of state. To M'Bow's critics, this kind of reception suggested that he was diverting funds to African nations in a way that Unesco itself would not have approved.

This is why many delegates to Unesco complained that the high percentage, approximately 78 percent,[46] of Unesco's budget in 1984 was spent on administrative operations in Paris, as opposed to being spent on the development of nations of the world that needed it most. Although M'Bow denied these charges, it was quite clear that his effectiveness had been damaged beyond repair. As Michael Massing put it, "if Unesco disappeared tomorrow, nobody would miss it except the army of drones who soak up a bloated budget with high salaries and trips to conferences held in such pleasant places as Paris."[47]

When M'Bow announced in 1986 that he would not seek a third six-year term, there was some hope that both the United States and Britain would reconsider their decision to withdraw from Unesco. But that possibility seemed remote when, in 1987, President Kenneth Kaunda, of

Zambia nominated him for a new term of office. At that time aides to M'Bow seemed to indicate that the director-general had never made a firm promise not to seek a third term. With an annual income of $160,000 and a rent-free apartment at Unesco headquarters, M'Bow could very well be persuaded to run for a third term. However he did not. That this was a prospect that Western nations did not want to consider is evinced by the reality that in 1987 Unesco's 158 members included 62 members from African nations.[48] Therefore, the problem that Unesco faced was that M'Bow himself had become a controversial figure among Western and Third World nations, especially Africa.

What has been discussed in this chapter leads to the conclusion that under M'Bow's leadership Unesco was experiencing major problems, not only in its financial resources or the direction it was moving to resolve major problems the world community was experiencing, but also in his personality, style of leadership, and the perception of Western nations that he represented elements of human and institutional structural relationships which they did not particularly like. The unfortunate part of this is that M'Bow was portrayed as the main problem that Unesco was facing. It would appear that in their actions Western nations were opposed to the principles of cultural diversity that M'Bow represented and that the United Nations recognized as the enrichment of the world community. How would such a contradiction be resolved?

While some observers believed that the financial resources of Unesco needed to be rechanneled into such projects as developing literacy programs, especially in Third World nations, instead of into the administrative operations in Paris, they failed to realize than an international organization such as Unesco needs considerable financial strength to run it efficiently. In criticizing M'Bow, Western nations must have been worried by what they saw as the erosion of their traditional role and ability to shape the policies of Unesco as membership dramatically increased in favor of representatives from Third World nations. The control of Unesco had therefore slipped from the hands of Western nations into those of M'Bow and Third World nations. Western nations regarded this shift in the balance of power as a development that was detrimental to their interests, the very line of thinking Unesco was created to eliminate. But because a larger portion of Unesco's budget came from Western nations, they were not persuaded to see larger world interests in accepting intended change.

The elements of solutions to the problems of Unesco lay in accepting the very idea of change itself, and that participation in Unesco's operation by members of the Third World under M'Bow did not in any way threaten the interests of Western nations. The little that he could have done to allay the fear of Western nations was to carry out his duties in accordance with the provisions of the charter. This he did, but Western nations failed to realize that the interests of the world community were more important than those of their own. It is here where their cooperation and understanding would have had the desired effect by expressing support of those projects that were considered to be in the best interest of the world as a whole.

Another problem that Unesco experienced during M'Bow's term of office is that Western nations accused Third World members of taking the side of the Soviet Union on critical issues. Since there was a fundamental difference in political ideology between Western nations and the Soviet Union, they automatically concluded that Third World nations had become satellite states of the Soviet Union at the expense of Western democracies. While Western roles and opinions on world issues became weakened by the sheer force of numbers from Third World nations, they felt that they had lost the influence they once exerted on policy and the conduct of operations of Unesco.

This was a situation which they felt M'Bow was quite capable of exploiting to his own advantage. As one Western official lamented in 1985, "M'Bow is openly and militantly forming a radical wing of the Third World and works hand in hand with the Soviet Union in an effort to make Unesco the most virulently anti-American of the UN style."[49] Of course, the official seemed to neglect the fact M'Bow was put in office by the democratic process that was always regarded as the hallmark of Western democratic values. Any organization based upon a biased forum in which minority opinion seems to outweigh that of the majority simply because of the influence of tradition undercuts the essence of the principles of human relationships and collective action. It was therefore important for Western nations to recognize that understanding in promoting cooperation among nations is best accomplished when collective action recognizes the principle of majority opinion through a voting system.

## POSSIBLE SOLUTIONS

Western nations need to understand that solutions to problems of Unesco lie in recognizing that the degree to which Unesco has been successful in promoting UN objectives has been limited by dissension within their own ranks simply because their behavior was influenced by national and regional interests, rather than by world interests. This has prevented Unesco from carrying out some of its basic responsibilities. Therefore, the first step that Unesco must take to resolve this problem is to improve its structure by seeking amendments to make it a more acceptable organization among nations.

In doing this Unesco would narrow its objectives so that it would concentrate purely on matters related to seeking knowledge, education,

and cultural enrichment of the world community. This would also eliminate the notion of it as an organization that is being directly involved
in the process of keeping world peace, a task that is clearly too big for
Unesco. By discharging a set of responsibilities that do not carry highly
visible political implications, Unesco could play a more positive and constructive role in designing strategies that could be employed pertaining
to peacekeeping and disarmament as the best way to ensure world peace
and cooperation. This would also eliminate controversy and would bring
its members closer in supporting those programs that they would agree
upon. This would make it possible for nations to support it in spite of
political bias.

In addition to this, Unesco also would allow a greater amount of funding and attention to move toward matters that directly relate to cultural
and educational development, especially those of less developed nations,
and still avoid the criticism that was leveled against M'Bow that he was
authorizing the funding of programs with a heavy bias in favor of countries of Africa. In the process of focusing on educational and cultural
matters, Unesco would also play a major role in formulating new methods of improving the health of the people of the world, and nations
would support this endeavor because all of them have problems with
illiteracy and poor health.

The next step in efforts to reform Unesco is that it should become less
controversial and, thus, more productive. This means eliminating the
political implications of its operations. Since politicizing and looking out
for one's national interests are not conducive to international objectives,
there is no reason to look at its functions from a political perspective.
This means that by making Unesco less political, there would be a greater
potential for forming a stronger international alliance for progress and
a forum for discussing an agenda to respond adequately to human needs.
Nothing would be more important than this function in reforming
Unesco to discharge this task.

Unesco would also become less political by taking away issues that,
by their nature, are political. For example, disarmament is a serious
global issue which carries heavy political implications that the Security
Council or the General Assembly can handle better than Unesco. In this
manner Unesco's charge and operational principles relative to international understanding and cooperation would need to be reemphasized,
possibly through encouraging developmental projects that would draw
traditionally opposing forces, such as the United States and the Soviet
Union, closer together by working side by side in areas of mutual interests, such as cultural exchange programs. In the era of *glasnost* this is
quite possible. The world has seen how Reagan and Gorbachev demonstrated that this is quite possible.

The question of establishing adequate representation for each of

Unesco's constituents is another problem that must be resolved to make it more effective. Because Western nations believe that they have lost both their influence and voice in the operations of Unesco, it is important to restore their confidence in its original goals. This necessitates an overhaul of the way countries are represented in it.[50] One way would be to set up a system that is compatible with the U.S. Congress in which there are two policy-making bodies, one in which each nation has equal representation, and one in which the number of representatives is determined by population distribution. While this would favor Third World nations, at least it is a method of representation that Western nations would understand. In this kind of structure, each house would be responsible for different aspects of Unesco's operations, with the ultimate approval of both houses required for action or implementation.

In addition to restructuring the method by which countries are represented, a general overhaul of Unesco's administrative structure also is necessary. Through the amount and intensity of the criticism that M'Bow received, it is quite possible that the administrative power that goes along with that position needs to be shared among several positions as opposed to being controlled by one person with almost unlimited power. This often provides a climate for the abuse of that power. A system of shared responsibility would provide a mechanism of checks and balances so critical in an effort to maintain the essential character of democracy.

In this manner the one-person position of the director-general would be turned into a board of directors that would consist of three to five members, each with a specific area of responsibility. The board members would serve staggered four-year terms, instead of the seven-year term the director-general serves. This would mean that some terms would expire every year or every two years, allowing the advantage of the board composed of both fresh and experienced members. This would eliminate the possibility of disruption caused by frequent change and the advent of new members.

In addition to working to eliminate political issues that work themselves into the operations of Unesco, the organization would need to reassess the ways in which its funds are spent. Obviously, less money should be used for central administrative procedures in Paris where Unesco has its headquarters, and more money should be put into the developmental programs. By placing a more prominent instrument for helping the world's education, rather than just another forum for political discussion, Unesco could salvage itself from the state of controversy it has fallen into.

## SUMMARY AND CONCLUSION

The solution to the problems that we have discussed in this chapter as characterizing Unesco can certainly be found if there is goodwill among all nations, and if they share a common belief that they should remove their national or regional interests from influencing their attitudes and actions. About the importance of this approach and line of thinking regarding Unesco, Walter Mertineit argues,

For all the current controversy, Unesco can still look back proudly on its achievements: literacy campaigns in many parts of the world, the preservation of cultural monuments, laying the foundations of modern educational systems, a free flow of information and communication, the exchange and transfer of science and technology, protection of the environment, and the battle to prevail against prejudice, intolerance, and discrimination. If the world community must share in the value of Unesco, its members must learn to place that value above that of the local or regional community.[51]

One must conclude that these accomplishments and attitude toward Unesco must remind all nations that the consequences of failing to sustain its basic goals and objectives would lead to a catastrophe much larger than the world experienced in 1914 and 1939. Acceptance of this line of thinking would demand that Unesco be restructured to recapture the effectiveness that it once had on the character of human and national relationships in the world. By reestablishing a more clearly defined action, principles, and goals, Unesco can once again serve the purpose of promoting understanding of the universal man as a condition of ensuring world peace. Realistically there is no other course of action for the international community to take.

In December 1990 Erwin H. Goldenstein, professor of educational foundations at the University of Lincoln, Nebraska, summed up the critical role that both the United Nations and Unesco have played in maintaining peace in the world: "The realization that the frequent regional eruption of violence has not been permitted to escalate into another world confrontation testifies to the soundness of the ideas that gave birth to the United Nations and its specialized agency Unesco and their potential for achieving genuine world understanding."[52] This is a record of service to humanity that the world cannot afford to lose, but must preserve at all costs.

## NOTES

1. Townsend Hoopes and Douglas Brinkley, *FDR and the Creation of the UN* (New Haven, CT: Yale University Press, 1997), p. 132.

2. Ibid., p. 133.

3. Ibid., p. 139.

4. Ibid., p. 140.

5. Robert Dullack, *Franklin Roosevelt and American Foreign Policy* (New York: Oxford University Press, 1979), p. 441.

6. Ibid., p. 442.

7. Ibid., p. 443.

8. Hoopes and Brinkley, *FDR and the Creation of the UN*, p. 148.

9. These were the United States, Britain, France, the Soviet Union and Nationalist China, later replaced by Red China.

10. Hoopes and Brinkley, *FDR and the Creation of the UN*, p. 136.

11. Ibid., p. 142.

12. It is ironic that the United States, as a major member of the United Nations and a permanent member of the Security Council, resorted to military force to address conflict with other nations. For example on October 25, 1983, its military forces invaded Grenada to stop its socialist system from taking control of the country. Since the war in the Persian Gulf with Iraq in 1992, the United States has frequently resorted to military campaigns against Iraq. On December 20, 1989, the United States invaded Panama to arrest Manuel Antonio Noriega for dealing in drugs. In 1999 the United States also resorted to military action against Slobodan Milosevic of Yugoslavia for his ethnic cleansing policy in Kosovo.

13. Hoopes and Brinkley, *FDR and the Creation of the UN*, p. 145.

14. This chapter discusses such an organization, Unesco.

15. Although German forces surrendered to the Allies on May 7, 1945, fighting in the Pacific continued until the United States dropped the atomic bomb on the Japanese cities of Hiroshima on August 9, killing 70,000 people, and Nagasaki on August 9, killing another 36,000.

16. United States, *Public Papers of F. D. Roosevelt: The Atlantic Charter.* Vol. 10, No. 359 (Washington, DC: Government Printer, August 14, 1941).

17. Charter of the United Nations: Preamble, 1945.

18. Charter of the United Nations, Chapter 1, Purpose and Principles: Article 1.

19. UN Charter, Article 2.

20. UN Charter, Chapter 2: Membership.

21. Since the founding of the UN, seven men have served as secretary-general: Trygve Lie (Norway) 1946–1952, Dag Hammarskjold (Sweden), 1953–1961, U Thant (Myanmar, formerly Burma), 1961–1971, Kurt Waldheim (Austria) 1972–1981, Javier Perez de Cuellar (Peru), 1982–1991, Boutros Boutros-Ghali (Egypt), 1992–1996), and Kofi Annan (Ghana), 1997–the present.

22. Kofi Annan: Biographical Note (New York: The UN, 1997).

23. Ibid.

24. UN Charter, Chapter 15: Article 97, The Secretariat.

25. UN Charter, Chapter 5, Article 3.

26. UN Charter, Chapter 9: Economic and Social Security Council.

27. In Africa Namibia, Tanganyika, Rwanda-Burundi, and the Cameroons, as former colonies of Germany, became trusteeship territories to be administered by Britain and France until they were deemed ready for independence.

28. UN Charter, Chapter 13, Article 87.

29. UN Charter, Chapter 14, Article 94.

30. Kofi Annan, "Water for Children, Peace for the World," *Time*, June 9, 1997, p. 75.

31. Hoopes and Brinkley, *FDR and the Creation of the UN*, p. 221.

32. Unesco's Charter, Paris, 1946.

33. George D. Stoddard, "Unesco," *Educational Digest*, Vol. 11, No. 7 (1984), p. 42.

34. Ibid., p. 43.

35. Marvin Stone, "The United States and Unesco: Had Enough?" *U.S. News and World Report*, December 10, 1984.

36. Ibid.

37. Malcolm G. Scully, "Unesco Future at Stake as Meetings Open in Bulgaria," *The Chronicle of Higher Education*, October 16, 1985.

38. Sally White, "Gadfly to the West," *World Press Review*, March 1984, p. 38.

39. "Eyeing the Long Term," *World Press Review*, March 1984, p. 27.

40. Walter Mertineit, "Beyond Power Rivalries," *World Press Review*, March 1984.

41. Stoddard, "Unesco," p. 43.

42. Stone, "The United States and Unesco."

43. Jerome Dumoulin, "Warning Gong or Death Knell?" *World Press Review*, March 1984, p. 41.

44. Ibid., p. 42.

45. Mertineit, "Beyond Power Rivalries."

46. Michael Massing, "Unesco under Fire," *The Atlantic Monthly*, July 1984, p. 90.

47. Ibid., p. 91.

48. *Time*, October 5, 1987.

49. Massing, "Unesco under Fire," p. 92.

50. Ibid., p. 93.

51. Mertineit, "Beyond Power Rivalries."

52. Erwin H. Goldenstein, "Unesco in Perspective" foreword to Dickson A. Mungazi, *International Education and the Search for Human Understanding*, Monograph Series, No. 2 (Flagstaff: Northern Arizona University, 1991).

# 7

# National Leadership and Understanding Causes of Conflict Among Nations

All human beings are born free and equal in dignity and rights. They are endowed with reason and conscience and should act towards one another in a spirit of brotherhood

UN Declaration of Human Rights, 1976

## EDUCATIONAL SYSTEMS AND THE SEARCH FOR UNDERSTANDING

Throughout the world there are few national programs that influence national character more than the educational system. The study of the system of education in any country reveals its economic system, social practice, political system, value system, legal practices, and its relationships with other countries. These combine to form national character. For example, a study of the system of education in the Soviet Union since the Bolshevik Revolution in 1917 shows how it has been transformed from seeking to strengthen national institutions to developing relationships with other nations based on its political practices and emerging socialist values.[1]

From the beginning of the government of Vladimir Ilyich Ulynov (better known as Lenin) in 1918 to the end of that of that of Joseph Stalin in March 1953, the Soviet Union operated its institutions by applying the philosophy that Lenin expressed at the beginning of the revolution: "Without teaching there is no learning, without learning there is no knowledge, without knowledge there is no Communism, without Com-

munism society degenerates into capitalistic decay."[2] Throughout the period of the Soviet Union before Mikhail Gorbachev came to power, the
leadership of the Soviet Union utilized this philosophy to shape its national programs to insure the security of the state. The question is: How
did the Soviet Union as a nation implement elements of this philosophy
to determine the nature of relationships it was having with other nations?

Chapter 2 presented evidence to show that when Lenin arrived back
in Russia at the time of the Revolution in 1917 to direct its course, he
had made a secret agreement with Germany to work against French and
British policy. This meant that the czar had to be eliminated. But when
the Nazi party came to power in Germany in 1933, Adolf Hitler and his
associates immediately adopted a policy hostile to Communists. Communists in Germany shared the same fate as Jews: extermination. The
power that the Bolsheviks thought they had by relegating the people to
a lower position than the state turned out to be their own undoing.
Although Stalin and Hitler signed a nonaggression treaty just before the
outbreak of the war in 1939, Hitler had no intention of honoring its
provisions.

As soon as Nikita Khrushchev came to power in 1958, he utilized
technology that the Soviet people had produced in form of launching
Sputnik to initiate a new kind of national leadership and to have relationships with other nations designed to promote the advantage of the
Soviet state. To create the impression that he was a different kind of
national leader, Khrushchev began to put a distance between his prede-
cessors and himself.[3] Until he was replaced by Leonid Brezhnev in October 1964, Khrushchev utilized his power to form what he considered
an appropriate dimension of national leadership. His introduction of a
ten-year schooling program in 1959 including twenty subjects, ranging
from the Russian language to foreign studies, was an extension of a national program that he believed would strengthen his approach to the
development of his leadership.

These foreign studies were purposely focused on the United States,
and included political ideology, economic system, and foreign policy
from the administration of Woodrow Wilson to that of Dwight D. Eisenhower. It was from these studies that the Soviet Union came to know
about the activities of the CIA and the flights of Francis Gary Powers in
1960, changing the nature of relationships between the two superpowers.
Only when he thought that his government was secure did he think of
returning what he considered benefits to the Soviet people. In this regard
Khrushchev was better than Stalin. But in the development of the ten-
year schooling, Khrushchev acted in much the same way as Stalin had:
he left no room for people to use their discretion in undertaking projects

to improve conditions of their lives as a prerequisite of serving the needs of their nation.[4]

The impact of Sputnik was felt more profoundly on the United States than on any other country in the world. The United States saw the success of Sputnik as a challenge to its leadership role in the world and decided to respond in two specific ways that would have a deep impact on relations between the two superpowers. The first way had to do with a change of attitude about the involvement of the federal government in education. Out of this new thinking emerged a national call for the federal government to think of new ways of encouraging development in key areas of research and technology. This required making a new start toward funding certain academic areas, especially mathematics and the sciences. President Eisenhower had opposed any federal role other than that of offering encouragement in education.

Eisenhower's reason for this position was that federal involvement would lead to federal control of education, a position the Constitution of the United States cautioned against by delegating education to the states. However, knowing that the era of the baby boom was placing considerable financial strains and demands on formulating strategies for action, conditions of the times compelled him to seek congressional action in initiating construction projects to improve education to match technological development that the Soviet Union was promoting through its own national leadership.[5] But many Americans saw the country's response to an educational call in terms of a number of political factors that included religion, gender, and race. That the southern states saw this effort as a way of seeking to impose the *Brown* decision accentuated the controversy surrounding Eisenhower's call for U.S. involvement in education, which he was now seeking to ensure its development as a response to Sputnik.

The second specific way in which the United States reacted to Sputnik was that as soon as it returned to Earth, President Eisenhower demonstrated a new level of national leadership by pushing through Congress the National Defense Education Bill. Due to congressional procedures the bill did not become law until September 1, 1958, still a relatively short period in the history of legislative action in the U.S. Congress. The first paragraph of the act stated clearly what its purpose was: "The Congress hereby finds and declares that the severity of the problems the nation faces requires the fullest development of the mental resources and technical skills of its men and women. The present emergency demands that additional and more adequate educational opportunities be made available. The defense of this nation depends upon the mastery of modern techniques developed from complex scientific principles."[6]

In 1959, while attempting to gain technological ground lost to Sputnik,

Eisenhower invited Khrushchev to visit the United States. The two leaders were playing the game of tag in leadership. In June of that year, Soviet First Deputy Premier F. R. Kozlov visited the United States to prepare for Khrushchev's visit. Khrushchev himself seemed to understand the impact that Sputnik was having on the thinking of people in the United States. On his return to the Soviet Union, Kozlov carried an official letter of invitation from Eisenhower to Khrushchev. Khrushchev reacted:

Our relations had been extremely strained. Yet here was Eisenhower, President of the United States, inviting us to head a government delegation on a friendly visit. America had been boycotting us completely, even to the point of issuing a special ban on the purchase of crab meat from the Soviet Union. They said our goods were manufactured by slave labor. They also refused to buy our caviar and vodka. How does one explain this sudden invitation? What did it mean? It was hard to believe. Recognizing Sputnik's success Eisenhower was being forced to listen to voices within the democratic circles and in the business community which advocated concrete measures to reduce tensions between the two countries.[7]

Conscious of the impact of the invitation, Khrushchev submitted the letter of invitation from Eisenhower to the Soviet Presidium for discussion and decision. It was decided to accept the invitation in principle, but to urge the United States to do more to reduce the tension that was building up between the two nations. M. A. Menshikov, the Soviet ambassador in Washington from 1958 to 1962, was instructed to relay the acceptance of the invitation to Eisenhower and to make appropriate arrangements for the visit. The trip lasted thirteen days in September 1959, shortly after the first anniversary of the passage of the National Defense Education Act. Khrushchev and his entourage would visit seven cities and the United Nations. His entire family, including his wife, his son Sergei, his daughters Yalia Gentor and Rada Adzhubei and her husband A. J. Adzhubei, and the editor of *Izvestia* were among the party. This raised the question in Moscow about the wisdom of taking the entire family to the United States in one plane during the height of tensions between the two nations.

Khrushchev's tour of the United States would have been completed without incident were it not for the remarks made by Norris Poulson, the mayor of Los Angeles, during a reception hosted by the World Affairs Council. Poulson chided Khrushchev for his "We will bury you" remark. Khrushchev recalled his reaction in an interview with his biographer, Strobe Talbott:

Everything was going fine until the mayor got up to make a speech. His remarks were brief but very offensive to us. He stuck all kinds of pins in the Soviet Union and our system, most in the form of comparisons with the United States. I was furious. I could not pretend that I did not know what he was really saying. So I decided to deal a counterblow as I said, "Mr. Mayor, I am here as a guest of the President of the United States. I did not come to your city to be insulted or to listen to you denigrate our great country and our great people. If my presence is unwelcome, then my plane is always ready to take me straight back to the Soviet Union." In my indignation I might have been a bit rude.[8]

Instead of returning to the Soviet Union with a favorable impression of the United States, Khrushchev returned with a strong suspicion that the United States was about to increase its anti-Soviet activity, including espionage. Indeed, Khrushchev did not have to wait too long to prove his suspicion correct. Early on May 1, 1960, Marshall Malinovsky, head of the Soviet national security system, called Khrushchev on the phone to report that an American U-2 reconnaissance airplane had crossed the border from Afghanistan into Soviet airspace and was flying toward Sverdlovsk, a strategic defense center. Khrushchev ordered the Soviet defense forces to shoot the plane down and not to allow it to get away as had happened in April when another U-2 plane had flown into Soviet airspace.

As soon as the plane was shot down, the pilot, Francis Gary Powers, a lieutenant in the U.S. Air Force who was also in the service of the CIA, parachuted to safety and was immediately placed under arrest. When Eisenhower refused to acknowledge espionage as the purpose of the flight, Khrushchev angrily denounced the United States and canceled the summit conference that was scheduled to begin in mid-May between himself, Charles de Gaulle, and Eisenhower to discuss postwar German issues and disarmament in general. This incident represented the lowest point in Eisenhower's presidency. He even reportedly considered resigning because he felt that he had not exercised proper leadership for the benefit of the country. This incident also witnessed the cold war take a dramatic turn for the worse. Neither leader could trust the intentions of the other. Khrushchev's recent visit to the United States was no more than a minor episode in the relationships between the two countries.

These developments had placed the United States in what a film documentary called the dangerous years.[9] By the time that the Cuban missile crisis presented itself in 1962, the United States was increasingly coming to the realization that the diplomacy it was initiating in order to improve relationships and reduce tension between the two nations must take a backseat to the need to strengthen its military forces. The arms race that followed represented a bold approach that included space exploration to counteract the prediction that Khrushchev had made during his tour of the United States. His expressed opinion was that the United States must abandon its capitalist policies in favor of adopting a socialist agenda, otherwise the country would fall further and further behind the Soviet Union. On February 20, 1962, John Glenn became the first American astronaut to orbit the earth in a spaceship. The arms race soon acquired expanding and perilous dimensions.

The American Federation of Teachers, like the rest of the world, became helpless participants in the doctrine known as MAD (mutually assured destruction) that these two superpowers obsessively embraced. Schoolchildren all around the world soon took part in two kinds of emergency classroom drills—fire and atom bomb.

## KENNEDY'S VISION OF THE NEW FRONTIER AS A NEW FORM OF NATIONAL LEADERSHIP

The tragic death of President John F. Kennedy on November 22, 1963, did not slow down the intensity of the competition in the arms race and the cold war in general. On the day he was assassinated, Kennedy planned to deliver a speech in which he was expected to say that national leadership and success in education are closely related. Kennedy's successor, Lyndon B. Johnson, continued to play a critical leadership role in the programs that Kennedy had initiated. The inauguration of the Kennedy administration had given Americans an opportunity to reevaluate the relationship that their country was having with other countries. This could be realistically done only in the context of posing fundamental questions about the U.S. own national leadership in the world and in domestic programs. This is why, on taking office on January 20, 1961, Kennedy recognized the need to develop a national program that would reach out for improved relationships with other nations.

Kennedy's concept of the "new frontier" was born out of this endeavor. It had the significance of acknowledging a basic tenet in human relationships which manifested the principle that the freedom of all people was essential to stability and peace among nations. For Kennedy the exploration of space was meaningful only within the context of seeking to recognize the exploration of the aspirations of all people, both in fulfilling their personal ambitions and to try new challenges leading to national enrichment. This is why in 1961 Kennedy enunciated new policies regarding the rise of African nationalism. The appointment of Dean Rusk as U.S. secretary of State brought a fresh new approach that witnessed a departure from past policies pursued by the State Department under John Foster Dulles. Until the Kennedy years, prior administrations believed that the consequences of the rise of African nationalism was the sole responsibility of the colonial governments.[10] But after 1961 new elements of national leadership were forming to influence new U.S. relationships with other nations based on the emergence of new values.

Kennedy also fully recognized the momentum that the U.S. civil rights movement was gathering. In it he saw a struggle that gave the United States an emerging national character that was necessary to enable the country to recognize its proper role in critical issues of relationships among nations. His basic conviction was that unless the United States found solutions to problems at home, it would not be able to play an effective role in developing meaningful relationships with other nations. Kennedy's national leadership style led to the conclusion reached by his administration that application of the principles of the new frontier demanded taking all pertinent factors into account in designing a domestic policy and agenda that were closely related to events abroad. This is the reason behind his submitting to Congress the most comprehensive bill on civil rights, which became law in 1964, one year after his tragic death.

The inauguration of the Peace Corps in 1961, under the direction of Sargent Shriver, Kennedy's brother-in-law, proved to be Kennedy's ultimate leadership in the new frontier. The Peace Corps was a cultural bridge that helped build new relationships among nations by providing the U.S. government and its people an opportunity to understand the nature of the culture and the problems of development that other countries were facing.

Under the Peace Corps Americans from all walks of life were called upon to participate in a national program to give Kennedy's vision and leadership of the transformation of the world a practical application to human understanding and cooperation. They were asked to live and work with people in other countries, studying and advising them on various aspects of their development. They would seek to understand the cultures of other people and avoid trying to persuade them to adopt the American culture. They symbolized mankind's ability to show appreciation of cultural diversity as a means toward enrichment of the world. Kennedy also demonstrated effective leadership in envisioning this enrichment as constituting an understanding that was a prerequisite in creating an atmosphere of peace and cooperation among nations. Nurses, teachers, agricultural specialists, engineers, and industrial workers all came forward in the spirit of Kennedy's call to offer their service in a national program designed to improve understanding between the United States and other nations.

In this rare and new venture Americans came to understand themselves within the context of understanding the world community. Kennedy's leadership also enabled participating Americans to rediscover themselves in an effort to refine a proper U.S. role in developing new relationships among nations. In this context the Peace Corps volunteers were found all over the world. The quest for human understanding came alive when agricultural specialists worked alongside people in Chile to raise food, when educators went to the Philippines to be both students of culture and teachers, when health workers helped establish health care facilities in Tunisia, and when geologists went to Tanzania and assisted in extracting minerals that were needed to harvest the benefits of natural resources without doing damage to the ecosystem. That there was no age limit to be a Peace Corps volunteer indicates the awareness that Americans had the potential for accepting an appointment in distant countries in the service of their nation. This allowed the Peace Corps teachers, for example, to return to American classrooms with a wealth of experience and knowledge to share with their students.

Kennedy's approach to national leadership and policy created an environment that helped define a new paradigm in relationships with other countries and which held new meaning for the United States. The new frontier manifested itself in a variety of national leadership programs initiated at home. The Higher Education Act of 1963 authorized $935 million in matching funds and $360 million in loans extended over a period of five years to institutions of higher education, both public and private, for building new educational establishments that included athletic and recreational facilities, and buildings for all purposes, even sectarian.[11] At the same time the Vocational Education Act, also passed in 1963, "extended and expanded all previous vocational programs including the Smith-Hughes Act of 1917."[12]

In 1965, having won the 1964 presidential election on his own merit against his Republican opponent, Barry Goldwater of Arizona, Lyndon B. Johnson set out to define in his own way the new frontier in which he played a critical national leadership role. On April 11, 1965, President Johnson initiated what he regarded as a new definition of the new frontier by signing the Elementary and Secondary Education Act. This legislation represented the most comprehensive provisions for education since the National Defense Education Act of 1958. The law provided for annual appropriations for education that enabled students from low-income families to avail themselves of educational opportunities. The implementation of this legislation began with $100 million for the 1965 academic year. It allowed for the purchase of textbooks, library resources, and other published materials needed in the promotion of education among the children of economically deprived families. States were required to insure that fiscal control of the funds was exercised to ascertain fair and equitable distribution of resources.

On November 8, 1965, President Johnson demonstrated another dimension of national leadership by expanding Kennedy's concept of the new frontier in the area of higher education. On that day he signed the Higher Education Act. Coming one year of the passage of the Civil Rights Act of 1964, this legislation prompted Johnson to acknowledge its importance by saying, "This is only one of more than two dozen educational measures enacted by the first session of the 89th Congress. History will forever record that this session did more for the cause of education in America than all the previous 176 regular sessions of Congress did put together."[13] There is no question that the purpose of the action was to seek better understanding of the Soviet Union.

While this was happening, African Americans were trying to define the new frontier in their own way. Since the *Brown* decision they were increasingly demanding their fair share of the educational pie. The constitutional conclusion of the Supreme Court in that decision, that separation of children on the basis of color gave them the stamp of inferiority, became the basis of a fresh approach to their quest for educational opportunities. Those who continued to argue that the black race was intellectually inferior, such as Arthur R. Jensen,[14] saw the earlier *Plessy* decision as supporting their line of thinking.

Those who argued that race was not a factor in human intelligence also used the *Plessy* decision to support their view. This brought the question of research into play. The *Brown* decision, however, validated a new line of thinking that environment plays a major and crucial role in academic achievement. This belief led African Americans to argue that society had a duty to provide an environment that was conducive to their learning. The reality of this aspect of the new frontier is that success or failure in both education and society in general must be measured by the guarantee of equality in all aspects of national life.

This line of thinking is why, from provisions of the Civil Rights Act of 1964 and of the Economic Opportunity Act of 1964, efforts were made to assist students from economically disadvantaged family backgrounds. They received special attention to help them overcome the effects of the denial of equal opportunity. Known as the antipoverty law, this legislation was intended to help students recognize their potential and to encourage them to use it in their educational efforts. In this connection Johnson's understanding of the new frontier was evident in his desire to initiate Head Start, a program for preschool children. The rationale behind Head Start was that students from culturally disadvantaged backgrounds were being placed in socially disadvantaged situations that made it hard for them to learn. This was due to the lack of racially integrated social interaction. This also deprived them of access to quality teachers and appropriate educational resources. As it did with the Peace Corps venture, the American Federation of Teachers and its president, Albert Shanker, lauded the implementation of Head Start as an important measure of national leadership.

We must now turn our attention to the discussion of national leadership of another country that was experiencing as much political trauma as Russia was under the Bolshevik Revolution, South Africa. In 1919 J. C. Smuts was elected prime minister of South Africa.[15] While he was attending the Versailles Peace Conference in that year, political events in his country were deteriorating rapidly as components of the policy of apartheid were being put in place. The practice of exclusion that the policy of apartheid meant to Africans was having a devastating effect on race relations in South Africa. Bitterness and rancor were felt in every aspect of national life as leadership was directed at protecting the position of whites. Africans were systematically eliminated from the election process as they were deprived of their citizenship, just as the Nazi government was doing in Germany beginning in 1933.

When the war broke out in 1914, it placed the leadership of South Africa on opposite sides of the conflict. Louis Botha, who served as prime minister from 1910 to 1919, and the leader of the opposition, B. J. Hertzog, did not agree on what had caused the war. Botha announced in Parliament a month after the war had started that as part of the British Empire South Africa would enter the war on the side of the Allies. He directed General Smuts to lead military campaign against German colonial administration in neighboring Namibia. Hertzog called on Afrikaners to join him in staging a demonstration against Botha's policy and action, arguing that Germany was acting in self-defense.[16]

It turned out that in their respective policy and action, Botha and Hertzog were aiming at prohibiting Africans from acquiring any role in the events that were unfolding in their own country. Like the Bolsheviks in Russia, both the South Africa party that Botha led and the Nationalist party that Hertzog led shared a common philosophical belief that Africans should not be allowed to claim the right to vote because they were presumed to be inferior.[17] Until the advent of the African majority government in April 1994, successive governments of South Africa practiced the policy of apartheid out of this belief. During those years the damage to the national character was so extensive that today it is going to take South Africa some years to repair. What one sees in the example of the Bolsheviks and of South Africa is that when national leadership is exercised for the exclusive benefit of a select group of people, the effect on the nation as a whole is often devastating. This is why the international community finally came to complete realization that the policy of apartheid was a crime against humanity and coordinated its effort to force it to an end. The reaction of the international community shows how national policy constructed under circumstance of bias such as Nazi Germany did can cause national disaster for the nation itself. Further, a nation cannot have meaningful relationships with other nations if it gives some of its own citizens preferential treatment over others.

While these developments were taking place in the Soviet Union and South Africa, the United States was having its own problems of national leadership, but from an entirely different background. The crisis that was unfolding in Little Rock, Arkansas, in 1957 over the question of desegregation of education compelled the Eisenhower administration to continue its soul search in order to develop elements of a new national character. The search had actually begun in 1954 with the U.S. Supreme Court ruling in *Brown vs. Board of Education of Topeka* that racial segregation of students was unconstitutional. It was quite clear that in 1957 Arkansas Governor Orval Faubus and President Dwight Eisenhower were on a collision course because they interpreted the meaning of the *Brown* decision from their own perspective of what it meant to the kind of leadership they wanted to project.

The crisis in Little Rock and the launching of Sputnik combined to create a national and international environment that required statesmanship in bringing the developments that ensued together to reduce the level of crisis so as to assure the people to see hope for the future. Both the United States and the Soviet Union wanted to avoid a new conflict in their relationships. In launching Sputnik and in seeking a resolution of the crisis in Little Rock, both the Soviet Union and the United States faced new challenges to their leadership. Although the crisis caused by integration in Little Rock took a back seat to the launching of Sputnik, President Eisenhower still focused on it as a manifestation of the quality of his national leadership. Only when he felt that this crisis was fully resolved did he pay attention to the aftermath of Sputnik. In his approach to the crisis in Little Rock and in Khrushchev's approach to Sputnik lay the fundamental difference in leadership styles between a socialist system and a democratic system. The former was intended to benefit the state, and the latter was intended to benefit the people.

## UN LEADERSHIP ROLE IN RESOLVING CONFLICT AMONG NATIONS

This section discusses examples of problems that existed in selected countries or conflict between them to illustrate the need to gain knowledge in order to find peaceful solution to them. The following examples also discuss how the United Nations functioned as a knowledge broker to resolve conflict peacefully. In his efforts to have the U.S. Senate ratify the U.S. involvement in the founding and operations of the League of Nations, President Woodrow Wilson furnished clear examples of what nations could do in this regard. In a political environment that was rapidly changing the nature of relationships among nations, knowledge of issues that caused conflict among them was the only viable means of maintaining peace. The League of Nations would have certainly enhanced the prospect of that peace. Even Germany, the pariah of relationships among nations, would have thought twice before it sent its forces to invade its neighbors.

In 1919, following the end of World War I, Georges Clemenceau, the seventy-eight-year-old prime minister of France, was asked if he had ever been to Germany. His answer was a surprise to those who heard it, "No, but the Germans had been to France twice in my life-time."[18] This answer suggests that Clemenceau expected the Germans to understand the French people but the French people did not have to understand the Germans. The French also considered the Germans the oppressor after the end of the Franco-Prussian war in 1871 and the beginning of World War I in 1914. Clemenceau did not feel particularly inclined to understand the Germans because the French did not feel that it was necessary for them to exercise understanding of any other people because they considered themselves an Aryan race and other people inferior species who did not deserve any understanding.

While Clemenceau might have good reason to express the views he did about Germany, it did not preclude him from seeking understanding of a functional knowledge that would have placed him and the French people in a better position in relating to Germans as a condition of peace. As the old expression goes, it takes two to tango. Ignorance of one's adversary on the assumption that knowledge about him would not be reciprocated cannot be justified on any ground. Even if national leadership in both Germany and France knew that there were historical reasons for the hostility that existed between them, they should have made efforts to understand the psychology of the people of each nation to minimize conflict between them. One can say that in this case, ignorance among the French about the Germans was no defense or reason for perpetuating it. This example of the lack of knowledge was itself an issue that caused conflict between them. One can reach the conclusion that both nations failed to exercise proper leadership that would have been utilized to solve that conflict.

Here are some examples of how the United Nations played a constructive leadership role in seeking knowledge of issues that caused conflict among nations and what it did to solve it. On June 26, 1945, fifty nations signed the UN Charter. On October 24, the U.S. Senate voted unanimously to ratify the United Nations, providing for the U.S. involvement in its operations. On December 10, the U.S. Congress voted unanimously to invite the United Nations to establish its permanent headquarters in New York City. One wonders how Senator Henry Cabot Lodge would have reacted to this development. However, unlike its action on December 19, 1919, the Senate did not want to be viewed as an important branch of the U.S. government that was against the exercise of reason to save humanity from future disaster caused by ignorance of the issues arising among nations. The United Nations accepted the invitation on February 14, 1946, at its general assembly in London. With these preliminary arrangements completed, the United Nations thought that it had created sufficient publicity to persuade nations to see the wisdom of resorting to peaceful means to settle dispute among themselves.

However, in 1947, while the United Nations was still settling in its new home, conflict broke out in Palestine. In that year Britain, which ruled it as its colony, asked the United Nations to investigate the breakdown of order and the fighting that was going on between Jews and Arabs. The UN General Assembly sent a special committee to Palestine to study the situation and make a recommendation for solution to the problem. On November 29, the committee recommended that Palestine be divided into an Arab state and a Jewish state. With this recommendation Britain began to withdraw from Palestine without taking formal steps to confer independence to either part of the country. While the Jews accepted the UN special committee's recommendation, the Arabs rejected it. On May 14, 1948, seeing an opportunity to fortify their position when Britain moved out, the Jews declared Palestine the state of Israel. President Harry S. Truman of the United States immediately extended U.S. recognition of the new state as fighting between Arabs and Jews intensified, creating a situation of conflict that has not been fully resolved to this day.[19]

Believing that the situation could be resolved to the satisfaction of both Arabs and Jews and that if it was unresolved it would threaten world peace, the General Assembly named Count Folke Bernadotte of Sweden as special mediator between the two sides. Bernadotte took his assignment seriously and tried hard to study the situation so he could make a recommendation for a fair solution to the problem. As he was coming close to submitting his report and his recommendation he was assassinated, plunging the whole situation into new chaos. Realizing that it had to find a solution to the problem, the United Nations named Ralph Bunche of the United States to complete Bernadotte's assignment. Bunche worked through 1949 to persuade the combatants to accept terms of a UN armistice. On June 24, Israel, Egypt, Lebanon, Jordan, and Syria signed the armistice agreement. For his efforts Bunche received the Nobel Peace Prize for 1950. Peace was temporarily restored between the Arab states and Israel although it did not last.[20] But the United Nations had made it possible for nations in conflict to realize that the acquisition of knowledge of issues causing conflict between them could yield some tangible results in an effort to resolve the conflicts and that before nations react to the conflict they are in they should always try to understand its causes objectively.

In July 1947 fighting broke out between the Netherlands and Indonesia over disputed territory in the Netherlands Indies. Indonesia wanted to unite all the Netherlands Indies into one nation. But the Netherlands and local rulers opposed the intended union. On August 1, the Security Council ordered both countries to stop fighting and start negotiations for a peaceful resolution of the problem under the supervision of the UN committee. When the parties continued to fight, the United Nations arranged a truce on January 17, 1948, and succeeded in persuading the parties to observe conditions of the truce so that a permanent solution could be found. The United Nations offered a peace plan that both sides could put into place. In the meantime the United Nations convinced the Netherlands that it was in its best interest to grant independence to the Netherlands Indies. But on December 18, 1948, the Netherlands resumed fighting, claiming that Communists were planning to take Indonesia. The United Nations arranged another truce and succeeded in convincing Communists that peace in the area was also in their best interest.[21]

As part of its strategy to create a climate in which nations in conflict had an opportunity to understand the concerns of the parties they were in conflict with, the United Nations worked out a plan for both the Netherlands and Indonesia to learn some important things about the other. Indonesia learned that the Netherlands had in the past invested considerable amounts of money in the development of the Netherlands Indies and expected return from that investment. Indonesia came to understand that this was why the Netherlands went to war to protect its economic interests.[22] The Netherlands learned that the spirit of nationalism that gripped many people in colonial domination could no longer be compromised. It had to take precedence over any other consideration. The Netherlands came to understand that this was why Indonesia was behaving the way it was.[23] In bringing knowledge of the issues that had caused conflict between the Netherlands and Indonesia, the United Nations found a solution to the problem.

On June 25, 1950, Communist armies of North Korea invaded the Republic of South Korea. The Security Council, in its characteristic response, met immediately and passed a resolution pleading both sides to stop the ensuing fighting in order to find a permanent solution to the conflict. It also urged North Korea to withdraw from South Korea in order not to aggravate the situation. When North Korea refused, the Security Council asked UN member nations to contribute military units to a UN military force to defend South Korea and to restore peace. Although the UN military force is only symbolic, it usually has the desired results, among them that a nation in disagreement with its policy is usually in the wrong.

Of the sixty nations that were UN members at that time, fifty-three supported the action against North Korea. Only seven that were part of the socialist system declined to support the measure to show solidarity with North Korea. The Soviet Union did not support the resolution because it had withdrawn its representative from the Security Council in protest of its action on North Korea. This was a major crisis that the United Nations faced. But resolutions had to be passed and action had to be taken in the interest of maintaining peace in the world. The Soviet Union learned an important lesson: not to boycott deliberations in an international forum because decisions could still be made without its participation. The United Nations also used the truce between North Korea and South Korea as a period for the parties to acquire knowledge about themselves. Although a stalemate and tension eventually developed between North Korea and South Korea, for many years both sides exercised caution based upon the knowledge that resorting to war to solve conflict usually becomes an exercise in futility as the United Nations stressed the importance of peaceful resolution of problems between nations.[24]

On October 23, 1956, hundreds of students and workers marched through the streets of Budapset demonstrating against Soviet Union's control of Hungarian government. Later, when the Soviet Union also controlled the Hungarian police, their units fired on the crowds. The United Nations thought that the situation was getting out of control. The Security Council could not take action to restore peace immediately because the Soviet Union exercised its veto power. Instead the General Assembly met in an emergency session on November 4 and voted to authorize the Security Council to act in the interest of restoring peace[25]

By end of November the Soviet Union had crushed the movement toward peaceful social change in Hungary, and the United Nations launched a campaign to inform members of the international community that the Soviet Union represented forces that were opposed to peaceful resolution of problems among nations.[26] Although the crisis in Hungary created 200,000 refugees from Hungary, the knowledge that the Soviet Union had caused this crisis brought other nations together to cooperate in finding solutions to problems of relationships among nations. From that point on the Soviet Union became increasingly isolated until Mikhail Gorbachev came to power in 1984, bringing a fundamental change in Soviet approach to its relationships with other nations by providing a different form of national leadership.

On July 26, 1956, while the crisis between Israel and the Arab states was going on, Gamal Abdel Nasser, the president of Egypt since the revolution that toppled King Farouk in 1952, nationalized the Suez Canal. After negotiations failed to resolve the issue, the Security Council was divided on the action that Nasser had taken. Britain and France, two major nations that had financed the construction of the canal and opened it for world trade in 1869, felt that Nasser had violated the international agreement that was reached at the beginning of the operation of the canal and threatened to use military force to force him to rescind the decision.[27]

But the Soviet Union argued that Nasser had the right to control the use of its territory as a practice of national principle and supported his action. President Eisenhower also opposed the intended move by Britain and France, forcing them to back down from their threat. In this regard Eisenhower showed more effective leadership and understanding of the issue than did Britain and France in solving the problems that had a potential of creating a real conflict on an international basis. For its part the United Nations did not have to debate and vote upon a resolution on the crisis about the Suez Canal because Eisenhower received support from an unlikely source.[28]

Lester B. Pearson of Canada, a former president of the UN General Assembly, suggested that the UN secretary-general be asked to set up a UN emergency force to end the crisis peacefully. Pearson also suggested that in the era of nationalism and self-determination among people struggling for independence, developed nations should show sensitivity when those people took action to promote their development in situations that appeared to go against the interests of developed nations. In this action Pearson also showed understanding and effective leadership in promoting knowledge of issues that caused conflict among nations. However, Britain was forced to withdraw its offer to build the Aswan High Dam on the Nile. Nasser immediately invited the Soviet Union to do so, creating a new era of relationships between Egypt and the Soviet Union.[29]

## NATIONAL LEADERSHIP AND UNDERSTANDING AMONG NATIONS

In his study, *Global Order: Values and Power in International Politics*, Lynn Miller of Temple University argues that future relationships among nations will be determined by the nature of national leadership that demonstrates understanding and knowledge of critical areas of national life that include national values.[30] Miller goes on to suggest that the acquisition of knowledge of conditions that influence these relationships among nations does not just happen, it is a product of good education. Like charity that begins at home, knowledge must have its basis in two critical aspects of human life: the material side and the spiritual side.

Miller also argues that a good national leader is one who utilizes a combination of common sense and intelligence to serve the needs of the people as a condition of establishing good relationships with other nations. This combination is also a product of good education. The effectiveness of a national leader depends upon his understanding of the meaning of both material and spiritual sides in the lives of the people. To be successful in establishing good relationships with his people, a national leader must promote the necessary balance between the material side and the spiritual side as a condition of happiness for the people.[31] No national leader can establish successful relationships with other nations unless he has established successful relations with his own people.

From Miller's conclusion one must ask an important question: What do these two sides of the human being mean in the life of the individual as a condition of establishing good relationships with other nations? Let

us take each at a time and discuss its importance to both the development of a national character and as a basis of establishing meaningful
relationships with other nations. The material side provides physical
comfort and well-being of the individual. It helps sustain the economic
base to ensure national development. It makes it possible for individuals
to participate in events of national importance. It brings people together
in an effort to develop common values that are utilized to minimize
conflict. It reminds people to see the importance of political activity in
the context of national goals and objectives.

In 1968 the Kerner Commission took this line of thinking in submitting
its report to President Lyndon B. Johnson in addressing the conflict that
emerged in the United States between African Americans and white
Americans caused by differences in the socioeconomic status between
them: "What white Americans have never fully understood, but what
the Negro can never forget, is that white society is deeply implicated in
the ghetto. White institutions created it, white institutions maintain it,
and white society condones it."[32] Responding to the report as a national
leader, President Johnson demonstrated his own understanding of the
socioeconomic crisis that gripped his nation as he said, "The only genuine, long-range solution lies in an attack mounted at every level upon
the conditions that breed despair and violence."[33] Johnson's understanding is what led to the introduction of the Great Society and War on
Poverty programs. There is no question that President Johnson was trying to address the material side of the human being as a condition of
developing relations with other nations.

The spiritual side helps to identify the essence of the human being. It
helps recognize the values of the deeper meaning of human existence. It
provides a knowledge of the importance of justice, fairness, and equality
in society. It makes it possible for society to see the importance of integrity and other positive attributes of the human person as the most important part of creation. It helps create a national frame of mind that it
is above temptation to erode away the qualities that sustain the supremacy of the human spirit. It helps bring people and their government
closer to cooperate in building new values needed to place their society
on the foundation of dedication to national causes.

In 1998 James Carville, a middle-of-the-road Democrat, expressed serious concern over what he saw as the purpose and the direction that
Kenneth Starr, independent Republican counsel appointed to investigate
wrongdoing by President Bill Clinton, was taking. Carville shared the
view of many Americans that Starr was motivated by partisan political
ideology in carrying out a campaign against Clinton and Democrats in
general. Carville observed,

I'm concerned that if we somehow let this man continue his jihad against the
President, my worst sweat-sheet nightmare will actually come true. Kenneth

Starr will never go away. The mean and menacing essence of him will remain with us like Strom Thurmond[34] or a cheap tattoo. Whenever the right wing does not like popularly elected officials, such as President Clinton, they will throw plenty of lies and money around just to get their way.[35]

There is no question that Carville was addressing elements of the deeper meaning of the spiritual side of human experience as an essential important component of relationships between people of the same country and among nations.

It is quite clear that these two sides of human experience can be developed to their fullest potential by the kind of education that one receives and the knowledge that one gains. Miller suggests that the application of these two sides of human experience can also be applied to efforts directed at seeking improvement in the relationships that must be developed among nations when they are made to improve relationships between people and their government.[36] This development gives national leadership an opportunity to realize that relationships between the people and their government constitute observance of critical elements of political behavior that are intended to sustain national principles needed to construct relationships with other nations.

National leadership will also have an opportunity to articulate and develop social values in an effort to strengthen the search for new political meaning in a far larger area of human activity that will not limit human creativity to less than its potential as an outcome of gaining knowledge that is cast in democratic values. For this reason those who seek positions of national leadership must make sure that they are properly educated and seek knowledge that is relevant to conditions existing in their nations and other nations. These developments are the outcomes of the combination of the material and spiritual sides of human experience that national leaders cannot take for granted. This combination also requires total commitment to principles of relationships among nations.

Miller also argues that a burglar who survives by robbing wields a kind of power as long as he is not caught. But he knows that because he is operating outside the values that society expects of all its people he is actually living on borrowed time because sooner or later he will be caught and brought to justice. In the same way national leaders who are corrupt rob their nations of the resources that people need to ensure their development. Like a burglar, they know that sooner or later they will be caught because they are operating outside the law.[37] In this national environment such national leadership cannot be effective both in their own nations and in building meaningful relationships with other nations.

Miller's conclusion that the quality of national leadership of the future will also determine the kinds of relationships nations will have with other nations leads him to suggest that there are two types of leaders among nations, idealists and realists.[38] We must ask the question: What are the characteristics of idealists and realists that will determine the kinds of relationships needed among nations in the future? Idealists tend to see the world in philosophical terms. They regard relationships among nations as they would like them to be. Idealists argue that by nature man is good, and with education he can be trusted with national responsibility. Idealists believe that man is capable of doing more good than evil. They also believe that the security of the world depends on the mutual trust and confidence that national leaders and their people place on each other nations because they share common values.[39]

Realists operate on the assumption that by nature man is selfish and greedy and that if man in position of leadership and power has an opportunity he will exploit his society for his own personal gain. Realists also believe that while those in positions of leadership have the potential for doing good, they need the law to guide and control their action and behavior. They argue that those in position of authority and power must not be trusted without checking their official action and conduct. Realists also argue that in designing relationships with other nations, national leaders must be guided and motivated by interests of the world community and national interests, rather than by personal interests. In order to accomplish this objective, national leaders must first insure the security of their own people. Once they have demonstrated their commitment to the security of their own people they are now ready to initiate collective action to insure the security of the world.[40]

In this line of thinking Miller seems to share George Schlid's view also that national leaders seem to be either realists or idealists.[41] Schlid considers Woodrow Wilson an idealist whose philosophy of U.S. involvement in world affairs, especially in the formation of the League of Nations, was absolute in every way. He refused to see things in any other way except the way he did. Miller and Schlid seem to reach four common conclusions about the importance of national leadership in the arena of relationships with other nations on issues of peace and security in the world. The first conclusion is that national leaders who have established good relationships with their own people are more likely to have good relationships with other nations. One can understand that Adolf Hitler, Benito Mussolini, Joseph Stalin, "Papa Doc" Duvalier, and Ferdinand Marcos, for example, failed to establish good relationships with other nations because they failed to establish good relationships with their own people.

The second conclusion is that national leaders who establish good relationships with their own people base them on democratic principles and values.[42] This makes it possible to translate the observance of these same values and principles into effort to develop good relationships with other nations. There is a definite connection between observance of democratic principles and values in designing relationships with one's people and establishing relationships with other nations. In this environment a national leader is better able to enhance the diplomatic process than those national leaders who do not.[43]

The third common conclusion is that national leaders who respect a collective system of values in their own nations are better able to understand and appreciate collective systems of values in establishing relationships with other nations. Respecting collective values in one's nation is a prerequisite of respecting collective values in relationships a national leader has with other national leaders. In the operations of the United Nations those national leaders who respect the position of their people understand better the concerns expressed by the international organization about the need to respect human rights in all countries better than those who do not. In recent years, for example, differences in understanding this basic principle have created problems of relationships between Iraq and other nations.

The fourth and last conclusion that Miller and Schlid seem to reach in common about national leadership and the kinds of relationships they have with other nations is that those national leaders who do not observe democratic principles in their own countries are always fearful of being removed from office by violent means. As a result they translate that fear into the kinds of relationships they have with other nations. They therefore exhibit erratic behavior because they do not know if they will hold office the next day, because they know that they do not have the trust of their people. In 1969, Kwame Nkrumah, president of Ghana, was removed from office while he was on a mission to help find a solution to the problems of Vietnam because he had lost the trust of his own people. Nkrumah was unable to complete his mission and died in exile in 1972.

There are other important considerations about national leadership in connection with developing relationships among nations. Those who hold positions of leadership must at all times remember that among important functions of governments they lead is to provide effective channels through which flow an equally effective system of communications to fulfill defined purposes. In this way national leadership becomes a means of serving national purpose. In May 1994 Nelson Mandela recognized the importance of this line of thinking when he argued that national leadership must regard itself as a public servant instituted to serve the needs of the people and must never regard itself as their master.[44] Some national leaders also tend to forget that nations create national institutions such as political systems, legislatures, and legal systems to serve the needs of the people, not the purposes of leaders themselves.

This reality suggests the conclusion that the people must at all times reserve the right to remove from office any leader who abuses his power. This must always be done by constitutional means, such as recall elections or impeachment.[45] Unless national leaders hold office under this provision, some are more likely to abuse the power they hold and the people pay the ultimate price. While it is important for national leaders and the people to remember that governments are a product of constitutional provisions and that governments in general influence the functions of legal systems, the people are the ultimate authors of both. This means that understanding the causes of conflict developing between the people and their leaders is greatly minimized.

It is by provision of the UN Charter that the International Court of Justice does not enforce its own decisions. Enforcement rests with the Security Council. If members of the Security Council have differences of opinion regarding the decisions of the International Court of Justice, they are required to eliminate them in seeking to implement those decisions in order to sustain the common good that the court sees in reaching its decisions. It is here where a national leader must rise to the occasion to exercise understanding that by supporting the decisions of the court, even if they are against his own nation, he is supporting the interests of his own people. This is what national leadership requires as a condition of establishing meaningful relationships with other nations. In the end establishing good relationships with other nations and establishing good relations with his own people become interdependent. That is what some people see when they say that the world has become a global village.

## SUMMARY AND CONCLUSION

This chapter has discussed the quest for knowledge of issues that cause conflict among nations as a basis of seeking solutions to problems among them. Unless nations endeavor to gain this knowledge they cannot find solutions to problems that arise in relationships among them. Today nations base their efforts to construct relationships with other nations on their understanding of what culture means. Things that people of one culture consider wrong are perfectly acceptable to those of another. This is why conflict between the leadership of Iraq and Western nations, for example, cannot be resolved over the treatment of the Kurds. Lynn Miller concludes that international corporations are both the products and agents of that cultural variation.[46] It is also a common belief among nations that political differences about where territorial waters end and international waters begin and violation of air space are among major causes of conflict among nations.

In recent years there have been other causes of conflict among nations arising from change of trade, distribution of national resources, and economic policy. These have been so delicate that a slight misunderstanding can cause a major conflict. For example, the production of oil from the Middle East has become so controversial that there is no ready agreement among oil-producing countries (OPEC) on price and shipment. Changes in political systems in which nations have tried to function in promoting their interests have come to influence trade relationships that did not exist before. Miller concludes that national leadership has played an increasing role in the function of technological momentum relevant to the production of materials that have brought sweeping changes in the economic structure and in transitional corporations that have rapidly emerged as powerful global actors.[47]

In carrying out their responsibilities both to their own nations and to the development of relations with other nations, national leaders must be reminded of the UN declaration of human rights in 1976: "All human beings are born free and equal in dignity and rights. They are endowed with reason and conscience and should act towards one another in a spirit of brotherhood."[48] Unless these new actors fully understand the dynamics of relationships among nations, cast in the environment of human rights that the United Nations so well defined, they are likely to cause new conflict in their desire or effort to complete their act.

## NOTES

1. Nigel Grant, *Soviet Education* (Middlesex, U.K: Penguin Books, 1979), p. 15.

2. Ibid., p. 25.

3. Ibid., p. 18.

4. Ibid., p. 29.

5. Ibid., p. 229.

6. U.S. Public Law 85–864, National Defense Education Act, 1958, 85th Congress, September 2, 1958.

7. Strobe Talbott (ed.), *Khrushchev Remembers: The Last Testament* (Boston: Little, Brown and Company, 1974), p. 369.

8. Ibid., p. 388. Twice in 1993 the author requested a copy of Poulson's remarks from the office of the mayor of Los Angeles, but he received no response.

9. A&E, "Eisenhower: The Dangerous Years," a documentary film, July 1988.

10. Dickson A. Mungazi, *The Struggle for Social Change in Southern Africa: Visions of Liberty* (New York: Taylor and Francis, 1989), p. 100.

11. Robert E. Potter, *The Stream of American Education* (New York: American Book Company, 1967), p. 406.

12. Ibid., p. 402.

13. U.S. Senate Committee on Labor and Public Welfare, *Enactments by the 89th Congress Concerning Education and Training* (Washington, DC: Government Printer, 1966), p. 18.

14. William van Til, *Education: A Beginning* (Boston: Houghton Mifflin Company, 1974), p. 346.

15. J. C. Smuts served twice as prime minister of South Africa, from 1919 to

1924, and from 1939 to 1948. This gave him an opportunity to participate in both the Versailles Peace Conference and the San Francisco Conference of 1945.

16. W. McIntyre, *Colonies into Commonwealth* (New York: Walker and Company, 1966), p. 22.

17. Ibid., p. 35.

18. Peter Jennings, "America's Century: A Documentary," The History Channel, July 27, 1999.

19. World Almanac, *World Almanac and Book of Facts* (New York: World Almanac, 1991), p. 721.

20. Ibid., p. 722.

21. Borgna Brunner (ed.), *Time Almanac* (New York: Time Inc., 1999), p. 269.

22. Ibid., p. 270.

23. Ibid., p. 271.

24. Ibid.

25. *The World Almanac and Book of Facts*, 1996, p. 771.

26. Ibid., p. 772.

27. This scenario was repeated in 1978 regarding the action that Panama took to control the Panama Canal. But in that case President Jimmy Carter exercised understanding by negotiating and signing a treaty, slowly turning control of the canal to Panama by 1999. As a Republican candidate for president two years later, Ronald Reagan argued that the United States should keep control of the canal because it built it. But he could not change the treaty that had been reached and signed during the Carter administration.

28. J. D. Hargreaves, *Decolonization of Africa* (London: Longman, 1988), p. 156.

29. Ibid., p. 157.

30. Lynn Miller, *Global Order: Values and Power in International Politics*, 2nd ed. (Boulder, CO: Westview Press, 1990), p. 73.

31. Ibid., p. 74.

32. United States, *Report of the National Advisory Commission on Civil Disorders* (Otto Kerner, Chairman). (Washington DC.: Government Printer, 1968), p. 2.

33. Ibid., p. xv.

34. Strom Thurmond is a U.S. senator from South Carolina who has served longer than anyone else. In 1998 Senator Thurmond was more than 90 years of age and indicated no intent to retire.

35. James Carville, *And the Horse He Rode On: The People vs. Kenneth Starr* (New York: Simon and Schuster, 1998), p. 11.

36. Miller, *Global Order*, p. 75.

37. Ibid., p. 77.

38. Ibid., p. 75.

39. Ibid., p. 74.

40. Ibid., p. 73.

41. George Schlid, *Between Ideology and Realpolitik: Woodrow Wilson and the Russian Revolution, 1917–1921* (Westport, CT: Greenwood Press, 1995), p. 15.

42. Ibid., p. 19.

43. Ibid., p. 23.

44. Dickson A. Mungazi, *The Mind of Black Africa* (Westport, CT: Praeger Publishers, 1996), p. 159.

45. This author does not understand why many nations do not make this pro-

vision in their constitutions. It is a necessary condition of protecting society and democratic values that are so critical to its survival.

46. Miller, *Global Order*, p. 155.

47. Ibid., p. 154.

48. Quoted in ibid., p. 175.

# 8

# Education and Understanding Among Nations: Summary, Conclusion, and Implications

When communication is between people with different world views, special skills are required if messages received are to resemble messages sent. The most important overriding skill is understanding the context within which the communication takes place. This context is to a large extent culturally determined.

H. Ned Seelye, 1993

If we cannot eliminate the causes and prevent the repetition of these barbaric events, it is not an irresponsible prophecy to say that this twentieth century may yet succeed in bringing the doom of civilization

Robert H. Jackson, Chief Prosecutor, Nuremburg Trials, 1946

## WILSON, EDUCATION, AND RELATIONSHIPS AMONG NATIONS

The purpose of this book is to present the evidence that shows that knowledge is critical to good relationships that must develop among nations. Some people believe that knowledge is synonymous with education. At the conclusion of the Russian Revolution in 1918, Lenin stated the relationships that he believed existed between knowledge and education. In conventional terms it is hard to differentiate education from knowledge because the two are closely related. But while education is the process of gaining knowledge, knowledge itself is usually the status of knowing something definite for a defined purpose. When the acquisition of knowledge does not lead to a resolution of the problem, it is not because education has failed, it is because human beings abuse it to suit their own selfish ends. They may ignore it completely in order to exercise power to have their own position prevail at the expense of others. For example, some members of the Nazi party in Germany were well educated. These include Hermann Goering, Joseph Goebbels, and Joseph Mengele.[1] But the action that some of them took proves they abused their education to sustain their position.[2]

This study began with a discussion of the legacy of Woodrow Wilson to the concept of seeking knowledge and understanding to ensure peace among nations to avoid conflict. Toward the end of his life Wilson predicted correctly that the world would encounter another serious conflict within a generation unless nations took extraordinary measures to avoid it. Within a space of twenty years from the end of World War I another major conflict broke out. In discussing Wilson's ideas of making the world safe for democracy and secure, one must appreciate the conditions that produced him and the kind of relationships he saw among nations of his time. As a student of history Wilson fully understood the trend that would lead to the outbreak of World War I. He studied how the wars of Napoleon shaped future relationships among nations, and how the Franco-Prussian war of 1870 changed those relationships. He understood how the illusive notion of the balance of power was destroying the ability of nations to come together in a collective action to stop conflict. He understood how the practice of secret alliances and treaties was handicapping nations from initiating realistic strategies to ensure peace.[3]

When Wilson was elected president of the United States in 1912, he was determined to initiate a new approach to relationships among nations. When he died on February 3, 1924, reasonable people all over the world regretted that the efforts he had made to create a climate of understanding and peace in the world through the functions and operations of the League of Nations had been rendered meaningless by the Senate's rejection of U.S. involvement in it, and that he was removed from the scene of constructing relationships among nations before his task was completed. His death was therefore considered the greatest tragedy in American national leadership since the tragic death of President Abraham Lincoln on April 15, 1865.[4]

In 1924, soon after Wilson's death, Josephus Daniels, who served as Wilson's secretary of the navy from 1913 to 1921, and so came to know him well, described the efforts that he made to create conditions of understanding and peace in the world:

Wilson spared himself no toil, no sacrifice of comfort, no affection, nothing that diverted him from the task which he set for himself. From early youth he always prescribed hurdles that called forth full absorption of all his power. In his boy-hood home his scholarly and critical father gave him the example of thorough-ness and accuracy. Wilson's style enabled him later to voice American idealism in such manner as to constitute him the spokesman of a new day in the world. He was a finished product of the preparation in the home of his preacher-father.[5]

This is a rare tribute to a rare national leader. Wilson measured up to expectations and gave more than anyone else at that time to the world struggling to find itself. Unfortunately he was cut short by an American institution that did not understand what he was trying to accomplish.

From his early life Wilson always overcame adversity to assert the superiority of the human spirit. He was born into a family that gave him what he needed to be successful in any endeavor. He was thoroughly prepared to solve serious problems. His education enabled him to adopt idealism that made him an efficient spokesman of a new era in the world that was searching for new meaning amid conflicting values that the Industrial Revolution of the nineteenth century had created.[6] As a stu-dent and later as professor and president of Princeton University, Wilson had a passion for the study of government function and its role in seeking improvement of the lives of the people. In his study of William Gladstone, Benjamin Disraeli, Herbert Asquith, and David Lloyd George,[7] men who served as leaders in Britain at different times, Wilson obtained the inspiration that he needed to carry out duties to his people and country.

Wilson's educational activity and scholarly endeavor as a student, pro-fessor, and president of Princeton University was a preparation for ef-fective service as governor of New Jersey and president of the United States. His participation in the Versailles Peace Conference made him into the principal architect of understanding peace among nations.[8] Other participants of the conference, including the remaining "Big Three," Lloyd George of Britain, Vittorio Orlando of Italy, and Georges Clemenceau of France, depended on him to shape the course of the con-ference as part of their new collective effort to shape the future security of the world. Having done his homework, Wilson responded with rare brilliance to the challenge. His Fourteen Points provided more than an adequate framework for the success of the conference. He believed that the security of the world depended squarely on observance of these points as fundamental operational principles.[9]

The legacy of Woodrow Wilson has been hard to match. When Con-gress convened in extraordinary session in the spring of 1913 to consider tariff regulations, Wilson was ready to outline the relationships he saw between the economy of the United States and the security of the world as a whole. He expressed hope and aspirations of the people of the world, saying that the United States must abolish everything that carried trappings of a provincial thought process and action unrelated to conditions in the world. He warned Congress not to become obsessed with protecting the U.S. economy to the extent that its actions would hurt the opportunity to carry on beneficial trade with other counties. He argued, "Only new principles of action will save us from a final hard stylization of monetary and complete loss of the influences that quicken free enterprise we need to shape the cause of understanding and peace in the world."[10]

Writing in 1956 in his book, *Profiles in Courage*, Senator John F. Kennedy paid tribute to Woodrow Wilson's courage in standing for the principles he believed in under difficult conditions created by the U.S. Senate. Kennedy quoted Wilson as giving his reasons why he could not accept the argument that some members of the Senate were advancing that neither the Versailles Treaty nor the League of Nations was of any benefit to the United States. Wilson responded, saying that he was not going to allow "a little group of willful men, representing no opinion but their own, that rendered the great government of the United States helpless and contemptible."[11]

Kennedy concluded that this kind of political courage requires strong leadership. In a foreword to the memorial edition of the book, Kennedy's brother Robert F. Kennedy wrote about how President Kennedy had admired those who exhibited the courage of leadership under stressed circumstances because it was a test of their character: "Courage is the virtue that President Kennedy most admired. He sought out those people who had demonstrated it in some way, whether it was on a battlefield or a baseball diamond, in a speech or fighting for a cause, that they had courage, that they would stand up that they could be counted on."[12] There is no question that both John F. Kennedy and Robert F. Kennedy greatly admired Wilson's courage.

Some historians have concluded that Wilson's tenure as president from 1913 to 1921 was also a time when he served as chief custodian of universal values that the world needed to embrace in order to insure that peace and security became a reality for the first time since the Industrial Revolution and the Franco-Prussian war of 1870.[13] He assumed the office of president when the influence of the Republican party was declining due to differences of opinion on how best to sustain Lincoln's legacy. This is why, by the election of 1912, Theodore Roosevelt and William Howard Taft had serious differences about the election platform and an agenda for action. Although Henry Cabot Lodge supported Roosevelt, the Republican party was divided right through the middle, making it hard to mount an effective election campaign. By serving as chairman of the Senate Foreign Relations Committee, Lodge hoped to exert influence on the election process. Instead he became so divisive that Wilson won the election with a substantial majority of the vote.

On the one hand, in all his opposition to the League of Nations and to Wilson himself, Lodge manifested the action of a leader who had neither the qualities of leadership nor the understanding of the issues that were becoming increasingly central to U.S. foreign policy and relationships with other nations.[14] Because he was not cast in a position of responsibility to see issues critical to the security of the United States, Lodge lacked the vision that Wilson projected in perceiving the U.S. role in a world that was rapidly changing. In his support for Roosevelt for president in 1912 Lodge did more harm to the Republican party than good. His partisan approach to issues portrayed him as an individual who lacked principles that were needed to serve the interests of the United States in a larger world of conflicting values.[15]

On the other hand Wilson saw the problems of Europe as problems of the entire world. This is why he believed that in finding solutions to problems of Europe, the world community as a whole, including the United States, must be involved. He also believed that to insulate Europe and set it apart from the rest of the world would compound the problems of relationships among nations. Such problems would be resolved only in the forum of interaction in an organization created among nations such as the League of Nations. This explains why he refused to give up the idea of forming such an organization.[16] Wilson also argued that from necessity to survive and to have an enduring peace, nations would support such an organization. George Schlid concluded that by 1939 it was so easy for nations to fall back to the notion of the balance of power, which was the major cause of the war, because there was no machinery for peace strengthened by effective leaders, such as Wilson, to remind them of the danger of taking that road.[17]

Wilson's observation just before his death in 1924 that the outbreak of the war in 1914 was a result of the lack of the practice of democracy led him to the conclusion in 1917 that the United States must play a major role in creating conditions for the introduction of democracy in the world. This is why he argued that the United States was entering the war to end all wars and make the world safe for democracy. He believed that this could be done collectively by utilizing provisions of the League of Nations Charter. In order to make this a reality he went to Versailles prepared to play a major role in the deliberations of the conference. He alone called for a peace treaty that included terms intended to uphold democratic values and principles.[18] He was in an extremely positive frame of mind as he believed that he would persuade other delegations to the conference to work out a peace treaty that was based on the Fourteen Points he so elaborately produced. He was to be disappointed.

## CONFLICT BETWEEN WILSON AND LODGE

When Wilson stood on the verge of great success in his effort to create the League of Nations at the conclusion of the Versailles Conference, his accomplishments so far were later reduced to nothingness by the action of the U.S. Senate, an institution that he thought would come to his assistance in sustaining principles of great interest to the country and the world. The rift that occurred in the Republican party caused by the candidacies of Theodore Roosevelt and William Howard Taft in the presidential election of 1912 led to Wilson's easy victory. The assassination of William McKinley in 1901, bringing Roosevelt to the presidency, had weakened the leadership of the Republican party considerably. Following the elections of 1908 and 1912 Republicans were left without a nationally recognized leader. During the years of the war in Europe from 1914 to 1918 they could not offer a viable alternative policy to the one Wilson was proposing.[19]

In an effort to fill the leadership void left by the conflict between Taft and Roosevelt, Lodge tried under very difficult circumstances to exert leadership influence using his position of chairman of the Senate Foreign Relations Committee. But his refusal to make an effort to see the importance of ratifying the League of Nations put him out of contention for the position of chairman of the Republican party. All he could do now was to become a rebel without a cause. His opposition to the League of Nations and to Wilson himself was well known. There was nothing that he could say that was considered new. William C. Widenor concluded that Lodge did not seem to understand the wider implications of his opposition to the League of Nations because he was heavily controlled by partisan political ideology, not by the consideration of the merits of the League itself.[20]

Widenor quotes Theodore Roosevelt as saying in 1917 about Lodge's personality, "He is an unmitigated Bostonian that one sees in his eyes robust, stiff-necked intolerant, bleak bad manners, tenacity in his beliefs to the end. Nothing outside ever really gets into him."[21] This is the Lodge that Wilson had to work with in developing national consensus in U.S. policy on Europe. Having Wilson ask Lodge to persuade the Senate to ratify the Treaty of Versailles was the same thing as asking the fox and the chicken to agree on how to ensure the safety of the coop. It might have been easier for Wilson to move a mountain than to ask Lodge to see the logic of ratifying the terms of the formation of the League.

Observers seem to conclude that Lodge appeared to approach the very issue that related to U.S. policy with an apparent self-righteous attitude. For example, in August 1876 he reviewed Jacob H. Patton's book, *Concise History of the American People* for *The Nation*, a leading journal of the time, and concluded that there was no theory, good or bad, in the book. Lodge concluded that the book was useless for Patton to search for cause and effect in presenting the history of the United States.[22] Suddenly Lodge had entered a new arena of controversy, the world of scholarship in which he had not developed an interest despite his receiving a doctorate in history from Harvard University that year. The assumption he made that Patton did not present a theory in his book suggests the conclusion that Lodge viewed the history of the United States from a narrower perspective than was generally accepted by scholars in the area.

Without prior research in history Lodge put himself in a position to judge the quality of the scholarship of a work that he was not qualified to judge. He would translate the same attitude into the arena of foreign policy of the United States. The combination of the two led to disaster. He became a critic of what others had written from his own perspective. He applied intellectual and academic litmus tests to suit his own tastes. Like some critics today he did not see diversity and a different approach to literature as an enrichment. If an educated individual from a prestigious institution was this narrow in his response to literature, how could he broaden his operational base on issues as important as U.S. foreign policy?

Widenor also concluded that in spite of his opposition to the League of Nations, Lodge was quite sensitive to some problems arising out of the process of formulating and implementing U.S. foreign policy in general. But he argued that defining the parameters of that policy must not be the prerogative of the president and the State Department; the joint responsibility must be shared with the Senate Foreign Relations Committee that he chaired. Lodge argued that this approach would insure that there was close consultation and cooperation in this important area of U.S. activity. Lodge made this suggestion when he felt that he was under considerable pressure to modify his opposition to the League of Nations. On April 18, 1919, Lodge tried to explain his position: "I am not opposed to the League. On the contrary, I should like to see the League among nations with whom we have been associated in the war which would tend to promote and secure the future of the world and sustain the interests of the United States."[23].

Of course, Wilson dismissed this claim and argued that even if Lodge had a change of heart over the League of Nations, his opposition had already done a great deal of damage, and Wilson wanted to know how Lodge was going to correct it. Wilson also argued that the use of force, which Lodge said worried him as an aspect of U.S. foreign policy, would not be a viable option. The use of force should be considered only in war situations, not in peacetime, and Wilson was talking about permanent peace in the world. To achieve this goal, dialogue would have to be utilized because peace terms could not be enforced unilaterally.[24]

The difference in political philosophy between Wilson and Lodge could not be resolved. Lodge had sufficient influence in the Senate to reject the League. Wilson's unwillingness to compromise any further than the modifications he had secured from European nations led him to the conclusion that Lodge was leading the Senate in a wrong direction.

He then decided to take the campaign for ratification of the Treaty of Versailles directly to Caesar, the American people. He believed that this appeal to Caesar would yield the results he wanted.[25] Speaking in Omaha, Nebraska, on September 8, 1919, Wilson used graphic language to make his case: "If I felt that I personally in any way stood in the way of this settlement, I would be glad to die so that it might be consummated. All the world is looking to us for inspiration and leadership, and we will not deny it to them."[26]

Throughout the tour Wilson returned frequently to address Article 10 of the League of Nations Covenant, which reads: "The Members of the League undertake to respect and preserve against external aggression the territorial integrity and existing political independence of all members of the League. In case of any such aggression or in case of any threat or danger of such aggression the Council shall advise upon the means by which this obligation shall be fulfilled."[27] The reason for Wilson's frequent return to Article 10 was that he had heard that as a result of implementing it the United States would be obligated to defend European nations by military means and that the European nations themselves would not do any thing in their own defense. He wanted to make sure that Caesar understood that this was not so and was a false impression deliberately created by those who were opposing the U.S. involvement in the formation and functions of the League.

Speaking in Los Angeles on September 20, 1919, Wilson addressed something that was not part of the experience of people in other countries, that the American people had always taken for granted because they lived in a truly democratic country, and that was the relationships that existed between the people and their governments:

This treaty is almost a discovery of international conventions that nations do not consist of in their governments, but consist of in their people. It seems to us in America to go without saying but it was never the leading idea in any other international congress that I ever heard of. They were always thinking of national policy, of national advantage, of the rivalries of trade, of the advantages of territorial conquest. There is nothing of that in this treaty. You will notice that even the territories which are taken away from Germany, like her colonies, are not given to anybody.[28]

Beginning in Columbus, Ohio, on September 4, 1919, Wilson spoke every day and night in campaigning for the ratification of the Versailles Peace Treaty until September 26, when he was stricken on the way to Wichita, Kansas. His spirits were rising high as his physical condition was declining due to extreme exhaustion. From that point until his death on February 3, 1924, his second wife, Edith Bolling Galt, assumed unofficially the responsibility of running his administration, acquiring the reputation that she was the first female president of the United States. In these tragic events Wilson's appeal to Caesar came to a sudden end and so closed a chapter of turbulent events in the history of the country.

Lodge's political fortunes also began to decline. In 1919 he did not seem to have the grip on his opposition to the League of Nations that he thought he had the previous year. On January 3, 1919, he admitted that he did not know what the president was doing in his policy about the League and said that he doubted that the president himself knew. What he knew about the issues was what he read in the papers. Although he repeated his claim that he was not opposed to peace arrangements between the United States and European nations, he wanted to see an agreement that would insure U.S. security and trade in Europe.[29] Beginning with the election campaign of 1912, Lodge and Roosevelt, who had been close friends and associates in their opposition to Wilson, became estranged because of their opposing positions on the candidacy of both William Howard Taft and Theodore Roosevelt for president.

Roosevelt saw the possibility of conspiracy between Lodge and Taft against him. Lodge thought that Taft would bring unity to the Republican party. That is why Roosevelt decided to run as candidate of the Progressive party. Lodge thought that Roosevelt was playing the role of spoiler, which Wilson would exploit to his advantage. Although Roosevelt and Lodge tried to patch up their differences, damage had been done to give Wilson an advantage and victory. When Roosevelt died suddenly on January 6, 1919, from a blood clot in the heart, Lodge felt that he had lost a friend whose support was crucial to his opposition of Wilson.

When Wilson died his wife sent a letter to Lodge, asking him not to attend his funeral. Lodge began to stay out of public events because his health was deteriorating and because he believed that the American people were blaming him for the Senate's rejection of the League of Nations. He died on November 9, 1924, ten months after Wilson, leaving behind a legacy of constitutional conflict the nation had to resolve at the end of World War II. In 1945 these two competing branches of the U.S. government decided that they did not want to subject the country to the power struggle that had derailed the League of Nations

## CONSEQUENCES OF U.S. SENATE REJECTION OF THE LEAGUE

This book has discussed the results of the U.S. Senate rejection of the League of Nations because it involved what it considered U.S. intimate involvement in European affairs. The book has also presented the reaction of European nations to the League, knowing that the United States would not be involved in its formation and functions. They also knew that without U.S. involvement any organization among nations was ineffective in carrying out its tasks. Japan's invasion of Manchuria in 1931, for example, was launched because Japan believed that having rejected the League, the United States was unlikely to respond in any way. Once Japan set this precedence other nations engaged in aggressive behavior of a similar nature and for the same reason.

A series of unfortunate events began to unfold following Japan's example in 1931. In 1935 Benito Mussolini ordered his troops to invade Ethiopia. In 1936 Adolf Hitler supported Francisco Franco in launching a revolution in Spain and establishing a dictatorship that lasted nearly half a century. In 1937 Japan attacked the U.S. gunboat, the *Ponay*, in the Yangtze River. On September 28, 1939, just about a month after Hitler sent his forces to invade Poland on September 1 to trigger the outbreak of World War II, Hitler and Stalin signed a nonaggression pact dividing eastern Europe between them. The greatest fallout of the U.S. Senate rejection of the League of Nations was felt in Germany, a nation that had been defeated in World War I. From the moment that Germany knew in 1919 that the U.S. Senate had rejected the League, it began a series of activities intended to make it a dominant nation in Europe and the world once more.

The formation of the National Socialist German Workers party (Nazi) in 1919 was the beginning of the new road to a major conflict in Europe only twenty years later. When Hitler joined the party as soon as it was formed, he steadily paved his way to the top rung of the leadership ladder. From that moment on a spiral of events began to unfold in a way that surprised leaders of other nations about the behavior of the Nazi party. From the terms of the Versailles Treaty Germany was forbidden to maintain or construct any military facilities on either the right or left banks of the Rhine River.[30] But, beginning in 1920, soon after learning that the U.S. Senate had rejected the League, the Nazi party began to prepare to take power in Germany by any means and started rearming Germany with little opposition from the League of Nations.

This book has also discussed examples to show that the Nazi party used the U.S. Senate rejection of the League of Nations to place Germany on the road to war by September 1939. On February 20, 1920, the Nazi party issued a statement consisting of twenty-five points outlining its operational principles and goals. Among these were demanding Germans to join in forming a union on the basis of the right to self-determination to the same extent that the Nazis said other nations were enjoying.[31] The Nazi party also stated that it demanded equality of rights for Germans in dealing with other nations, and the abolition of the Versailles Treaty because its members said it was detrimental to Germany's interests. The Nazi party also stated that it demanded land or territorial space to settle Germans. It extended citizenship only to those who were members of the Nazi party and said that anyone who was not a citizen lived in Germany as a guest.[32] The Nazi party took these measures to provoke reaction from other nations in Europe in order to enforce its will on them by military means. Germany was getting ready for war.

On April 12, 1932, Adolf Hitler gave a speech in Munich to a Nazi meeting, saying that he accused the 100,000 Jews in Germany of greed. He concluded,

The Aryan looks upon work as the foundation of the national community. The Jew looks upon work as a means of exploiting others. The Jew never works as a productive creator but rather with the idea of becoming master. As a Christian and as a man with boundless love, I read that passage which told how the Lord finally gathered His strength and used the whip in order to drive the money-changers, the vipers, and the cheats from the temple.[33] Today, some two thousand years later, I understand with deep emotion Christ's tremendous struggle on behalf of the world against the Jewish poison.[34]

For Hitler to compare himself with Christ is like a hyena claiming that he is as good as a German shepherd dog in ensuring the safety of the flock. There was no question that Hitler was deliberately distorting Christ's position to justify his hatred of the Jews.

When Paul von Hindenburg was reelected president of Germany in 1932 in accordance with provisions of the Weimar Republic constitution, Hitler issued a call for the Nazi party members to get ready for an intense and decisive struggle to gain the power he said was rightly theirs. During the remainder of 1932 von Hindenburg and Hitler failed to come to agreement on any issue because Hitler wanted power for the Nazi party on his own terms. For example, on August 13 von Hindenburg asked Hitler if the Nazi party was willing to participate in the existing government for the good of the country. Hitler responded, "We are willing to take over full responsibility for German political policy in every form provided that means unequivocal leadership of the government. If that is not the case, then the National Socialist movement can accept neither power nor responsibility."[35] Hitler never considered the question of coming to power through the electoral process; he wanted power regardless of the method he used to get it. This was a very bad omen for both Germany and Europe.

When von Hindenburg suggested a compromise that all political parties convene a conference to seek a solution to political problems in the interest of the country, Hitler turned him down, arguing that the Nazi party was entitled to nothing less than total power. Von Hindenburg finally realized that this was not the behavior of a leader of a political party that was concerned about the welfare of the people and the country, but was merely interested in assuming power to serve its own purposes.[36]

The next few months, knowing that at eighty-seven years of age von Hindenburg was rapidly losing control of his own government, Hitler and the Nazi party did everything in their power to cause chaos in both the government and the country. Suddenly, in January 1933 Chancellor Franz von Popen and his administration resigned, leaving von Hindenburg with no choice but to invite Hitler on January 30 to be the next chancellor. Hitler readily accepted because he knew that he had eliminated every opposition to his quest for supreme and total power. By the summer of that year Hitler had made himself dictator.

When von Hindenburg died on August 2, 1934, his final testament, dated May 11, 1934, was published two weeks following his death. Although von Hindenburg stated that he did not want Hitler to succeed him as president or chancellor, Hitler abolished the titles of president and chancellor, and named himself head of the government creating for himself a new title, *fuehrer*. At last after a fanatical struggle lasting more than a decade, Hitler was at the top position of power. He immediately adopted the policy the Nazi party had been formulating since its founding in 1919: anti-Marxist, anti-Bolshevik, anti-Catholic, anti-democracy, anti-Versailles Peace Treaty, and anti-Semitic. Hitler and the Nazi party also adopted a hostile policy toward other nations because they were inhabited by people who did not belong to the Aryan race.

From reading his book *Mein Kampf*, which Hitler wrote while he was in prison for leading an attempted coup in 1922, one gets a clear picture of what he intended to do in the future. He told of his life, his education, and suffering in Vienna and blamed the Jews for it all. Born on April 2, 1889, in the Bavarian-Austrian town of Braunau, the son of a pensioned customs official, Hitler attended the Realschule School in Linz. At the age of 11, he told his father that he did not wish to follow in his footsteps. Instead he wanted to become a painter and architect.[37] It turned out that he became an architect of the horror he later perpetrated against those he considered less than human. Hitler went on to add, "When I look back now after so many years, I see two things of importance in my childhood. First, I became a nationalist. Second, I learned to understand and grasp the real meaning of history. When I was fifteen years old, I understood the difference between dynastic patriotism and racial nationalism."[38] The ideas he expressed in *Mein Kampf* became the guiding principles of his government and relationships with other nations.

In 1934 Hitler held all the cards. He began to implement a program that he believed would bring the entire world under his control using the machinery that the Third Reich created to last at least a thousand years. He believed also that he would succeed where Alexander the Great, Hannibal, Napoleon, and Chaka the Zulu had failed in their efforts to bring the entire world under their control. Developing diplomatic relationships with other nations was not his way of relating to them. Confrontation and conquest was the way. But in April 1945 he and the Nazi party paid the ultimate price. In the end they took the easy way out and left the world in chaos for others to solve.

On November 20, 1945, the international community sought justice by putting members of the Nazi party on trial in Nuremberg, the center of the Nuremberg Laws of 1935. On July 20, 1946, the chief prosecutor, Robert H. Jackson of the United States, summed up the charges against the Nazi members: "These deeds are the overshadowing historical facts by which generations to come will remember this decade. If we cannot eliminate the causes and prevent the repetition of these barbaric events, it is not an irresponsible prophecy to say that this twentieth century may yet succeed in bringing the doom of civilization."[39] All major Nazi leaders were found guilty and sentenced to various terms of imprisonment or death.

## CONCLUSION

Appearing on television in the United States in August 1999 to discuss what he saw as the outcome of World War II, Oskew Schnolling, a German citizen who was sixteen years of age on D-Day on June 6, 1944, concluded that World War II did little to bring the Allies and the Axis powers closer to understanding each other because they were enemies before the war and they remained enemies after the war.[40] It is true that the two sides went to war because they did not understand that they had common objectives that could have been met without going to war. Schnolling concluded that the lesson that could have been learned is for nations to make an effort to understand each other to avoid war.[41] This book has presented a line of argument that reflects Schnolling's point of view.

This book has also concluded that it is not possible to exercise understanding without acquiring a functional knowledge of a people by studying its culture. The study of culture is important because culture is the foundation of national institutions. The economy, political activity, family structure, relations among members of society, and social relations are all based on culture. When cultural functions in any society are transmitted into the arena of relationships among nations, they acquire powerful dimensions that determine how successful those relationships are. Conflict between Germany and other nations in Europe was caused by an attitude and policy that regarded Germans as an Aryan race and the rest of the people as inferior. This attitude is an example of a powerful cultural dimension that influences relationships among nations. When the Nazi government tried to structure relationships with other nations, it operated under an environment created by this dimension. In Germany itself certain people were considered less than human. Thus, conflict became inevitable.

This book has also suggested that among aspects of education that people in various nations should acquire in order to have understanding is the study of various features of culture. H. Ned Seelye takes this line of thinking when he argues, "When communication is between people with different world views, especial skills are required if the messages received are to resemble messages sent. The most important overriding skill is understanding the context within which the communication takes place. This context is to a large extent culturally determined."[42] Seelye goes on to add that without understanding the culture of a people it is not possible to have meaningful communications with it. Without communications conflict becomes inevitable.[43]

In contemporary world situations understanding has become so important that some national leaders have risked their lives or lost them in order to improve relationships with other nations. We have only enough space in this section to discuss briefly three examples to substantiate this conclusion. The first example relates to the continuing saga of conflict in the Middle East. In November 1977 Anwar Sadat, president of Egypt since he succeeded Gamal Abdel Nasser who died of a heart attack in 1970, made an official visit to Israel to break the stalemate that had existed between the two countries and spoke eloquently to the Knesset about the need to demonstrate understanding in order to find solutions to problems of conflict in the Middle East. Sadat decried the violence that was paralyzing the entire Middle East and called for the exercise of reason to stop it.

On March 30, 1979, Sadat and Menachem Begin, prime minister of Israel, signed a formal peace treaty sponsored by President Jimmy Carter of the United States at Camp David, ending 30 years of hostility and establishing diplomatic relations between the two countries for the first time.[44] As a result of this peace treaty Israel returned control of the Sinai to Egypt. However, the treaty between Sadat and Begin created a new level of tension between Muslim fundamentalists in Egypt and Sadat. On October 6, 1981, Sadat was assassinated by his own people for visiting Israel and making peace with what they considered an enemy. But both Israel and Egypt began to have a sense of real peace.

The second example also relates to the Middle East. On June 23, 1992, the Labour Party led by Yitzak Rabin won a clear victory in the elections that were held in Israel. As soon as he took office Rabin became convinced that Israel would never enjoy peace and security unless Palestinians had a homeland. He began to make overtures of that possibility to Yasir Arafat, the Palestinian leader. The two men began negotiations that finally led to an agreement signed at the White House under the sponsorship of President Bill Clinton, raising hopes among members of the international community that at last permanent peace in the Middle East was possible. But on November 4, 1995, Rabin was assassinated by an Orthodox Jewish Israeli as he was leaving a peace rally in Tel Aviv. Both Sadat and Rabin were assassinated by their own people who did not understand the need for peace in the region for the benefit of all. Although, on September 5, 1999, individuals in two cars tried to stage a suicide attack on Israel while officials of both sides were discussing peace plans, spokesmen for both sides indicated that peace discussions would continue.

The third example relates to tragic events that began to unfold in the Philippines during the time that Ferdinand Marcos was in power. For a number of years Marcos was head of the government that was known all over the world for corruption. On September 21, 1972, Marcos declared martial law and ordered the arrest of hundreds of his political opponents, claiming that Communists were trying to take over the government. On January 17, 1973, Marcos proclaimed a new constitution that made him virtual dictator. He outlawed all political opposition and gave his wife, Imelda, wide powers to plan and supervise national programs. Those who continued their opposition activity disappeared without trace. Within the space of a few years the Marcoses became extremely rich.[45]

One of Marcos' political opponents was Benigno S. Aquino, Jr., a very popular and respected man of high principle. Realizing that his life was in danger, Aquino went into exile for a number of years in the United States. During this time opposition leadership persuaded him to return to the Philippines to oppose Marcos in the presidential election due to be held in 1974. After seriously considering the invitation Aquino decided to accept the challenge, knowing that the interests of his people and country required dedication and sacrifice. He therefore decided to return. On August 21, 1983, he arrived back home, but he never had a chance. As soon as his plane landed at the airport in Manila, Aquino was assassinated in broad daylight.[46] It was believed that Marcos ordered his elimination because he posed the most serious threat to his power and corruption.

However, the assassination sparked a worldwide condemnation of Marcos and called for his resignation. Aquino's widow, Corazon, stepped forward to launch an effective campaign against Marcos, forcing him to resign after losing the election to her. He went into exile in the United States, where he died a few years later. At last the Philippines got rid of a ruthless dictator and democracy was restored although at a high cost.

These three examples explain two things. The first is that demonstrating understanding under difficult circumstances of accomplishments is best exercised by those in positions of responsibility to set a good example for the rest of the people in a country to follow. The important thing to remember is that there are risks that those who show understanding must be willing to take, including death, for a cause. It is a risk that must be taken to insure common good for humanity. The second thing that these three examples show is that because in a world of conflict there is no adequate substitute for understanding, nations have a responsibility to insure that their people are adequately educated to insure successful relationships among nations. If nations fail to do this they will pay the ultimate price of the conflict that ensues from ignorance.

## IMPLICATIONS

When President George Bush of the United States and President Mikhail Gorbachev of the Soviet Union signed the nuclear arms reduction treaty in Moscow on July 31, 1991, they ushered in a new era of relationships between the two superpowers and members of the world community. This event suggested the changing character of relationships among nations. Gorbachev understood that in 1992 the Soviet Union, as it had been known since the Bolshevik Revolution of 1917, could go out of existence if that was what the people in the Soviet Union wanted, to be substituted by a federation of independent republics as a condition of peace. The attempted coup in the Soviet Union, August 19–21, 1991, convinced Gorbachev that his government would have kept the Soviet Union together by resorting to brute force such as Stalin used. He did not want to subject the country to that course of action.

Indeed, the world of 1991 and 1992 was experiencing enormous problems that seemed to defy solution. The rapidly increasing population, estimated at 5.3 billion people with an annual growth rate of 1.8 percent and with per capita income of $3,470[47] complicated the problems of poverty and declining resources. The inability of nations to find solutions to national and international conflict accentuated the age-old myth that military power ensures national security. This is why designing national priorities by some nations has been influenced by huge military spending that has robbed the people of their legitimate access to resources they need to ensure their development and security. The end of the cold war has come to mean that national priorities have to be reset. By the beginning of 1992 this had not been done, creating a climate among nations that raised questions about the nature of relationships among them.

One sees two disturbing aspects about resorting to military power as the ultimate illusion of national security. The first aspect is that it gives politicians a false sense of national security and an intransigence that makes them arrogant and refuse to see issues of relationships among nations from their proper perspective. The world witnessed the tragedy of this thinking in the crisis that broke out in the Persian Gulf caused by Iraq's invasion of Kuwait on August 2, 1990.[48] The extent of destruction that is always evident in wars does not seem to influence the thinking or the action of national leaders; all they think of is the political gain they hope to make in the pursuit of their own political agenda and purpose. The behavior of the Nazi party in Germany serves as a clear example.

Quite often, as the world saw in 1991 when hostilities escalated between Iraq and the Western coalition forces, national leaders whose own political positions were weak took advantage of the conflict to improve their standing with the people. In this way an opportunity was lost to put in place elements that are needed to find genuine solutions to the problems of conflict among nations. With ready availability of various means of communication made possible by advances in technology, ranging from the ordinary airmail system through the E-mail to the fax, there is no reason for nations to fail to develop an effective system of communication to insure understanding and so avoid conflict. The age of the jumbo jet makes it possible for many people to reach every corner of the world within hours on any day. In recent years the United States has participated in joint space exploration endeavors with people of other nations to ensure that there is no hostile intent on its part. This is an encouraging development. In 1961 the first U.S. astronauts were known as Friendship Seven to signify that exploration of space was intended to benefit all mankind.

To achieve their own political objectives, many national leaders deny their people the opportunity to utilize resources to insure their development. Instead, they use those resources to strengthen military forces in order to bolster their own political positions. It really does not make any difference whether national leaders are democratically elected or whether they impose themselves on their people, their political behavior is quite often identical. They often claim that the pursuit of military objectives is in the national interest. They portray the party with whom they are in conflict as the aggressor. They convince the military establishment that theirs is a mission to save the world. They rarely think in terms of seeking knowledge of the causes of the rising tensions and subsequent conflicts. The action that the United Nations took on December 3, 1992, to send a multinational military force to Somalia to enable relief agents to distribute food to the starving masses caused by internal conflict, seems plausible. But it must be recognized that it also carried a serious potential for greater conflict than was acknowledged.

The United Nations did not consider the question of what would happen to Somalia if the international peacekeeping force left before solutions to political problems were found. This suggests the conclusion that UN efforts would have been better directed at bringing much needed education to the parties in conflict and the country as a whole to find a lasting peace. Further, the United Nations would have helped Somalia by giving it the educational assistance it desperately needed when its people were struggling for development. One must regret the military action taken on January 13, 1993, by Western coalition forces against Iraq for what President Bush said was Saddam Hussein's failure to comply with the UN resolution forbidding his forces from violating the no-fly zone which was imposed in southern Iraq following the conclusion of hostilities that had broken out two years earlier.

One is also led to the conclusion that in this action Western leaders who were part of the coalition against Iraq neglected some important considerations, among them that military action often robs leaders of the ability to utilize human reason to resolve conflict. How did the coalition forces hope to create a climate of peace through dialogue under conditions that made Iraq an occupied country? The sad part of all this is that people often regard national leaders who take them into war as heroes. This is why President Bush's popularity rose sharply at the conclusion of hostilities in the Persian Gulf in 1991. People tend to believe anything that their national leader says and give him the support he says he needs to carry out a national policy he claims to be in their interests.

In this setting any action that may question the policy of such leaders is often considered unpatriotic. These are characteristic features found in all national leaders, but they do not contribute positively to national purpose. In January 1992, for instance, the economy of the United States was weakened by a combination of powerful factors that included the aftermath of the war in the Persian Gulf. This contributed to President Bush's defeat by Bill Clinton, his Democratic opponent, in the elections held on November 3, 1992.[49]

The second disturbing aspect of the illusion of military power is that because national leaders are not able to see their own errors, they operate on the assumption that the party with which they are in conflict is always wrong and that they are always right. This is the environment in which President Saddam Hussein convinced his followers to see President George Bush as the ultimate threat to the world of Islam. This is also the same environment that President Bush utilized to convince his fellow Americans to believe that Hussein was the embodiment of Moslem extremism that must be stopped to deny him an opportunity to become another Adolf Hitler.

The frequent use of such terms as "the Great Satan" and "the Infidel" to characterize Western leadership, "the brutal dictator" to characterize Saddam Hussein, and "the evil empire" to characterize the Soviet Union contributed nothing to the creation of a climate of real knowledge of the issues that caused conflict among nations and the need to initiate dialogue to resolve problems. To refrain from using extreme language would have enabled the parties to learn, understand, and appreciate the concerns of the other side. The process of understanding and appreciation requires knowledge and education. Indeed, the conflict in the Persian Gulf underscores the importance of education for leaders to understand the essence and the art of diplomacy.

Another critical problem that stood in the way of seeking a peaceful resolution to the crisis in the Persian Gulf was the enormous ego manifested in the attitudes and actions of both President Hussein and President Bush. This problem was caused primarily by previous international events that had the impact they sought to turn into an advantage. On the one hand, having come out of the six-year war with Iran, Hussein, seeking to fill the regional leadership void left by the death of Anwar Sadat, wanted to assert himself as the undisputed leader of the Arab world. On the other hand, President Bush, recognizing that the United States had endured the humiliation of the war in Vietnam and the tragic drama of the hostages held in Iran and Lebanon in 1979, sought to assert his own leadership role in the Western world.

The personality of both men left no room for dialogue or accommodation. Instead, they acted in ways that accentuated rhetoric that was partly carried out by the media. This is why, at the conclusion of the war with Iraq in 1991, Bush proudly proclaimed that the Vietnam syndrome was finally over, suggesting that he used the war with Iraq to eliminate the residual effect of the demise the United States had endured in that conflict. President Bush's proudest moment was his claim that the Patriot missiles had elevated the American spirit to a new level of national pride and self-confidence. He appeared to neglect the importance of developing the ability to reason things out, rather than to utilize military power to seek solutions to international problems.

Indeed, it is quite clear that both Hussein and Bush needed a new level of knowledge and education to help them understand that humility and self-restraint are distinct qualities of national leaders and that they do not diminish the power of leadership and the office they hold simply because they seek to understand the concerns of their potential adversary as a condition of dialogue. This suggests that education is the essence of political behavior and action. To neglect its development in favor of building military forces is to undercut the very essence of national endeavors.

The situation discussed above is a reality that delegates in San Francisco in 1945 took into account in their deliberations. But by 1992 too many leaders had already forgotten this basic principle. The world of 1991 showed much that could be related to events of earlier times. The change of leadership in Britain from Margaret Thatcher to John Major, the continuing saga of apartheid in South Africa, the conflict between Mikhail Gorbachev and the Baltic states, the political crisis in East European countries, and the end of the Soviet Union—all were manifestations of conditions that could easily lead to a major global conflict unless nations learn what they must to bring about a lasting peace.

The sad part of the tragedy in the Persian Gulf is that in this kind of environment the real causes of the conflict were not addressed. On the one hand, Hussein, claiming to be the guardian of the Palestinian cause, wanted linkage to that cause interpreted in his invasion of Kuwait. On the other hand, Bush, believing that he was the guardian of Western democratic values, rejected the idea of linkage and argued that the invasion was nothing less than naked aggression that must not be allowed to stand.

Failure to resolve this difference through dialogue is what caused the war in the Persian Gulf in 1991. Must one assume that differences of opinion on issues of international relationships and human existence could be resolved only by military means and not by applying reason? It would be a sad day for the international community to be forced to accept such thinking. Yet, in 1991 this kind of thinking became the norm of international relationships when the United Nations itself voted to authorize military use to force Iraq out of Kuwait. Then, on January 12, the U.S. Senate voted 52 to 49 and the House of Representatives 250 to 183 to authorize President Bush to use military means to force Iraq out of Kuwait. While this action yielded considerable political support, it had its dark side, a lingering and devastating effect that would last for years. Victorious in military action, the United States entered a new phase of economic decline that forced Bush to undertake a mission to Japan in January 1992 in an effort to revive the economy.

In examining the role that education must play in helping nations seek an improvement in the human condition and international relations, one must remind oneself of the diagnostic approach that the world community made at the conclusion of the war in 1945. This is the place and time that this study begins. Painful as this exercise was, the delegates to the San Francisco conference concluded that rather than blame the Axis powers for causing the war, all nations must share the responsibility for its outbreak. If they had come to this conclusion in 1939, the war would have been avoided in the first place. And if nations had come to this realization in 1991, the devastation caused by the war in the Persian Gulf would have been avoided and the billions of dollars used to wage the war could have been directed toward the much-needed social services that not all countries have been able to extend to their people.

Neither the U.S. Senate nor the House of Representatives predicted the setting on fire of oil fields in Kuwait and the displacement of the Kurds as outcomes of the Gulf war. If the restoration of Kuwait was accomplished at the price of the displacement of the Kurds and the destruction of natural resources in Kuwait, then one must conclude that the victory that allied coalition forces thought they scored against Saddam Hussein must be considered a disaster. This means that using military force to force Iraq out of Kuwait had a much darker side in the form of human cost that it could not be measured.

There is another cost to this tragedy: Prospects for peace in the Middle East, which Western nations thought would become possible with the defeat of Iraq, have remained as distant as ever. The shuttle diplomacy that Secretary of State James Baker initiated at the conclusion of hostilities did not yield any tangible results. Indeed, Baker's efforts amounted to a reincarnation of Henry Kissinger's shuttle diplomacy but with its weak side. As the presidential campaign got under way in August 1992, President Bush removed Baker from the State Department and appointed him manager of his reelection efforts. This created more doubt than confidence in the minds of Americans about his ability to design a good foreign policy.

The fears that Israel and its Arab neighbors have had about the intention of each other even intensified as both sides hardened their respective positions, refusing to see the critical issues they faced from the other's perspective. Only new elections in Israel in 1999 would resolve that deadlock when a more flexible national leader was returned to office. With Baker out of the negotiations, the crisis in the Middle East took a dramatic turn for the worse. On January 20, 1993, President Bill Clinton inherited from the Bush administration a critical foreign issue complicated by Israel's decision to expel a hundred Palestinians from occupied land in December 1992. The continuing crisis between Saddam Hussein and George Bush added a perilous twist to an already difficult situation.

There is yet another disturbing aspect of the war in the Persian Gulf that the Western forces had not anticipated. As it progressed and allied forces were reported to be within striking distance of victory, social and economic conditions in the United States began to deteriorate rapidly. In his PBS television program on June 2, 1991, Bill Moyers gave the following facts as an outcome of the war: Nearly a million Americans were lining up for welfare benefits that were not there. The recession was having a devastating impact on education as nearly 54 percent of the programs were being cut. Hospital care and other services were being reduced. The scourge of homelessness was rapidly increasing and the plight of the less fortunate was deteriorating. In New Jersey the Office of Social Services was advising those fifty-five years and older to seek economic and financial help from their children in order to survive.[50]

Many American servicemen returned home from the Gulf to find their families in a state of economic ruin. Some experienced family trauma that they had not anticipated, such as divorce. Even conservative journalist George Will argued in June 1991 that the war with Iraq had left behind "broken homes, broken hopes, and broken hearts" in both Iraq and the United States.[51] Tom Foley, the Speaker of the U.S. House of Representatives, added on June 16 that the preoccupation with the war in the Persian Gulf had created an array of problems at home that the nation was now finding hard to resolve.[52] On August 2, ABC published the results of a poll that indicated that those Americans who had supported going to war with Iraq now questioned the decision to do so by a margin of 54 to 46 percent. While this was happening, controversy between the president and the Democrats in Congress over the civil rights bill of 1991 was having a paralyzing effect on the political process.

Can one conclude that all these adverse effects justified going to war with Iraq over Kuwait? Why was it not possible to utilize human reason to resolve the problem of Iraq's invasion of Kuwait? Yes, the Bush administration argued that it had tried to resolve the problem through dialogue, but the conditions Bush specified for such dialogue undercut the very essence of its universal meaning.

This is why on May 16, 1991, Baker returned to the United States to report to President Bush that he had accomplished nothing with his shuttle diplomacy. On May 18, during a television broadcast, Bruce Morton of CBS concluded that the comprehensive peace that the United States had hoped would result from the defeat of Iraq remained as distant as ever, and suggested that what may be needed to find solutions to the problems of the Middle East was a new strategy—education.[53]

The tragedy in the Middle East shows that there is always a price to pay for conflict as long as nations refuse to learn about the concerns of other nations and as long as they see issues exclusively from their own point of view. To reach this realization and alter their thought processes, all nations require an education that creates a climate of understanding so that problems can be resolved. The truth of the matter is that conflict exists in human existence only because people do not know what it takes to avoid it. In May 1991 Bush came close to recognizing this reality when he addressed another unexpected fallout of the war with Iraq.

Speaking to the graduating class of the U.S. Air Force Academy on May 24, 1991, President Bush decried what he saw as the proliferation of weapons of massive destruction in the Middle East, and indicated that his administration would do everything in its power to stop it.[54] However, Bush's decision to continue supplying weapons to what he called "our friends in the Middle East" manifested a classic example of the kind of behavior that has always been one of the major causes of conflict between nations. He failed to emphasize the importance of understanding and dialogue as principal pillars that sustain the edifice of lasting international peace.

The sad part of this unfortunate development is that neither Bush nor any other world leader could do anything to stop it. Although Bush outlined his plan to eliminate weapons of massive destruction in the

Middle East, he fell short of explaining the need to initiate an international approach to the development of an educational system as a strategy to enable all people to understand the importance of the mutuality of trust through utilization of knowledge. In stating, "we are committed to stopping the proliferation of weapons of massive destruction in the Middle East," Bush neglected to put all relevant aspects into proper perspective.

In October 1999 the drama of controversy was once more developing in the United States between President Bill Clinton and the U.S. Republican-controlled Senate over the question of the ratification of the international nuclear test ban treaty. In 1999 Republican senators were opposed to the treaty while Democrats and President Clinton supported it. This is precisely the same scenario that developed between Republicans and President Wilson in 1919. The question that was asked in 1999 was the same question that was asked in 1919: Can the world be expected to keep any peace treaty without the involvement of the United States? The relationship between Jesse Helms, chairman of the U.S. Senate Foreign Relations Committee, and Trent Lott, Senate majority leader, presents a haunting reminder of the relationships in 1919 between Senator Henry Cabot Lodge and Theodore Roosevelt. It is quite clear that in 1999 history was repeating itself.[55] When CBS-TV Anchorman Dan Rather reported on October 12, 1999, that Lott wanted to bring the matter to a vote in the following few days unless President Clinton agreed not to bring the issues up again for the rest of his term of office, the political motives for Lott's action became quite obvious.

The knowledge that before the war in 1939 educational opportunity was the privilege of a few individuals, the reality that economic development was not possible without adequate education, the reality that poverty and urban decay were products of the Industrial Revolution, the knowledge that political and economic power were inherited rights of a few—all these factors combined to create an international climate that, by 1939, made conflict on a global scale inevitable.

In 1992 this conflict took a perilous twist when a multinational military force was sent to Somalia to protect UN agents who were distributing food to starving masses. It did not occur to the United Nations that the best course of action would have been to help Somalia develop an educational system that would have helped them achieve a national character compatible with their aspirations.

The balanced and objective approach the delegates to the San Francisco conference took to seek solutions for the world was also evident in other areas of their endeavors. They concluded that the environment of conflict was created because people of the world did not know each other and because they were not sufficiently educated to understand the causes of human conflict. That they placed the responsibility for this situation squarely on the shoulders of national leaders substantiates the conclusion that leaders design policies that, while seeming to serve the interests of their nations, actually serve their own political interests.

However, one must not negate the reality that the delegates to the San Francisco conference took into account in concluding that educational development was the best means of resolving conflict, both international and national. As it lay in ruins, Japan realized in 1945 that before the war it had a fully developed industry which it gambled away in military adventure. Now, it was time to start all over again.

In this context it is interesting to note that the delegates to the San Francisco conference saw a definite relationship between the effort to create ideal national conditions and international peace and security. They readily recognized that when people of any nation had the right to education, economic security, political participation, and basic civil liberties that include freedom of speech, self-expression, and association, they provide a stable environment that eliminates national conflict. This environment translates into the creation of international peace and security. The delegates emphasized that the journey to this international destination must begin with a single educational step and underscored their belief in the value of education as a relevant factor of the human condition.

In spite of the enthusiasm of the delegates to the San Francisco conference to utilize education to create a brave new world order in which the position of the individual would supersede the political interests of the national leaders, there were enormous problems that they did not anticipate. The rapid increase in population translated into a rapid increase in school enrollment. The poor facilities then in existence combined with poor resources to limit the effectiveness of the new thrust in seeking improvement in education.

The new level of enthusiasm among parents to provide their children with an opportunity for education as a preparation for the future accentuated the hope among the dispossessed that the route to a better future lay in their pursuit of education. Decline in economic programs also combined with rising inflation and declining national resources to severely impinge on the efforts nations were making individually and collectively to plan a future different from the past.

In spite of recognizing these problems, the delegates to the San Francisco conference established an impressive set of objectives to guide their actions. They set 1960 as a target date for all nations to achieve 100 percent literacy. They decreed that every child in every country must be allowed to attend school. They passed a resolution calling on all nations to establish adult literacy programs to combat illiteracy on all fronts. They called on all nations to cooperate in building economies and national institutions in order to meet the varying dimensions of human need and to serve the educational purpose of their people.

As the year 2000 came to an end, the hope and enthusiasm that had been part of its beginning turned into dark shadows of despair as new conflict broke out in the Middle East. The limited success that Ehud Barak of Israel and Yasir Arafat of Palestine had achieved with the aid of the United States during the previous few months suddenly turned into a new wave of violence among their people as new fighting broke out in October. U.S. President Bill Clinton was deeply disturbed by the deterioration in this situation, but appeared helpless to do anything further to resolve the conflict.

It is important to remember that the problems that the world faces today are so complex that no single nation has enough national resources to solve them alone. International terrorism, increase in crime in general, AIDS epidemic, population explosion, trade imbalance, ethnic or cultural conflict, and negative influence of global warming on agricultural production are big problems that require a well-coordinated effort to solve. Without cooperation among nations these problems continue to increase. But to have that cooperation nations must understand each other first. Without understanding, nations will always have conflict. Within an environment of conflict, problems will always gain an advantage over any effort to solve them.

This is why the participants at the San Francisco conference called on all nations to reform their educational and political systems so that they would become more representative in their operations in order to sustain democracy as a condition of understanding and peace demanded by the times. They reminded national leaders that they held office as a public trust, and that if they violated that trust they must be removed from office by constitutional means. They called on national leaders to observe at all times that sacred democratic principle Thomas Jefferson so eloquently enunciated that "governments are instituted among men with the express consent of the governed." They created Unesco as an agent of the world organization to coordinate scientific, cultural, and educational programs throughout the world to bring about improvement in the conditions that influence human life and relationships among nations. In the words of the Prophet Isaiah, "Nations shall beat their swords into plowshares and their spears into pruning hooks. Nation shall not lift up sword against nation, neither shall they learn war any more."[56] This is the challenge that nations face today.

## NOTES

1. It is a historical fact that Joseph Mengele, a medical doctor, carried out various experiments with Jews to prove Nazi theories. One such experiment was to see how long Jews would live without oxygen.

2. Ian Kershaw, *Nazi Dictatorship: Problems and Perspectives of Interpretation* (London: Edward Arnold, 1985), p. 6.

3. George Schlid, *Between Ideology and Realpolitik: Woodrow Wilson and the Russian Revolution, 1917–1921* (Westport, CT: Greenwood Press, 1995), p. 27.

4. History recorded that on the evening of April 14, 1865, while Lincoln was watching a performance of *Our American Cousins* at Ford's Theater, John Wilkes Booth, one of the best actors of the day, shot him. Lincoln died at 7:22 a.m. the next day, April 15.

5. Josephus Daniels, *The Life of Woodrow Wilson, 1856–1924* (New York: Will H. Johnson, 1924), p. 13.

6. Ibid., p. 20.

7. For detailed discussion of these men, see, for example, Dickson A. Mungazi, *The Last British Liberals in Africa: Michael Blundell and Garfield Todd* (Westport, CT: Praeger Publishers, 1999), pp. 81–102.

8. Daniels, *The Life of Woodrow Wilson*, p. 14.

9. David Steigerwald, *Wilsonian Idealism in America* (Ithaca, NY: Cornell University Press, 1994), p. 21.

10. Daniels, *The Life of Woodrow Wilson*, p. 15.

11. John F. Kennedy, *Profiles in Courage* (New York: Harper and Row, 1956), p. 174. Kennedy was elected president of the United States in 1960 and served from 1961 until he was assassinated in Dallas on November 22, 1963, by Lee Harvey Oswald.

12. Ibid., p. ix.

13. Steigerwald, *Wilsonian Idealism in America*, p. 62.

14. The author was quite surprised to learn on October 3, 1999, from an ABC-TV program stating that the Republican majority leader in the U.S. Senate, Trent Lott, opposed President Bill Clinton's initiative to ensure peace among nations by bilateral agreements. The similarity between Lodge's opposition to Wilson and Lott's opposition to Clinton is striking.

15. Steigerwald, *Wilsonian Idealism in America*, p. 66.

16. Daniels, *The Life of Woodrow Wilson*, p. 320.

17. Schlid, *Between Idealism and Realpolitik*, p. 161.

18. Ibid., p. 162.

19. Daniels, *The Life of Woodrow Wilson*, p. 322.

20. William C. Widenor, *Henry Cabot Lodge and the Search for an American Foreign Policy* (Berkeley: University of California Press, 1980), p. 72.

21. Ibid., p. 3.

22. Ibid., p. 51.

23. Ibid., p. 319.

24. In 1999 the world saw this reality in operation in seeking a solution to problems in Yugoslavia between Slobodon Milosevic and NATO forces over Kosovo. *World Almanac and Book of Facts* (New York: 1999), p. 860.

25. Daniels, *The Life of Woodrow Wilson*, p. 327.

26. Ibid., p. 326.

27. Article 10 of the League of Nations Covenant, quoted in ibid., p. 329.

28. Ibid., p. 328. Indeed, Wilson was quite correct. Germany lost its colonies in 1915. Those colonies were designated mandated territories to be administered by nations appointed by the League of Nations, which were to prepare them for independence when they were ready.

29. Widenor, *Henry Cabot Lodge*, p. 302.

30. Louis L. Snyder, *Hitler's Third Reich: A Documentary History* (Chicago: Nelson-Hall, 1969), p. 17.

31. Ibid., p. 23.

32. Ibid., p. 24.

33. Hitler was referring, of course, to John 2: 14–16, which states, "And he found in the temple those who sold oxen and sheep and doves and the money-changers doing business. He made a whip of cords and drove them all out of the temple with the sheep and the oxen and poured out the changers' money and overturned the tables. He said to those who sold doves, 'Take these things away! Do not make my Father's house a house of merchandise' " *The Holy Bible, The New King James Version*, (New York: Thomas Nelson, 1983).

34. Snyder, *Hitler's Third Reich*, p. 29.

35. Ibid., p. 75.

36. Ibid., p. 197. Synder quotes von Hindenburg as saying in his "Political Testament," published on August 16, 1934, "Once again the old German spirit will assert itself victoriously, but only after it has been purged in the flames of passion and suffering" to which the Nazi party was subjecting it. Von Hindenburg did not think that Hitler and the Nazi party were genuinely interested in serving Germany.

37. Synder, *Hitler's Third Reich*, p. 43.

38. Ibid., p. 44.

39. Ibid., p. 561.

40. Oskew Schnolling, "Comments about World War II," The History Channel, August 8, 1999.

41. Ibid.

42. H. Ned Seelye, *Teaching Culture: Strategies for Intercultural Communication* (Lincolnwood, IL: National Textbook Company, 1993), p. 1.

43. Ibid., p. 2.

44. *World Almanac and Book of Facts*, 1999, p. 801.

45. Eventually the world knew Imelda Marcos as having bought 2,000 pairs of shoes as a symbol of her wealth. In 1999 she was sued for $15 million for her part in the deaths that occurred while her husband was in office. Imelda was reported to indicate that she would pay that amount from his estate. This showed how rich she was.

46. *World Almanac and Book of Facts*, 1999, p. 833.

47. *World Almanac and Book of Facts*, 1992, p. 775.

48. Ibid., p. 776.

49. *World Almanac and Book of Facts*, 1999, p. 930.

50. Bill Moyers, PBS television program, June 2, 1991.

51. George Will, Reaction to the War in the Persian Gulf, on ABC-TV, June 14, 1991.

52. Tom Foley, Reaction to the War in the Persian Gulf, U.S. House of Representatives, June 16, 1991.

53. Bruce Morton, Reaction to the War in the Persian Gulf, CBS-TV, May 18, 1991.

54. President George H. W. Bush Speaking About Weapons of Mass Destruction, May 24, 1991, CBS-TV.

55. The background of the developing crisis in the nuclear test ban treaty of 1999 was that some Third World countries that included India, Pakistan, Israel, and Iraq were reported to be developing their own nuclear arms. As in 1919, unless the United States was part of the treaty the rest of the nations would not be able to maintain it by themselves. The increasing tension between India and Pakistan required the involvement of the United States to ease. As in 1919, neither Jesse Helms nor Trent Lott seemed to understand this reality in their opposition to President Clinton's peace plan.

56. Isaiah 2:4.

# Selected Bibliography

Asgood, Robert Endicott. *Ideas of Self-Interest in American Foreign Policy*. Chicago: University of Chicago Press, 1971.

Azarov, Yuri. *Teaching: Calling and Skills*. Moscow: Progress Press, 1988.

Bahai Assembly. *The Vision of Race Unity: America's Most Challenging Issue*. Wilmette, IL: Bahai Publishing Trust, 1991.

Baker, Ray Stannard. *Woodrow Wilson: Life and Letters: Princeton, 1890–1910*. New York: Doubleday, 1927.

Battle, V. M., and Lyons, C. H. (eds.). *Essays in the History of African Education*. New York: Teachers College Press, 1970.

Berg, J. Otto. "America Faces a Choice." Lecture to a graduate class in education at Northern Arizona University, December 3, 1992.

Biber, Barbara. "Understanding Mankind Through Preschool." In Robert Ulich (ed.), *Education and the Idea of Mankind*. Chicago: University of Chicago Press, 1964.

Bloom, B. *Human Characteristics and Learning in School*. New York: McGraw-Hill, 1976.

Boyer, James. *Administration's Checklist for Ethnic and Multicultural Curriculum*. Manhattan: Kansas State University, 1978.

Brezhnev, Leonid. *Following Lenin's Course*. Moscow: CPU, 1972.

Brown, G., and Hiskett, M. (eds.). *Conflict and Harmony in Education in Tropical Africa*. London: Allen and Unwin, 1975.

Bruner, J. S. *The Process of Education*. Cambridge, MA: Harvard University Press, 1960.

Brunner, Borgna (ed.) *Time Almanac*. New York: Time, Inc., 1999.

Bush, George, President of the US, Speaking About Weapons of Mass Destruction, New York, ABC-TV, May 24, 1991.

Carville, James. *And the Horse He Rode On: The People vs. Kenneth Starr*. New York: Simon and Schuster, 1998.

Castle, E. B. *Education for Self-help: New Strategy for Developing Countries*. London: Oxford University Press, 1972.

Clinton, Bill. *Putting People First: A National Economic Strategy for America*. Little Rock: Clinton for President Committee, 1992.

Coffin, Charles (ed.). *The Complete Poetry and Selected Prose of John Donne*. New York: Modern Library, 1952.

Coleman, J. S. *Equality of Educational Opportunity*. Washington, DC: U.S. Office of Education, 1966.

Coles, E. K. *Adult Education in Developing Countries*. Oxford: Pergamon, 1977.

Coombs, Philip. *World Crisis in Education: The View from the Eighties*. New York: Oxford University Press, 1985.

Corsini, Raymond, and Ignas, Edward. *Alternatives to Educational Systems*. Itasca, IL: F. E. Peacock, 1979.

Corsini, Raymond, and Edward Ignas (eds.). *Comparative Educational Systems*. Itasca, IL: F. E. Peacock, 1982.

Cowan, L., et al. *Education and Nationalism in Africa*. New York: Praeger, 1965.

Craig, Gordon. *Germany, 1866–1945*. New York: Oxford University Press, 1978.

Curle, Adam. *Educational Strategy for Developing Societies: A Study of Educational Social Factors in Relation to Economic Growth*. London: Tavistock, 1963.

Curle, Adam. *Education for Liberation*. New York: John Wiley and Sons, 1973.

Cusick, P. A. *The Egalitarian Ideal and the American High School: Studies of Three Schools*. White Plains, NY: Longmans, 1983.

Daniels, Josephus. *The Life of Woodrow Wilson*. New York: Will H. Johnson, 1924.

Daniels, R., and H. Kitano. *American Racism: Exploration of the Nature of Prejudice*. Englewood Cliffs, NJ: Prentice-Hall, 1970.

de Klerk, F. W. Address to the South African Parliament, Cape Town, SABC-TV, February 2, 1990.

Desmond, Cosmos. *The Discarded People*. Baltimore: Penguin, 1971.

Dewey, John. *Experience and Education*. New York: Collier, 1938.

Dickerman, M. "Teaching Cultural Pluralism," in J. Banks (ed.), *What Educators Are Saying*. Washington DC: National Council for Social Studies, 1973.

Dodd, W. H. *Primary School Inspection in New Countries*. London: Oxford University Press, 1968.

Dore, R. *The Diploma Disease: Education Qualifications and Development*. London: Allen and Unwin, 1976.

Douglass, Frederick. *Narrative of the Life of Frederick Douglass: An American Slave Written by Himself*. New York: New American Library, 1845.

Dullack, Robert. *Franklin Roosevelt and American Foreign Policy*. New York: Oxford University Press, 1979.

Dumoulin, Jerome. "Warning Gong or Death Knell?" *World Press Review*, March, 1984.

Duthie, George. "Education in Rhodesia," *British South Africa Association for the Advancement of Science*, Vol. 4, 1905.

Emmerson, D. K. *Students and Politics in Developing Nations*. London: Pall Mall, 1968.

Fagerburg, Joan. Director, Office of Education for Students from Other Countries at Northern Arizona University. Statement of Mission. Flagstaff, Arizona, October 27, 1999.

Fantini, M. D. *Alternative Education.* Garden City, NY: Doubleday, 1976.

Faure, E. et al. *Learning To Be: The World of Education Today and Tomorrow.* Paris: UNESCO, 1972.

Feinberg, Walter, and Soltis, Jonas. *School and Society.* New York: Teachers College Press, 1985.

Foley, Tom, Speaker of U.S. House of Representatives. Reaction to the War in the Persian Gulf. New York: ABC-TV, June 16, 1991.

Freire, Paulo. *Pedagogy of the Oppressed.* Trans. Myra Bergman Ramos. New York: Continuum, 1982.

Gardener, R. (ed.). *Teacher Education in Developing Countries: Prospects for the Eighties.* London: University of London Institute of Education, 1979.

Gershunsky, Boris. *Russia in Darkness on Education and the Future.* Moscow: Gaddo Gap Press, 1993.

Goldenstein, Erwin H, "Unesco in Perspective," Foreward to Dickson A. Mungazi, *International Education and the Search for Human Understanding* (Monograph Series, No. 2). Flagstaff: Northern Arizona University, 1991.

Gorbachev, Mikhail. *Towards a Humane and Democratic Socialist Society.* Moscow: Novosti Press, 1990.

Grant, Nigel. *Soviet Education.* Middlesex, U.K.: Penguin Books, 1979.

Gray, J. H., and Cole, M. *The Cultural Context of Learning and Thinking.* London: Methuen, 1971.

Grayson, Gary, *Woodrow Wilson: An Intimate Memoir.* New York: Holt. Rinehart and Winston, 1960.

Grayson, K. "Human Life vs. Science." Thomas Weaver (ed.), *To See Ourselves: Anthropology and Modern Social Issues.* Glenview, IL: Scott, Foresman, 1973.

Gutek, Gerald. *American Education in a Global Society: Internationalizing Teacher Education.* New York: Longman, 1993.

Hansen, J. W., and Brembeck, C. S. (eds). *Education and the Development of Nations.* New York: Holt, Rinehart, and Winston, 1960.

Hargreaves, John D. *Decolonization of Africa.* London: Longman, 1988.

Hargreaves, John D. *The End of the Colonial Rule in West Africa.* London: Macmillan, 1979.

Hasbulatov, Ruslan. *Perestroika as Seen by an Economist.* Moscow: Novosti Press, 1989.

Hawes, H. R. *Lifelong Education: Schools and the Curriculum in Developing Countries.* Hamburg: UNESCO, 1975.

Hicks, David, and Tawnley, Charles (eds.). *Teaching World Studies.* New York: Longman, 1982.

Holmes, Brian. "Education in the U.S.S.R." In Edward Igans and Raymond Corsini (eds.), *Comparative Educational Systems.* Itasca, IL: F. E. Peacock, 1982.

Hoopes, Townsend, and Douglas Brinkley. *FDR and the Creation of the U.N.* New Haven, CT: Yale University Press, 1997.

Jarolimek, John. *The Schools in Contemporary Society: An Analysis of Social Currents Issues and Focus.* New York: Macmillan, 1981.

Jolly, R. (ed.). *Education in Africa: Research and Action.* Nairobi: East African Publishing House, 1969.

Kennedy, John F. *Profiles in Courage.* New York: Harper and Row, 1956.

Kershaw, Ian. *The Nazi Dictatorship: Problems of Perspectives of Interpretation.* London: Edward Arnold, 1985.

King, Martin Luther, Jr. *Why We Can't Wait.* New York: New American Library, 1964.

Kliebard, Herbert. *The Struggle for the American Curriculum, 1893–1958.* New York: Routledge and Kegan Paul, 1987.

Knock, Thomas. *To End All Wars: Woodrow Wilson and the Quest for a New World Order.* New York: Oxford University Press, 1992.

Krupskaya, N. K. *Education.* Moscow: Foreign Language Publishing House, 1957.

Kuzin, N., and Kondokov, M. *Education in the U.S.S.R.* Moscow: Progress Press, 1977.

La Guma, Alex (ed.). *Apartheid: A Collection of Writings of South Africa by South Africans.* New York: International Publishers, 1971.

Lappe, Frances Moore. "Democracy and Dogma in the Fight Against Hunger," *The Christian Century,* December 10, 1986.

Link, Arthur S. *Wilson: Campaign for Progressivism and Peace, 1916–1917.* Princeton, NJ: Princeton University Press, 1965.

Link, Arthur S. *Wilson the Diplomatist.* Chicago: Quadrangle Books, 1957.

Luria, A. R. *Cognitive Development: Its Cultural and Social Foundations.* New York: Longman, 1989.

Machel, Samora. "Leadership Is Collective Responsibility, Responsibility Is Collective." Speech given at the Joint Meeting of Frelimo in Maputo, Mozambique, February 2, 1972. Mozambique Ministry of Information.

Mandela, Nelson. Statement to the Press, SABC-TV, March 2, 1990.

Marquard, Leo. *The Peoples and Policies of South Africa.* London: Oxford University Press, 1969.

Marten, Clyde. *A Venture in International Understanding.* Austin: The University of Texas Press, 1985.

Martin, Laurence W. *Peace Without Victory; Woodrow Wilson and British Liberals.* New Haven CT: Yale University Press, 1932.

Massing, Michael. "Unesco under Fire," *The Atlantic Monthly,* July 1984.

M'Bow, Amadou Nahtar, Unesco Director-General. "Unesco and the Promotion of Education for International Understanding." Address to the New York Association of African Studies, Albany, October 29, 1982.

McIntyre, W. *Colonies into Commonwealth.* New York: Walker and Company, 1966.

McLaren, Peter. *Life in Schools: An Introduction to Critical Pedagogy in the Foundations of Education.* New York: Longman, 1989.

Mertineit, Walter. "Unesco Power Rivalries," *World Press Review,* March 1984.

Miller, Lynn H. *Global Order: Values and Power in International Politics,* 2nd ed. Boulder, CO: Westview Press, 1985.

Montgomery, L. "The Education of Black Children." In N. Wright (ed.), *What Educators Are Saying.* New York: Hawthorne Books, 1970.

Morton, Bruce. Reaction to the War in the Persian Gulf. New York: CBS-TV, May 18, 1991.

Mueller, Robert. *New Genesis.* New York: Doubleday, 1982.

Mungazi, Dickson A. *Annotated Bibliography of Multicultiethnic Conceptual Litera-ture*. Lincoln: Nebraska Department of Education, 1978.

Mungazi, Dickson A. "Educational Innovation in Zimbabwe: Possibilities and Problems," *The Journal of Negro Education*, 54, no. 2, 1985.

Mungazi, Dickson A. *Educational Policy and National Character: Africa, Japan, the United States, and the Soviet Union*. Westport, CT: Praeger Publishers, 1993.

Mungazi, Dickson A. "Education and the Quest for Human Completion: The African and Afro-American Perspectives Compared." In *ERIC Clearing-house for Social Studies and Social Science Education*. ref. Ed 292/713/MF01/PCO2. Bloomington: Indiana University, 1987.

Mungazi, Dickson A. *The Evolution of Educational Theory in the United States*. West-port, CT: Praeger Publishers, 1999.

Mungazi, Dickson. "Global Curriculum: Teaching Freedom to Think." Paper Pre-sented at the National Social Science Conference, New Orleans, November 2–4, 1989.

Mungazi, Dickson A. *The Honored Crusade: Ralph Dodge's Theology of Liberation and Initiative for Social Change in Zimbabwe*. Gweru: Mambo Press, 1992.

Mungazi, Dickson. *International Education and the Search for Human Understanding*. Flagstaff, Northern Arizona University Monograph Series, No. 2, 1991.

Mungazi, Dickson A. *The Last British Liberals in Africa: Michael Blundell and Garfield Todd*. Westport, CT: Praeger Publishers, 1999.

Mungazi, Dickson A. *The Last Defenders of the Laager: Ian D. Smith and F. W. de Klerk*. Westport, CT: Praeger Publishers, 1998.

Mungazi, Dickson A. "The March to the Promised Land: The Progress of Black Education in the U.S., 1875–1975." Paper wriiten for graduate class, Uni-versity of Nebraska, 1975.

Mungazi, Dickson A. "Perceptions of Culture: The Basis of Human Understand-ing." Paper presented at the Black School Educators Conference, Las Ve-gas, Nevada, March 4–6, 1993.

Mungazi, Dickson A. *The Struggle for Social Change in Southern Africa: Visions of Liberty*. New York: Taylor and Francis, 1989.

Mungazi, Dickson A. *To Honor the Sacred Trust of Civilization: History, Politics, and Education in Southern Africa*. Cambridge MA: Schenkman, 1983.

Mungazi, Dickson A. *The Underdevelopment of African Education: A Black Zimbab-wean Perspective*. Washington, DC: UPA, 1982.

Mungazi, Dickson A. and Walker, L. Kay. *Educational Reform and the Transfor-mation of Southern Africa*. Westport, CT: Praeger Publishers, 1998.

Mutumbuka, Dzingai, "Zimbabwe's Educational Challenge." Paper presented at the World Universities Conference, London, 1979. Zimbabwe: Ministry of Information.

Myrdal, Gunnar. *An American Dilemma: The Negro Problem and Modern Democracy*. London: Harper and Brothers, 1944.

National Commission on Excellence in Education. *A Nation at Risk: The Imperative for Educational Reform*. Washington, DC: Government Printing Office, 1983.

Nebraska Department of Education. "Position Statement on Multicultural Edu-cation." Lincoln, 1980.

Pai, Y. *Cultural Foundations of Education*. Columbus: Merrill Publishing Company, 1990.

Payne, Charles. "Preparation of Multicultural Teachers." Paper presented at a conference on multicultural education, Lincoln, Nebraska, June 12, 1978.

Potter, Robert E. *The Stream of American Education*. New York: American Book Company, 1967.

Putintsev, A. *U.S.S.R: Perestroika*. Moscow: Novosti Press, 1990.

SABC-TV. "The Search for Sandra Lainge: Apartheid and Education in South Africa." A documentary film, 1981.

Scanlon, David. *International Education: A Documentary History*. New York: Teacher's College Press, 1960.

Scanlon, David. *Traditions of African Education*. New York: Teacher's College Press, 1964.

Schlid, George. *Between Ideology and Realpolitik: Woodrow Wilson and the Russian Revolution, 1917–1921*. Westport, CT: Greenwood Press, 1995.

Schnolling Oskew. "Comments About World War II." New York: History Channel, August 2, 1999.

Scully, Malcolm G. "Unesco's Future at Stake as Meetings Open in Bulgaria," *Chronicle of Higher Education*, October 16, 1985.

Seelye, H. Ned. *Teaching Culture: Strategies for Intercultural Communication*. Lincolnwood, IL: National Textbook Company, 1993.

Shields, James, and Greer, Colin. *Foundations of Education: Dissenting Views*. New York: Wiley, 1974.

Sithole, Ndabaningi. Interview with the Author. Harare, Zimbabwe, July 22, 1983.

Smith, Fenier. *The Great Departure: The United States and World War I*. New York: Cambridge University Press, 1964.

Smith, Gene. *When the Cheering Stopped: The Last Years of Woodrow Wilson*. New York: Time, 1964.

Snyder, Louis L. *Hitler's Third Reich: A Documentary History*. Chicago: Nelson-Hall, 1981.

Southern Rhodesia. *Report of the Commission of Inquiry into Discontent in the Mangwende Reserve* (James Brown, chairman). Salisbury: Government Printer, 1961.

Spring, Joel. *American Education: An Introduction to Social and Political Aspects*. New York: Longman, 1985.

Steigerwald, David. *Wilsonian Idealism in America*. Ithaca, NY: Cornell University Press, 1994.

Stoddard, George. "Unesco," *Education Digest*, Vol. 11, No. 7, 1984.

Stone, Marvin. "The U.S. and Unesco: Had Enough?" *U.S. News and World Report*, December 10, 1984.

Straightforward, David. *Wilsonian Idealism in America*. Ithaca, NY: Cornell University Press, 1984.

Tagore, Rabindranath. Letter dated September 16, 1934, addressed to Professor Albert Murray. By courtesy of the United Nations.

Tagore, Rabindranath. "The Unity of Education," in Robert Ulich (ed.), *Education and the Idea of Mankind*. Chicago: University of Chicago Press, 1964.

Talbott, Strobe (ed.). *Khrushchev Remembers: The Last Testament*. Boston: Little, Brown and Company, 1974.

Thornbrough, E. T. *Booker T. Washington*. Englewood Cliffs, NJ: Prentice-Hall, 1969.

Ulich, Robert (ed.). *Education and the Idea of Mankind*. Chicago: University of Chicago Press, 1964.

Unesco Charter, Paris, 1946.

Unesco. *Education and Cultural Exchange*. Paris, 1976.

"Unesco Inefficient and Wasteful." *Chronicle of Higher Education*, September 19, 1984.

United Nations. Article 22 of the League of Nations. New York, January 20, 1920.

United Nations. "Kofi Annan: Biographical Note." New York, 1997.

United States. *Brown et al. v. Board of Education of Topeka*, 347 US 483. Washington, DC, 1954.

United States. *Congressional Record: First Session of the Sixty-Sixth Congress of the United States*. Washington, DC: Government Printer, November 19, 1919.

United States. *The Public Papers of F. D. Roosevelt: The Atlantic Charter*, Vol. 10, No. 359. Washington, DC: Government Printer, 1941.

United States. Report of the National Advisory Commission on Civil Disorders. Washington, DC: Government Printer, 1968.

United States. Senate Committee on Labor and Public Welfare. *Enactments by the 89th Congress Concerning Education and Training*. Washington, DC: Government Printer, 1966.

Van Til, William. *Education: A Beginning*. Boston: Houghton Mifflin Company, 1974.

Waldon, John W. *The Universities of Ancient Greece*. New York: Charles Scribner's Sons, 1910.

Washington, Booker T. *Up From Slavery*. New York: Doubleday, 1916.

Washington, James (ed.). *Testament of Hope*. New York: Harper and Row, 1986.

Weinstein, Gerald, and Fantini, Mario. *Toward a Humanistic Education: A Curriculum of Affect*. New York: Praeger Publishers, 1970.

White, Sally. "Gadfly to the West," *World Press Review*, March 1984.

"Why Africans Go Hungry." *Scholastic Update*, January 27, 1989.

Widenor, William C. *Henry Cabot Lodge and the Search for American Foreign Policy*. Berkeley: University of California Press, 1980.

Will, George. Reaction to the War in the Persian Gulf. New York: ABC-TV, June 14, 1991.

Willice, H. "Government Advised to Stay in Unesco," *Times Higher Educational Supplement*, July 26, 1985.

Wilson, T. *Towards Equitable Education: A Handbook for Multicultural Consciousness for Early Childhood*. Palo Alto, CA: Ujama Developmental Education Publication, 1976.

World Almanac. *World Almanac and Book of Facts*. New York: Funk and Wagnalls, 1990, 1991, 1992, 1996.

Yagodin, Gennadi. *Towards Higher Standards in Education Through Its Humanization and Democratization*. Moscow: Novosti Press, 1989.

Zimbabwe. *First Women's Seminar*. Harare: ZANU Information Office, 1981.

Zinovyev, M., and Pleshokova, A. *How Illiteracy Was Wiped Out in the U.S.S.R.* Moscow: Language Publishing House, 1981.

# Index

**About the Author**

DICKSON A. MUNGAZI is Regent's Professor of Education and History at Northern Arizona University. Born in Mutare, Zimbabwe, he first came to the United States in 1961 to attend college. After returning to Zimbabwe, he taught high school social studies. He returned to the United States in 1971, receiving graduate degrees in history and the philosophy of education. He is the author of many books and articles, the most recent being *In the Footsteps of the Masters* (Praeger, 2000) and *The Journey to the Promised Land* (Praeger, 2001).